FAITH, CLASS, AND LABOR

Intersectionality and Theology Series

This series is a home for theologies that weave in the strands of gender, race, and class. Because weaving involves stripping the strands, this series makes room for plaiting sub- and minor- strands. Each volume of the series, as such, will exhibit the interwoven and intersectional natures of theology—theology is a weaving or intersection where words, images, schemes, stories, bodies, struggles, cultures, and more, meet and exchange. At this weaving/intersection, traditions, standards and ideals inspire, transpire, and some even expire.

EDITORIAL ADVISORY BOARD

Kuzipa Nalwamba, World Council of Churches (Switzerland)
Mahsheed Ansari, Islamic Science and Research Academy (Australia)
Miguel De La Torre, Iliff School of Theology (USA)
Miguel M. Algranti, Universidad Favaloro (Argentina)

"This collection of essays represents a fine addition to the growing juncture of religious-theological studies and economic studies. Its particular focus is on the significance of labor and class for the study and practice of religion and theology, and vice versa. Toward this end, the volume draws on an excellent group of scholars. . . . The result is a keen reading of the problematic from a broad variety of angles of vision. A creative and sophisticated interdisciplinary exercise; well done!"
—FERNANDO F. SEGOVIA, Vanderbilt University

"I thank the authors for laboring to connect work, faith as deep solidarity, and class realities as ways to breathe new life into labor struggles and the revitalization of religion. As long as people have to work for a living, this text is required reading for all who hunger and thirst for justice, and for those labor and are heavy-laden. They are in fact, one and the same."
—ANGELA COWSER, Louisville Presbyterian Theological Seminary

"This volume opens many lines of inquiry to redress one of the greatest failures of Christian theology, ethics, and biblical studies over the past few decades: not adequately engaging labor, class, and capitalism as such, in right proportion to the immense power the capitalist class exercises over every dimension of life. And the volume does so fully immersed in the intersections of class, gender, and race, thereby showing how each is indispensable for a full understanding of the others."
—JEREMY POSADAS, Austin College, Sherman, Texas

"*Faith, Class, and Labor* is a thoughtfully conceived anthology. Through the lenses of history, Bible, gender, and organizing and activism, authors representing eight geographical contexts present complex and nuanced readings of class that describe how intersectional circumstances influence and reveal the meaning of class in what people experience. . . . This book is a must-read for academic and practical engagement in Christian ethics as well as for all of us who sometimes are befuddled by the absence of concrete discussions of class as we witness its diverse, disappointing manifestations in our own communities and in communities around the globe."
—ROSETTA E. ROSS, Spelman College

FAITH, CLASS, and LABOR

Intersectional Approaches in a Global Context

EDITED BY
Jin Young Choi & Joerg Rieger

☙PICKWICK *Publications* · Eugene, Oregon

FAITH, CLASS, AND LABOR
Intersectional Approaches in a Global Context

Intersectionality and Theology Series

Copyright © 2020 Wipf and Stock Publishers. All rights reserved. Except for brief quotations in critical publications or reviews, no part of this book may be reproduced in any manner without prior written permission from the publisher. Write: Permissions, Wipf and Stock Publishers, 199 W. 8th Ave., Suite 3, Eugene, OR 97401.

Pickwick Publications
An Imprint of Wipf and Stock Publishers
199 W. 8th Ave., Suite 3
Eugene, OR 97401

www.wipfandstock.com

PAPERBACK ISBN: 978-1-7252-5716-0
HARDCOVER ISBN: 978-1-7252-5717-7
EBOOK ISBN: 978-1-7252-5718-4

Cataloguing-in-Publication data:

Names: Choi, Jin Young, editor. | Rieger, Joerg, editor.

Title: Faith, class, and labor : intersectional approaches in a global context / edited by Jin Young Choi and Joerg Rieger.

Description: Eugene, OR: Pickwick Publications, 2020. | Intersectionality and Theology Series. | Includes bibliographical references and index.

Identifiers: ISBN: 978-1-7252-5716-0 (paperback). | ISBN: 978-1-7252-5717-7 (hardcover). | ISBN: 978-1-7252-5718-4 (ebook).

Subjects: LCSH: Religion and sociology. | Social class. | Ethics. | Marginality, Social—Religious aspects—Christianity.

Classification: BT78 F15 2020 (print). | BT738 (epub).

Manufactured in the U.S.A.

Contents

Acknowledgments | vii
Introduction | ix

1. The Multiple Intersections of Faith, Labor, and Class | *Joerg Rieger* | 1

SECTION I: HISTORY OF CLASS AND LABOR

2. Christianity and Socialism in China: Allies or Strange Bedfellows | *Kwok Pui-lan* | 25
3. The God That Never Failed: Black Christian Marxism as Prophetic Call to Action and Hope | *Juan M. Floyd-Thomas* | 44
4. With Our Hands We Will Build Machines, with Our Hearts We Build the Future: Religion, Labor, and Class Consciousness | *Marcus Trammel* | 69

SECTION II: READING BIBLE, READING CLASS

5. People's Money, Women's Precarious Life, and Empire | *Jin Young Choi* | 87
6. A Trans-textual and Trans-sectoral Gender-economic Reading of the Rape of Tamar (2 Sam 13) and the Expropriation of Naboth's Land (1 Kgs 21) | *Gerald O. West* | 105
7. Ruth as Esperanza?: A Trans-textual Reading of Ruth with Foreign Domestic Workers in Singapore | *Chin Ming Stephen Lim* | 122

SECTION III: GENDER, RACE, AND CLASS

8. Proletarianized Sexuality of Soldiering and Prostitution: Making a Christian Ethic of Peace Countering Necropolitics of War | *Keun-Joo Christine Pae* | 143
9. Class and Privilege-Salient Racism: The Case or Curse of Being Black! | *Sifiso Mpofu* | 164

SECTION IV: ORGANIZING AND ACTIVISM

10. Deep Solidarity: A Pre-requisite to Resisting Capitalism and Building Economic Democracy | *Rosemarie Henkel-Rieger* | 185
11. Invited, Invigorated, and Invented Spaces: A Trans-development Approach | *Sithembiso S. Zwane* | 212
12. Transcendence in the Time of Neoliberalism: A Theological Reflection on the Employer–Employee Relationship and the Theological Struggle for Everyday Life | *Karl James E. Villarmea* | 234

List of Contributors | 261
Scripture Index | 263
General Index | 266

Acknowledgments

THIS PROJECT WOULD HAVE been impossible without the tremendous support of the Council for World Mission through the Discernment and Radical Engagement (DARE) initiative. We would like to thank General Secretary Rev. Dr. Collin Cowan, Mission Secretary Dr. Sudipta Singh, and Program Associate Ms. Maria Fe Labayo for providing a space in which the contributors, as a working group, have engaged in a discussion of issues of class and labor that demand the church's missional responses and theology's public witness. Our special appreciation goes to Dr. Jione Havea for his support of this project from the conception stage to publication both as an architect of the DARE program and as the series editor of the Intersectionality and Theology Series of Pickwick Publications (Wipf and Stock Publishers). We thank Dr. Aaron Stauffer for his editorial support and for preparing the index. Finally, we would like to thank our contributors for their outstanding collaboration, which consisted of meeting in person in Taipei, Taiwan, constructively engaging each other's presentations, and being in correspondence with the suggestions and queries of the editors of this volume. As a result, this book is not merely a collection of individual essays but a product of collective *labor* that embodies our commitments to and hope for a just society where working people, which means the majority of people with all of their differences, become more effective agents and are treated with respect, dignity, and equity.

Introduction

WHAT IS GAINED WHEN activists and scholars of religion, theology, and the Bible begin to address matters of economics, labor, and class? Despite the fact that 99 percent of us have to work for a living and even though our work shapes us to the core, labor and class are topics that are underrepresented in the work of scholars of religion, theology, and the Bible. In recent decades, labor and class have rarely been addressed in-depth even in the growing number of explorations of theology, religion, and economics.[1] One way to frame this conversation is to observe that labor relations impact, and are impacted by, all other relations. This includes religion, which can also be defined in relational terms, as relationships among people, religious traditions, and the divine.

With this volume, an international group of scholars and activists at various stages in their careers presents a concerted effort to bring issues of labor and class back into the discussion. The twelve contributors have roots in eight different countries including (in alphabetical order) Germany, Hong Kong, South Korea, the Philippines, Singapore, South Africa, the U.S., and Zimbabwe. They currently reside and work in five different countries and are connected through various academic, ecclesial, and activist networks. Some are in positions to provide long and deep assessments of their fields, others are making provocative statements about how things might be different if the next generation of scholars would pick up one of the key topics of our age.

---

1. See Rieger, "Capitalism and Christian Theology." This includes even the work of many Latin American liberation theologians, who have critiqued economic inequalities but have often focused more on broader relationships between the global North and the global South. Note that emphasis on poverty does not equal closer investigations of labor and class.

While each of the various contributions covers new ground, taken together they provide even deeper layers of insight and inspiration. One reason for this synergy is that matters of economics, labor, and class affect virtually everything, both people and the planet: no one and nothing can exist for very long in a vacuum. Many of the other struggles that mark our age (race, ethnicity, gender, sexuality, age, colonialism, etc.) are also negotiated here. Labor relations—relationships of power at work—are inextricably tied to race relations, for instance, so much so that leaders of African American emancipation in the United States such as W. E. B. Du Bois and Martin Luther King Jr. articulated in their own ways that the organizing work done by labor unions in the U.S. was essential in the struggle against racism.[2] In the fight against gender oppression, long traditions of socialist feminists and some African American womanist scholars have emphasized the importance of liberation along the lines of class. And a good deal of the pushback against ethnic minority groups is linked to the challenges of labor migration in the U.S. and elsewhere, which is why efforts to welcome immigrants without paying attention to labor issues are so limited.

Another reason for the synergy that emerges in these chapters is that the authors themselves are deeply involved in matters of labor and class and are genuinely interested in engaging and learning from each other. What can activists learn from scholars and scholars from activists? What can biblical scholars learn from theologians and theologians from biblical scholars? What are the implications for the study of religion and theology, and what are the implications for activism and organizing? These questions and concerns, brought together in this volume, are the foundations of intersectional, transdisciplinary, trans-textual, transactional, transnational, and transgressive work in our time.

In the following chapters, historians and theologians investigate how new images of God, people, and the world emerge and what difference they can make, in conversation with traditions and practices both ancient and contemporary. Biblical critics develop new takes on ancient

---

2. Martin Luther King, speech at the Highlander Folk School, 1957: "Organized labor has proved to be one of the most powerful forces in removing the blight segregation and discrimination from our nation. Labor leaders wisely realize that the forces that are anti-Negro are usually anti-labor, and vice versa. And so organized labor is one of the Negro's strongest allies in the struggle for freedom." King, *All Labor Has Dignity*, 14. W. E. B. Du Bois: "Probably the greatest and most effective effort toward interracial understanding among the working masses has come about through the trade unions." Du Bois, *Writings*, 68.

texts that are not only unexpected and surprising but lead to the reversal of readings that are seemingly stable, settled, and have been taken for granted in past decades. Activists and organizers are identifying fresh sources of power and energy that have been neglected in recent history but have never gone away and are returning in new force, and they are reporting about results and transformation that are happening but often go underreported.

Focal Points

The efforts to address matters of labor and class in this volume have two focal points. One has to do with analysis and a deeper understanding of how labor is part of our being human, affecting and being affected by all other areas of life. Since most people are spending the bulk of their waking hours at work—this includes those who are casually employed, in the gig economy, or even those who have not given up looking for work—labor shapes us more deeply than is commonly realized. While it may come as a surprise to some that labor also shapes, and is shaped by, religion, we are only beginning to understand what that actually looks like and all that might be implied. How might labor shape religion, and how might religion shape labor, for good and for ill, for better or for worse?

The second focal point has to do with the question of agency. Working people, no matter how exploited and oppressed they may be, continue to maintain some agency in their lives, however limited. Unlike certain types of colonization in both past and present, capitalism still cannot do without people who do the work, because even in a time of increased automation it remains true that without working people "not a single wheel can turn."[3] How does the power of working people shape up today, how is it being organized, and how might it be making a difference in the world?

To be sure, the reflections on the importance of labor and work offered in this volume do not mean to suggest that work is everything. In a climate where work continues to be the ground of exploitation and where work allows the few to build their fortunes on the basis of the labor of the many (why else would labor and work be policed so consistently and harshly around the world, despite the gains of financial capitalism?), we also need to acknowledge the problems and limits of work. So-called

---

3. From the song "Solidarity Forever," by Ralph Chaplin, *Socialist and Labor Songs: An International Revolutionary Songbook.*

anti-work theory has made the point that work under the conditions of capitalism needs to be questioned and some of it perhaps cannot be redeemed.[4]

Nevertheless, we maintain that labor is not merely the place of exploitation and oppression but remains a prime place of resistance, agency, and the fertile ground for the construction of alternatives. Labor movements, both past and present, cooperative enterprises and businesses, and the growing development of economic democracies all over the world speak for themselves. Religious scholars and communities overlook the generative combinations of labor and religion at their own peril. Picking up on those dynamics, the contributors intend to demonstrate what theological discourses and religion-involved engagements can do to promote another world that is shaped by the values of human dignity, justice, and genuine creativity that brings together the divine, people, and the world.

Summary of the Volume

As Joerg Rieger argues in chapter 1, the concerns of labor have the potential to deepen the experience and practice of religion, while engaged religion can help refocus and radicalize the labor movement. Examples are drawn from the Abrahamic religious traditions (Judaism, Christianity, and Islam) in various locations, with a focus on the southern parts of the U.S., where religion has often become part of the problem rather than the solution. These dynamics are linked to the emergence of fresh engagements of class as (asymmetrical) relationships of power rather than stratification, shaping up in the force fields of the intersectional concerns of race, ethnicity, caste, gender, and sexuality.

In the first section of the book, historical perspectives on class and labor are presented. In chapter 2, developments in China further broaden the horizons of both scholars and organizers. Kwok Pui-lan recalls the complex history of labor organizing in China and the various transformations that took place. Under the current regime, it is fair to say that even in China inequality is on the rise and the rich get richer and the poor get poorer. Add to that the situation of 300 million migrant workers and the situation of female workers in China. New challenges not only for economists and organizers but also for theologians arise from these developments.

4. See, for instance, Weeks, *Problem with Work*.

Juan M. Floyd-Thomas, in chapter 3, examines the Black Manifesto that was introduced by civil rights activist James Forman in New York City's Riverside Church on May 4, 1969. At the core of the Manifesto is the relation of religion, racism, and reparations. Since structural poverty is part of the problems that haunt the African American community, and since the demand for reparations is still on the table, issues of labor and class must necessarily become more central parts of the ongoing conversations. After all, slavery, which is at the basis of race relations in the U.S., might be considered one of the most distorted forms of labor relations and might guide our thinking about reparations.

Chapter 4, authored by Marcus Trammell, investigates how Pentecostal and other religious traditions that are usually classified as more conservative shape up in a context where working people of different racial and religious backgrounds begin to organize and gain influence in the worlds of politics and economics. What emerges is a fascinating picture of how the agency of working people is supported by (and shapes) seemingly unlikely religious traditions. Trammell's account addresses broader historical developments in the northeastern United States in the early decades of the twentieth century with a focus on Detroit, interspersed with recollections of his own family history. Some of what moved his grandparents in their involvement in the United Autoworkers union (UAW) and Pentecostal traditions continue to move Trammell's own current involvement as an organizer and his engagement in theological education.

In the second section, three biblical scholars provide trans-textual and/or trans-sectional readings of the Jewish and Christian Scriptures, engaging issues around class and labor and intersections of gender/sexuality and race/ethnicity in the global and postcolonial contexts. In chapter 5, Jin Young Choi rereads the story of the poor widow (Mark 12:41–44) through the lens of her precarious life in the Roman imperial context, as well as in the context of Mark's narrative, in which Jesus appears to be concerned with economic transactions against the multitude (*ochlos*). This reading not only reveals how women's destitute living conditions are aggravated by the entangled structures of patriarchy, religion, and imperial/colonial politics, but also affirms the widow's agency by interpreting her act as a social commentary depicting the fate of poor women in times of colonial oppression and war. Choi's interpretation invites the reader to watch through Jesus's eyes poor women's precarious work and lives within today's neoliberal capitalism.

Chapter 6, written by Gerald O. West, reflects on the capacity of trans-textual and trans-sectional resources to forge alliances across gender, race, and class. Employing Makhosazana Nzimande's intersectional imbokodo (grinding-stone) interpretive frame, West provides a trans-textual reading of 2 Samuel 13:1–22 and 1 Kings 21:1–16 in the postcolonial context of South Africa. First, his trans-textual reading discloses not only Jonadab's activation of the (hetero-) patriarchal system but also Jezebel's complicity with patriarchy. Second, as economic agendas are central to the patriarchal expropriation in both cases of Jonadab and Jezebel, West's trans-textual reading develops into gender-economic trans-sectional readings. Last, the belated presence of the prophet of God in 1 Kings 21 (Elijah) trans-forms Tamar as the immanent prophet of God in 2 Samuel 13, thus constituting a theological economic-gender trans-sectional reading of each text.

Chapter 7 is another trans-textual reading, by Chin Ming Stephen Lim, of the book of Ruth with a play produced in Singapore, *Esperanza*, which centers on a Filipina domestic worker. Lim begins by situating Christians within class hierarchies of the wider society and the home in Singapore, particularly in relation to the foreign worker who provides "intimate labor." While both Ruth and Esperanza are viewed as sharing similar plights in that they are relocated to a foreign land in hope of a better life, Lim argues that the narrative of Ruth, which seems to affirm inter-marriage, ironically intensifies the alien nature of Moab. Finally, he examines the possible discursive effects of the text on Christian readers in Singapore so as to disrupt class desires that transform Ruth into a model worker while ignoring the systemic issues with her being a poor, foreign woman.

Chapters 8 and 9 in the third section focus on issues of class and labor that intersect with gender/sexuality, race, and powers manifested in the forms of militarism and white privilege, respectively. In chapter 8, Keun-Joo Christine Pae analyzes war and militarism through the two distinctive forms of necropolitical labor—military prostitution and soldiering. With a focus on America's military presence in East Asia, Pae investigates the state's recruitment of the racialized and sexualized poor into its war business, which creates the complex and antagonized relationship between American soldiers and Asian prostitutes despite their shared class backgrounds. Notwithstanding the long historical presence of prostitution in the global war theater, poor women's sexualized labor has been generally ignored in Christian discourse on war and peace.

Thus, Pae constructs a class-sensitive Christian ethic of peace transected with gender/sexuality and race, asking the practical question of how "God's preferential option for the poor" can critically inform transnational solidarity for peace.

In chapter 9, Sifiso Mpofu's interrogation of the intersection of race and class begins with the universal phenomenon that even the success of black people is treated not as being based on merit or hard work but as being stolen from white people. In addition to demonstrating that this ill derives from white privilege, Mpofu examines economic marginalization of black people as a social process, particularly as the result of slavery and colonialism. As class structures and Christian colonialism together have destroyed the spirit of *ubuntu* in Africa and the legacy of the structures of privilege have dominated Zimbabwe's society and church alike, the author argues that the church should speak out against institutionalized economic divisions that cause these social frictions.

The final section of the book deals with organizing and activism. In chapter 10, Rosemarie Henkel-Rieger discusses how addressing economic realities, such as growing inequality, that affect workers and people of faith alike, can contribute to building relationships of solidarity. Projects include intersectional organizing that acknowledges and appreciates differences in terms of race, ethnicity, gender, and sexuality, and expanding worker-ownership as a means of building community wealth and power, as well as democratic control to the workplace.

Sithembiso S. Zwane, in chapter 11, contrasts the "invited spaces" of neoliberal capitalism that undermine working people and the "invigorated spaces" that build agency among working class religious and social movements through engagements with the Bible. These invigorated spaces are found, for example, in religious communities such as the African Initiated Churches (AIC) and Abahlali Basemjondolo (the shackdwellers movement).

In the final chapter (12) Karl James E. Villarmea investigates the employer–employee relationship as part of neoliberal capitalist construction of problematic forms of transcendence that are violent and destructive. In this context theologians have an opportunity to use the tools of their trade in order to develop alternatives, not merely in the field of knowledge but in engaging the world of social movements and political organizations.

Bibliography

Du Bois, W. E. B. *Writings*. Edited by Herbert Aptheker. Milwood, NY: Kraus-Thomson, 1982.
King, Martin Luther, Jr. *All Labor Has Dignity*. Edited by Michael K. Honey. Boston: Beacon, 2011.
Rieger, Joerg. "Capitalism and Christian Theology." *Religion Compass*, February 2020. https://doi.org/10.1111/rec3.12350.
Socialist and Labor Songs: An International Revolutionary Songbook. Oakland: Kerr, 2014.
Weeks, Kathi. *The Problem with Work: Feminism, Marxism, Antiwork Politics, and Postwork Imaginaries*. Durham: Duke University Press, 2011.

1

The Multiple Intersections of Religion, Labor, and Class[1]

Joerg Rieger

Introduction

LABOR AND CLASS ARE topics crucial to much of life: 99 percent of us need to work in order to make a living, and in the twenty-first century much of the natural environment has been affected by processes of human labor. Another crucial topic in many places around the world is faith. Still, few things can derail a conversation in the United States faster than mentioning labor and class, with topics combining labor and religion coming in as a close second. This is true not only for casual conversations, it is also true in the theological academy and even more true for most religious communities.

The reasons are multiple. In many cases, any reference to class is seen as irredeemably Marxist, as if it would be impossible to come up with the notion of class without the help of Karl Marx. This is very strange, considering the fact that class differentials are directly experienced on a daily basis by those who feel the humiliations of power at their workplace. This is not only a problem in the United States and other countries in the proverbial West; even many Chinese intellectuals have turned away from

---

1. This chapter builds on some material published in Rieger and Henkel-Rieger, *Unified We Are a Force*, chapters 4 and 5, used by permission.

the question of class, as I found when lecturing in academic settings in China in 2015. In addition to the term class, terms like labor and even work also tend to be seen in a negative light; conversations about worker cooperatives, for instance, are easier when reframed in terms of employee cooperatives.

My question as a theologian is how we might reclaim discourses on labor and class as well as discourses on religion. My suggestion is that this happens by bringing the two together, as concerns of labor and class can revitalize religion, and some of the concerns of religion can revitalize the engagement of class and labor.

In the following, I will talk about labor and class in the same breath, as class describes the basic relationship of people at work. At the most basic level, class is determined by the power that people have at work and over their own work. This power relates not only to how much money people are making—although this is a significant factor when profits are rising in times of "mean and lean production"—it also relates to how much of a say people have in the work process. Moreover, the power that people have at work also influences and shapes how people embrace and embody power in many other areas of their lives. Since most people are spending the majority of their waking hours at work, and since work is the fundamental pillar of people's livelihoods, it can be argued that class relationships tend to shape us all the way down. According to some estimates, two-thirds of Americans are working class due to their limited power at work,[2] but we should not forget that 99 percent of us have to work for a living and that even many traditional middle-class jobs are being downgraded and offer even less power than they once did. Working people are no longer confined to those who wear blue collars—today they wear also white collars, lab coats, and in many cases even clerical and professorial gowns.

Note that this definition of class in terms of relationships of power stands in contradistinction to other definitions of class in terms of social stratification.[3] Stratification theories examine class as layers of a social system but not necessarily in relation to each other. This definition of class also questions the usefulness of the common notion of "classism," which seems to assume that the problem of class is linked with prejudices

---

2. See Zweig, *Working Class Majority*.
3. See Rieger, "Introduction," in *Religion, Theology, and Class*.

of one class against another and that the problem can be overcome by doing away with the prejudice rather than the structure of class.

Unfortunately, there is no room in this chapter for more extensive discussions of race, ethnicity, caste, gender, and sexuality. Labor is crucially related to all of these categories, as exploitation and oppression along these lines is a major factor of racism, ethnocentrism, caste hierarchies, sexism, and heterosexism. The workplace is where all of these elements come together most intimately, as workplaces are typically more diverse than other social spaces, including the practice of religion. This is the foundation for the formation of solidarity, which does not have to be understood as homogenizing the various identities but as providing space for bringing to bear different identities (as well as different religious traditions) in constructive ways. This is what, together with co-authors Kwok Pui-lan and Rosemarie Henkel Rieger, I have called deep solidarity elsewhere.[4]

Religion Needs Labor

When engaging a group of undocumented Latino construction workers in the United States a few years ago, many expressed concern that religion was more of a problem than a help. They pointed out that their employers were religious people as well, and that this made little positive difference at work. Moreover, they argued, religion might be harmful for workers because it tended to make them more docile and submissive. To these construction workers, the conventional values they connected with religion, like humility, service, and love of neighbor, was bound to make things worse for working people. Another way of understanding religion, however, caught their attention. What if religion is not primarily about ideas, conventional values, or about the sort of things that people do in private, when they are off work? What if religion is about the experience of struggling communities, deep solidarity that includes racial/ethnic and sexual identities without erasing difference, the formation of alternative power, and the fight for a better life for everyone? In these examples, religion is not defined by the pious ideas of the status quo but by people of different identities bonding together with the divine in order

---

4. See Kwok and Rieger, *Occupy Religion*; and Rieger and Henkel-Rieger, *Unified We Are a Force*, chapter 3.

to make use of their abilities (including their disabilities, to be sure) for the common good.

Ancient Traditions on the Side of Labor

Religion shapes up differently when seen through the lenses of labor and class. When connecting with the issues of real life, religion has an opportunity to return to its sources, which in many cases are linked to the lives of ordinary working people. The three Abrahamic religions have deep roots in the struggles for liberation of the Hebrew slaves in Egypt, where God is portrayed as involved in the movement. Elsewhere in the traditions of Judaism, Christianity, and Islam, God is presented as a working person who forms the human being from clay (Gen 2:7; Qur'an 15.26; 15.28) and plants a garden (Gen 2:8–9). In these traditions, God goes about the creation of the world just as working people would do, rather than as a supervisor or a manager who puts others to work. When religion is viewed from the perspective of labor and class, images of God as ruler can be called into question. Coincidentally, a search for the notion of God as king in the Bible produces surprisingly few results outside of the book of Psalms.[5] In the prophetic texts of the Hebrew Bible, God is even portrayed as opposing the power of kings because of the exploitation and oppression that so often goes with the office. Jews and Christians share these traditions.[6]

To be sure, there are other traditions where God's act of creating is seen as less hands-on, for instance in the so-called first creation story (Gen 1:1—2:3), but this does not erase the traditions of God as worker. And even in that story, God rests from work after six days (Gen 2:2), a gesture which has been an inspiration for working people through the ages, who usually had to fight for time off work even on weekends even in the "Christian" nations of the West.

---

5. Most of the references are found in the Psalms, which is probably why so many people are familiar with the notion of God as king. The apostle Paul, on the other hand, never refers to God as king, and his references to Jesus as Lord can be seen as subversive of the Roman emperor. See Rieger, *Christ and Empire*, chapter 1.

6. See, for instance, 1 Sam 8:11–18, where God is opposed to giving the people a king because this means that they are rejecting God as their king. The kings on earth are very different kinds of kings than God, as they tend to exploit and oppress the people.

Christian traditions go one step further yet when they hold that God joined the workforce as a human being in the form of a day laborer in construction—no doubt a distinct class position—in the incarnation of Jesus Christ. As a result, Christians who believe that Jesus Christ is both fully human and fully divine have to deal with an image of God in Christ that does not easily fit in with widely held ideas of God as a heavenly monarch or as a transcendent manager.

Unfortunately, most religious communities are unaware of the deep implications of these and other religious traditions that tie religion to the everyday lives of working people. Instead, religions in colonial and postcolonial times have often been lured into understanding themselves as matters of otherworldly affairs, having mostly to do with another world, with grandiose ideas, or with private concerns. In the process, religions have been domesticated and lost most of their meaning and almost all of their bite. So great is the confusion that many religious people now assume that religion equals religious rituals and cult, something that happens off work, in the evenings or on one of the days of the weekend.

Yet few of the key figures of the Abrahamic religions spent the bulk of their time in worship or dealing with matters of religion in such a narrow sense.[7] Abraham, Moses, the Hebrew prophets, Jesus, and Muhammad were down-to-earth people who were interested in the well-being of their communities, in how covenantal relationships with God shape up in relation to other human beings, and all of them were concerned with how religion transforms the world. This is true even for supposedly more ethereal figures like the apostle Paul. As recent research has shown, Paul's message was grounded in alternative ways of life in the midst of the Roman Empire.[8]

Religion Awakened by Labor

Taking the concerns of labor seriously can help people of all religions and identities rediscover these and other ancient traditions and reclaim them, including images of God, the self-understanding of religious communities, and key religious ideas and concepts across the religious traditions.

---

7. This modern understanding of religion is increasingly being deconstructed in the contemporary study of religion. See, for instance, Masuzawa, *Invention of World Religions*.

8. See, for instance, the work of Elsa Tamez, Neil Elliott, and Richard Horsley.

Consider, for example, notions of sin and salvation: If sin is not merely a private matter between the self and God but a matter of the distortion of broader relationships that include workers, employers, and God, then salvation is no longer merely a private matter either but has to do with the restoration of these relationships.

Moreover, in the encounters of religion and labor, the idea of religion itself changes. Informed by matters of labor and class, religion is linked to matters of politics, economics, and everyday life and it can provide positive inspiration without needing to dictate the outcomes. As religion is reshaped in the tensions of life that affect working people, it can reclaim its roles as an agent in the struggle for the common good. Without being reshaped in these ways, religion may well support a social concern here and there, as often happens, but it will remain a matter of peripheral interest and not be able to make much of a difference.

Labor can help us sort out two of the most burning issues that affect us today and that are closely connected: capitalism and religion. Christianity has a special place in this discussion because it is the religion most closely connected with the development of capitalism.[9] Unfortunately, despite this history, religion in general and Christianity in particular is often unaware of the role it plays in matters of labor and class. In fact, much of the support it gives to the capitalist status quo happens unconsciously. Even when it appears to be withdrawing from the world and spiritualizing religion, religion endorses the status quo, as it provides room to the dominant powers to do as they please. Furthermore, by envisioning God in terms of the dominant powers—another move that often happens unconsciously—religion provides a justification for the status quo without necessarily being aware of what is going on.

Worst of all, unlike many other communal projects, much of religion today is unclear about its purpose. As a result, religion has become equated either with some aloof spirituality or with some form of dated morality that is tied to conventions of the past for good or for ill. In this situation the encounter with labor can help religion find its purpose again. The Abrahamic spiritualities or moralities that are emerging in this encounter are not vague, and neither are they primarily otherworldly or narrow. Spirituality here describes a way of life that values labor, productivity, and creativity (both human and nonhuman), with a focus on what

---

9. Sociologist Max Weber has analyzed the legacy of Protestantism in particular as it relates to the development of Capitalism. See Weber, *Protestant Ethic and the Spirit of Capitalism*.

benefits the world as a whole, both human communities and nonhuman communities.

There is one more issue where religion needs help. Religious people often lack an understanding of how to distinguish friend and foe. The only distinction many are able make is between people of religion and people who reject religion—insiders and outsiders—or between theists and atheists. But this is by no means the most interesting distinction. Class struggle—which is how the class relationship has shaped up in capitalism—is generally not waged between people of religion and people who reject religion; it is waged by corporations whose CEOs in the United States are likely to be members of a religious community (whose board meetings begin with a prayer) against working people who are members of religious communities as well. The most interesting question for religion, therefore, is not whether one is religious or not, but what kind of religion they practice (or refuse to practice).

For the most part, religions have not much of a clue what to do with these tensions, or with tensions in general. In fact, many religious people refuse to acknowledge tensions within their families and communities, which is why in religious communities sexual abuse often goes unreported, racism is not challenged, and economic exploitation is so often overlooked. The result is that in these settings those who represent the dominant powers win out. And because the depth of the tensions is not acknowledged, religious calls to reconciliation and love are not only shallow but likely perpetuate the problem.

In these cases, labor presents another challenge to religion that is not foreign to many of our traditions, raising the following questions: What would it mean to side with those who are exploited and oppressed rather than to stay neutral in situations of injustice? What would it mean to confront sin and evil rather than to accommodate to the status quo? Organizers know that they need a target. What if religion could help us with that, but without the need to demonize individuals, according to the old saying "Hate the sin, love the sinner"?

In sum, religion that has been awakened by labor does not necessarily have to serve the capitalist status quo; traditional religious notions such as sin and salvation or conversion and repentance do not have to be abandoned. Just the opposite: in the struggle against the capitalist exploitation and oppression of labor, religions gather new steam and can make a difference. Liberals might be surprised to find that even the fire-and-brimstone sermons of yesterday, which they seek to leave behind, might be useful again, although their target would now be different. Instead of proclaiming judgment against the masses of working people, judgment can now be proclaimed on a sinful status quo—the absolute maximization of profit at all cost—that is harming both working people and the globe in unprecedented ways. The goal of this religion is not feeling guilty but acts of repentance and conversion, which in the Hebrew traditions always implied practical responses: the Hebrew word *shub* connected to concepts of repentance and conversion literally means turning around and going the other way.

The Future of Religion

Religion ebbs and flows. In the United States, religion has enjoyed great success for many years, seemingly defeating developments of secularization that marked Europe. Today, however, even in the United States interest in organized religion is waning, especially among the younger generation and particularly in the mainline denominations of Christianity. Because much of the public image of religion in the United States is tied to a religious landslide that was engineered by the Religious Right with the support of corporate America, it stands and falls with this relationship.[10] For decades now, the Religious Right has managed to present itself as more faithful to religion and orthodox, more concerned about traditional religious values, and it has managed to create the impression that it is closer to the origins of Christianity. This method, to be sure, betrays a false logic: upholding what amounts to the family values of the 1950s (heterosexual nuclear families, gender stereotypes, etc.) does not necessarily mean returning to the values of Jesus.

A recent study by the Brookings Institution provides another framework for the future of religion:

> The religious right spoke to the country's worries about social change. The religious progressive movement speaks to the country's desire for economic change. In the late 20th century, 'family values' were invoked in opposition to what many saw (and feared) as a cultural revolution. In the early twenty-first century, family stability is most threatened by an economic revolution that has created a growing gap between the economy's

---

10. For the history, see Kruse, *One Nation under God*.

productivity gains and the wage growth of most American workers.[11]

What might be the prospects of the other framework of religion described in this passage? What if the Brookings Institution is right and the concerns of economic justice prove to be the fertile ground of this era?[12]

As people are concerned about increasing inequalities and injustices, particularly in the world of work and labor where it affects them the most (and race, ethnicity, gender, and sexuality are part of this), they are also paying attention to how these things play out in the churches. People judge their religious communities in terms of economic justice as well: forty-five percent of those who had been raised Evangelical, forty-three percent of those raised Catholic, and thirty-one percent of those raised in a mainline Protestant denomination said the focus on "money and power" was an important reason they no longer associated with a church.[13]

In other words, even though religion in the United States has gained prestige by accommodating to the interests of the ruling class, it has also lost a great deal. More and more people seem to be getting tired of religion playing the wingman of the status quo. And, what is perhaps most surprising, those getting tired of dominant religion might be the ones who actually care more about religion than those who continue to go through the motions without asking questions. If religion keeps losing those who care and retains those who don't, it does not have much of a future.

When religion gets involved in the tensions of real life and engages with labor and class, things change. Far from being just one more outlet for socially engaged people of religion, engaging in the struggles of labor and class can help reclaim the heart of various religions. If images of the divine set the stage in these struggles, as many of religious traditions insist, religious people will only find God if they look for God in these struggles rather than in the vestiges of dominant religion.[14]

---

11. Davis et al., *Faith in Equality*, 49.
12. Davis et al., *Faith in Equality*, 50.
13. Davis et al., *Faith in Equality*, 26.
14. This insight was powerfully expressed by a German theologian who fought the false religion of German fascism, Dietrich Bonhoeffer. See the monumental biography by Bethge, *Dietrich Bonhoeffer*.

While the future of religion will depend on how it deals with the struggles of life, religion in the past has also been decided along these lines. How has religion been able to maintain an edge amidst innumerable temptations to assimilate to the status quo? It seems that joining people and the divine in the grassroots struggles has kept alternative forms of religion alive. Alternative religion has been deeply shaped, for instance, through the efforts of a St. Francis who sought to reconnect the dominant church with the poor of the Middle Ages, through taking a stand with the peasants of early modernity that shaped Protestant reformers like Thomas Müntzer, and through the experiences of the African slaves in the United States, shaping both alternative Christianity and alternative Islam.[15] These movements have been so powerful that some of their traditions are still used in worship today, from Francis' prayer to the spirituals and the gospel hymns.

The close relationship between labor and religion is not a new idea but goes back to the origins of the Abrahamic religions. Slightly over a century ago, even mainline churches in the United States had the good sense to support the concerns of working people in the fights against child labor, for the eight-hour workday and the weekend, for the respect of women at work, and for collective bargaining.[16] Today, the official documents of many mainline denominations still support collective bargaining, but only a small percentage of members are even aware of this. What might religion have learned in these efforts to support labor? Did the God worshipped by these religions look different than the God of capitalism, whose main goal is the maximization of profit?

The future of religion may depend on whether it manages to develop an edge or whether it continues to accommodate to the status quo. Today this edge shapes up perhaps nowhere more clearly than in the relation of religion and labor. After a seminar on religion and labor with the statewide Texas AFL-CIO, a young organizer asked whether I was suggesting that labor should begin to lobby religion, just like it was lobbying politics. A better way to phrase this concern might be to talk about organizing religion: people of faith—many of which are working people—can pull together and organize so that religion can reclaim its edge and recover some of its most powerful traditions. How else are we going to prevent the dominant powers from continuing to shape religion in their image?

15. See Raboteau, *Slave Religion*. Recall that the Nation of Islam was founded in the 1930s, still under the impression of the ongoing struggles of African Americans.

16. See Fones-Wolf, *Trade Union Gospel*.

Labor Radicalized by Religion

Just as labor can help us rediscover and reclaim the edge of religion, religion can help us rediscover and reclaim the edge of labor. This is not merely a matter of revitalizing labor unions, just like merely revitalizing existing religious communities would be missing the point. What would it take to reclaim the significance, the energy, and the power of labor? How would this be linked to reclaiming the significance, the energy, and the power of religion?

None of this can happen when religion is treated like a cheap date for labor organizing. Religion needs to be more than a place where labor organizers can recruit and mobilize warm bodies or "rent a collar," as the saying goes. To begin with, religious traditions can provide important resources that help clarify the importance of labor and class at a time when these topics have become taboo. Next, religions can help generate a kind of critical thinking by asking questions about what really matters in life. In these ways, religions can help question the dominant powers of the age and identify alternative powers.

Production—still the basis for the accumulation of profit in the capitalist economy—may serve as an example for what is at stake. When viewed from the perspective of labor and religion, the perspective of production changes: Productive labor matters not just in terms of profit but in terms of the actual contributions that working people make to the community, shaping history from the bottom up. This perspective is supported by religious traditions that remind us that God stands with working people in the exodus from Egypt and, in Christianity, becomes human as a member of the working class.

Abrahamic Perspectives on Labor

Religion, and the Abrahamic traditions in particular, can provide a broader perspective for labor and the labor movement. Note that refusing to address religion does not mean it will stop interfering with labor and wither away; it means that religion will be used in service to the dominant powers and the corporations, as it often is.[17]

---

17. "When people experience sociopsychological strain, but lack the cultural or theological resources to make sense of it, they turn to the predominant ideology" (Bloomquist, *Dream Betrayed*, 47).

In many of the Abrahamic religious traditions, the view from the perspective of working people is not only enlightening, but indispensable. For example, the legacy of Moses, shared in different ways by Judaism, Christianity, and Islam cannot be conceived without his solidarity with the Hebrew slaves in Egypt. The liberation from Egypt is deeply anchored in all three Abrahamic traditions. The legacy of Jesus cannot be conceived without his solidarity with working people of his own time and which drew the ire of status quo religion. The legacy of Muhammad is likewise tied to a concern for the wellbeing of the working people of his time, many of whom were being defrauded in the transition from a tribal to a mercantile society where traders gathered substantial fortunes at the expense of the masses.

Core religious holidays of the Abrahamic religions may demonstrate what is at stake. Judaism's celebration of the Passover, for instance, is an annual reminder of the liberation from slavery in Egypt. Few other religious rituals are as strongly grounded in an act of liberation. This liberation is not merely a spiritual matter but affects everything, including economics, politics, community, and personal relationships. The Passover begins with the Seder, a ritual meal during which the story of the exodus from Egypt is retold. If religion is understood in terms of people's daily lives, it is not hard to see the many connections of this struggle to the struggle of working people today. Exploitation and oppression are still real-life experiences, as are stories of liberation. These connections are made explicit today especially in the so-called "Labor Seders" organized by the Jewish Labor Committee, which serve as reminders that the struggle for liberation is ongoing. The following parallels between ancient times and today are highlighted: persecution, oppressive taskmasters, impossible work demands, work quotas, and a struggle for freedom.[18]

In Christian traditions, Christmas is a holiday deeply connected with work and labor. In the birth of Christ, God chose to become a day laborer in construction who would have known the realities of labor firsthand. This arrangement was certainly not the most advantageous for the spread of any dominant religious message, and so it appears to be more than a historical accident. Why make a spectacular announcement of this birth to lower working-class shepherds—sending the heavenly choir

---

18. See the concerns expressed in the Jewish Labor Committee Passover Haggadah, Third Edition: Spring 2002. On the web: https://org2.salsalabs.com/o/5483/images/onlinehaggadah2014.pdf/. See also Jews United for Justice (http://jufj.org/content/labor-seder), now also augmented by a Social Justice Seder and a Racial Justice Seder.

of angels no less—rather than to the upper crust of the country, including the high priests and the vassal kings (Luke 2:7–10)? The symbols of Christmas, including shepherds and sheep, are not romantic adornments of a mystical event. They serve as reminders of God's unflinching solidarity with working people. And so it appears that even the angels join in solidarity with working people. In this spirit, the common critiques of consumerism leveled around Christmastime need to be redirected: rather than blaming consumers, what about challenging those who fuel consumerism?

In Islam, the month of Ramadan mandates fasting, observed for twenty-nine or thirty days in a row, from dawn to sunset. Ramadan is the commemoration of the first revelation of the Qur'an given to the prophet Muhammad and a time of increased self-discipline, prayer, and charity (the latter two are added to fasting, resulting in three of the five pillars of Islam). One interpretation of fasting during Ramadan is that it helps the faithful experience what it might feel like to be poor and to be in solidarity with the poor. Empathy and support for the poor is not merely another moral commandment in Islam—it is tied to the heart of faith because it reflects the will of God. Muslims continue to work during Ramadan, as balance between worship and work is encouraged by the Prophet, yet the celebration of Ramadan can inspire resistance to the capitalist ethos of limitless growth and the infinite accumulation of profits.[19]

The celebrations of Passover, Christmas, and Ramadan each teach important lessons about God's solidarity with exploited working people, through acts of liberation from enslavement (Passover), acts of identification with the working class (Christmas), and acts of solidarity with the poor and resistance to limitless profit (Ramadan). Moreover, these three major religious celebrations can provide safe spaces for exploring alternative ways of life both in the imagination and in practice. In the rituals of Passover, Christmas, and Ramadan, religion is public, pushing beyond the narrow boundaries of what is commonly considered the "sacred" and working towards the transformation of the world. The solidarity with and among working people that develops here is strengthened rather than undercut by the diversity of religious expression and—by the same token—reminds us of the necessity to incorporate the related struggles along the lines of race, ethnicity, gender, and sexuality. The result is a move from minority politics to a different kind of majority

---

19. See, for instance, Ramadan, *Radical Reform*, 239.

politics, where the majority can resist exploitation and oppression while maintaining its diversity.

Justice

One of the key theological terms in the Abrahamic religions is justice, even though this is often overlooked or even repressed. Even working people seem to identify religion with charity rather than justice. The notion of justice in the Abrahamic traditions contradicts the meaning of justice in capitalist societies. According to capitalist economist Friedrich von Hayek, for instance, justice is defined as "the fair and impartial application of legal, moral and perhaps customary rules."[20] One of the fundamental premises of capitalism is that all participants in the market are equal. This is evidently not the case, however, in the real world. There is a substantial difference between large and small participants in the market, as the largest corporations have a significantly stronger position than smaller corporations or even workers. The key problem is that justice defined as fairness is unable to deal with situations of grave power differentials.

Alternative perspectives on justice emerge from those who lack power in the current situation, like workers, small business owners, and the growing masses of those who cannot find a job or who lack job security. Here is a significant parallel to the Abrahamic religious traditions, which also derive from the perspective of people under pressure. In these traditions, God is not neutral like Lady Justice, the Roman goddess who is traditionally portrayed with a blindfold, and a pair of scales and a sword in each hand. In situations of grave power differentials, divine neutrality amounts not to justice but to injustice. As Farid Esack, a South African Muslim liberation theologian has pointed out, neutrality or objectivity in the context of oppression is a sin according to the Qur'an.[21]

In the Jewish traditions on which Christianity and Islam are building, justice means not being neutral but being in solidarity with those who experience injustice and taking the sides of those who have been marginalized and excluded from the community. In many texts of the Hebrew Bible, for instance, justice refers to a covenant, that is, to a relationship between God and humanity initiated by God. This relationship

---

20. Hayek, *Fatal Conceit*, 116–17.
21. Esack, *Qur'an, Liberation and Pluralism*, 106.

is expressed in terms of God's faithfulness, which implies God's special concern for those pushed to the margins and excluded by some who are under the mistaken impression that their way of life is favored by God (or who simply don't care).[22] In the New Testament, Jesus often takes the sides of the oppressed over and against the oppressors (see, for instance, his biting critique of dominant groups like the ones made up by certain Pharisees in Matt 23:1–36). In Islam, the Qur'an expresses a similar concern when it gives the following advice: "And if two factions among the believers should fight, then make settlement between the two. But if one of them oppresses the other, then fight against the one that oppresses until it returns to the ordinance of Allah (49:9)."[23] In sum, Judaism, Christianity, and Islam all share special concerns for the oppressed.

What the Abrahamic notions of justice have in common is their focus on community and solidarity, the latter a term that resonates with the labor movement. The Hebrew verb *sdq* (to be just) means to be faithful to the community that was established by the covenant with God.[24] The Greek term *dikaiosyne* (justice or righteousness) as used in the New Testament, also reflects this emphasis on communal relationship, and justice tends to include both the relations between human beings and the relation to God.[25] In Islam, likewise, justice (the Arab terms for justice, *quist* and '[set ayin]*adl*, are used interchangeably in the Qur'an) is defined in relation to the divine (as a witness to Allah)[26] and has implications for how people treat each other (Qur'an 4:135). As Jewish scholar Aryeh Cohen points out from a Rabbinic Jewish perspective, the fundamental problem is the unequal relationship between worker and employer, which is never merely a private matter since the community has an interest in it as well.[27] In sum, the restoration of relationships with the oppressed is not merely another social issue or the moral consequence of religion; rather, the quality of religion itself, and the quality of the relationship with the divine, is closely tied to the restoration of relationships among the people.

These insights are helpful in various ways. First, rather than talking about justice in terms of a grand idea, particular experiences of injustice

---

22. See, for example, Marshall, *Beyond Retribution*.
23. Qur'an 49:9, Sahih International Translation, on the web at Quran.com.
24. Koch, "sdq, gemeinschaftstreu/heilvoll sein."
25. Lührmann, "Gerechtigkeit III."
26. Esack, *Qur'an, Liberation and Pluralism*, 103.
27. Cohen, *Justice in the City*, 120, 123.

and power have to be examined. Who wins and who loses in a particular situation? What would it take to turn things around in this particular relationship? Note that notions of fairness and balance are unlikely to be strong enough to resist injustice that has become institutionalized, and so more engaged notions of justice are required.

Second, injustice in relation to labor issues under capitalism is tied to the dramatic differences in the valuation of productivity. Working people, both blue and white collar, make hundreds of times less than upper-level managers. Is this really just? Wages cut precisely at a time when workers are becoming more productive all the time, how can this be justified? Justice in this case will lead to a revaluation of the productivity of workers and to a reconstruction of the class-based relationships between those who work and those who manage.

Third, justice that deals with the specific injustices experienced by working people requires rethinking solidarity in the face of distorted economic relations. The experience of economic pressures tend to weld together people who differ along the lines of race, ethnicity, gender, and sexuality. The labor movement cannot function without such solidarity, and neither can religion. Religious people could be ahead of the game if they realize that distortions of economic relations—class struggle waged not from the bottom but from the top—are a central issues in the sacred texts of the Tanakh, Bible, and Qur'an, not merely as a social or ethical issues, but also in terms of the distortion of our relations to each other and to the divine.

Taking Sides

These reflections on justice point to one of the most interesting convergences between the traditions of labor and the Abrahamic religions: an understanding of the need to take sides in situations of injustice and grave power differentials. Taking sides does not have to mean narrow partisanship or mindless radicalism, it means to support the wellbeing of the 99 percent who have to work for a living starting with those at the very bottom, leaving open the possibility that the 1 percent at the top will see the light and join in this project as well. Some may consider it impossible for 1 percenters to take sides and join the movement, but this has happened time and again.[28]

28. See, for example, the Occupy Wall Street movement, where 1 percenters did in fact join the 99 percent: http://westandwiththe99percent.tumblr.com/.

The labor movement's tradition of taking sides has waxed and waned through the decades. Many working people today assume that taking sides is unnecessary and that it is possible to make everybody happy. As a result, they try to please the company by working extra hard, giving up vacation, and never speaking up, while hoping for the best. On the whole, however, the fortunes of working people are hardly on the rise, and individuals will never be able to balance the growing inequality of power. Even representatives of labor unions have at times forgotten that it is necessary to take sides, instead searching for middle roads between workers and employers. Yet, as the Abrahamic religious traditions and the experiences of most working people in recent times, remind us, there is no safe middle ground.

In this situation, religion can provide some unexpected inspiration. As we have seen, in the Abrahamic traditions, God engages in the struggles of the world on the side of the oppressed, challenging the oppressors. Any god who sides with the dominant powers is an idol and not the God of Abraham, Moses, Jesus, and Muhammad.[29] This insight is expressed in different ways. In Islam, God's Otherness is a central theme.[30] This means that God is not envisioned in terms of human beings. In Judaism and Christianity, on the other hand, God is often portrayed as a worker, although there are also Jewish and Christian traditions where God is seen as different from humanity. The parallels, however, should not be overlooked: in all three religions, God is not easily envisioned in terms of the ruling class, although efforts to domesticate God in this way start in the sacred texts themselves.

Some of the Jewish and Christian images of God as worker can help us deepen these insights. God is envisioned, for instance, as construction worker, builder, craftsman, metal worker, potter, or garment maker. The latter two images also challenge gender stereotypes because in the early history of Israel these were mostly the work of women. God is also envisioned as gardener or farmer, watering plants and sowing. God is depicted as shepherd, and sheep herding is common in all three Abrahamic religions as a marginal and less valued job. Elsewhere, God is spoken of as a tentmaker—a profession that was looked down upon by Greek and

---

29. The critique of idolatry is one of the central concerns of Ellis, *Toward a Jewish Theology of Liberation*, 163–76, 205, developed in conversation with Christian liberation theologies.

30. Dabashi, *Islamic Liberation Theology*, 254.

Roman elites.[31] These images can help us value work and workers more, encouraging us to take sides in particular with those among the working 99 percent who are often discounted and belittled.

In Islam, the need to take the side of the oppressed is equally clear. In the Qur'an 4:75, the faithful are asked this question: "And what is [the matter] with you that you fight not in the cause of Allah and [for] the oppressed among men, women, and children who say, 'Our Lord, take us out of this city of oppressive people and appoint for us from Yourself a protector and appoint for us from Yourself a helper?'" The divine cause is to take sides in the fight against oppression, and the faithful are expected to be part of it. This fight is not a minor matter. Khali Ur Rehman, Chairman of the All Pakistan Federation of Labor, argues that Islam helps us understand that exploitation and usurpation are the causes of all of the world's problems.[32]

God-talk shifts sides here. Too often have dominant religions claimed God to be on their side in order to shore up their power. Labor can learn from these mistakes, but one might wonder whether working people are committing the same mistakes when they claim that God is on their side? History shows that we should not presuppose too quickly that God supports certain causes over others. Nevertheless, not discussing where God is found does not solve the problem, as those who refuse to take sides altogether typically endorse the dominant status quo without being aware of it. From the Abrahamic traditions one might learn that neutrality is not an option, as any vacuum will quickly be filled by the dominant forces—even when it comes to God-talk and certainly when it comes to movement politics.

In sum, three things ought to be clear: First, God is never on the side of those who exploit others, no matter how respectable they appear. Second, God's concern for the community demands that a stand be taken against whatever destroys it. Images of God's judgment, common in all three Abrahamic religions, are not bad news but good news for the exploited and oppressed. Third, the Abrahamic traditions insist that God is at work in the world, in places where we least expect it. That God is working alongside working people is significant, even though it does not mean that working people own God or control God. There are lessons here for the labor movement that will need to be explored further.

31. See Banks, *God the Worker*.
32. Rehman, *Concept of Labor in Islam*, 59, 60: "[Islam] tells the capitalist and the wealthy, that all they have is in due to their workers."

Conclusions

At a time when the future of religion is open, the future of the labor movement is open as well. Neither religion nor labor should be limited to particular organizations. If religion is the quest for something bigger that we cannot control as individuals or institutions, so is labor. It might be argued that everybody who works for a living is part of labor in some form or fashion—expanding the notion of the working class—even though not everybody realizes this and even though the current legal situation in the United States obscures this.

It is no surprise that labor unions, like most religious institutions, are hesitant to challenge the dominant system. It is much easier to critique moral or legal transgressions, including wage theft, unfair labor practices, or clear violations of safety regulations; easier also to denounce malpractice in business like embezzlement or noncompliance. The fundamental problem in capitalism, however, is not moral or legal transgressions or malpractice; the problem is that corporations are responsible for the maximization of profits. As a result, they are accountable only to their stockholders and not to their workers. And a time-honored way to maximize profits is to cut working people's wages and benefits, and to reduce whatever power they might have over themselves and their work. This now happens even in organizations like universities, churches, and community groups that were once considered off limits. In this climate, labor and religion have the potential to become allies in dealing with these systemic issues, and their futures depend on how well they are able do this.

At the same time, labor and religion can become allies in very practical matters. Labor can help religious people understand the importance of organizing, which is essential because religious communities will hardly change from the top down. But neither will labor. Religion also has ways to get people involved. In what seems to be a surprising turn, studies have found that "religious organizations are three to four times more likely to mobilize a person politically than a union."[33] This is not about party politics but about joining the struggle for the common good. Moreover, in both labor and religious communities working people are able to prove themselves in leadership roles: they can practice public speaking, preside over meetings, and negotiate with official representatives, developing civic skills and technique. This development of skills and technique needs to be tied to a deeper awareness of why all of this is

---

33. Snarr, *All You That Labor*, 151.

important, not limited to the mind but incorporating the heart and bodies as well. This is what religion can do, and what it has done throughout the ages. In the United States, neither the abolitionist movement, nor the Civil Rights movement, and not even the labor movement can be envisioned without the contributions of religion and its abilities to shape people holistically.

The most important issue of all, however, is the question of power. Too often, both in past history and at present, leaders in both labor and religion assume that there is only one sort of power that will be successful, namely dominant power that operates from the top down. Some have wielded such power very well and with great success. The problem is, however, that in these cases both labor and religion often assimilated to the status quo. Union leaders, clergy, and even images of God adapted to the model of the powerful CEO. In these cases, both labor and religion gained power by giving up the ability to challenge dominant systems and to make a real difference.

As we have seen, many strands of the Abrahamic religious traditions promote alternative images of power. In these traditions, the true leaders do not shape up in the image of the "strong man" (usually white and straight as well); rather, leaders shape up in relations of solidarity from within the working majority. This is true even for images of God, which need to be rethought from within the movement. Ultimately, the power of the people always differs from that of the elites, and both labor and religion may have a brighter future if they manage to embrace, pursue, and develop this sort of power. The good news—of labor and of religion—is that some of this is already happening.

Bibliography

Al-Qur'an. https://quran.com.

Banks, Robert. *God the Worker: Journeys into the Mind, Heart, and Imagination of God*. Valley Forge, PA: Judson, 1994.

Bethge, Eberhard. *Dietrich Bonhoeffer: A Biography*. Rev. ed. Translated by Eric Mosbacher. Revised and edited by Victoria J. Barnett. Minneapolis: Fortress, 2000.

Bloomquist, Karen L. *The Dream Betrayed: Religious Challenge of the Working Class*. Minneapolis: Fortress, 1990.

Cohen, Aryeh. *Justice in the City: An Argument from the Sources of Rabbinic Judaism*. New Perspectives in Post-Rabbinic Judaism. Brighton, MA: Academic Studies, 2012.

Dabashi, Hamid. *Islamic Liberation Theology: Resisting the Empire*. New York: Routledge, 2008.

Davis, Korin, et al. "Faith in Equality: Economic Justice and the Future of Religious Progressives." Brookings (blog). November 30, 2001. https://www.brookings.edu/research/faith-in-equality-economic-justice-and-the-future-of-religious-progressives/.

Ellis, Marc H. *Toward a Jewish Theology of Liberation: The Challenge of the 21st Century.* Waco, TX: Baylor University Press, 2004.

Esack, Farid. *Qurán, Liberation & Pluralism: An Islamic Perspective of Interreligious Solidarity against Oppression.* Rockport, MA: Oneworld, 1997.

Fones-Wolf, Ken. *Trade Union Gospel: Christianity and Labor in Industrial Philadelphia, 1865–1915.* Philadelphia: Temple University Press, 1989.

Hayek, Friedrich A. von. *The Fatal Conceit: The Errors of Socialism.* London: Routledge, 1988.

Khalīlurraḥman. *The Concept of Labour in Islam.* Karachi: Arif, 1995.

Koch, Klaus."*sdq*, gemeinschaftstreu/heilvoll sein." In *Theologisches Handwörterbuch zum Alten Testament.* Edited by Ernst Jenni and Claus Westermann. Zürich: Theologischer Verlag, 1971.

Kruse, Kevin Michael. *One Nation under God: How Corporate America Invented Christian America.* New York: Basic Books, 2015.

Kwok, Pui Lan, and Joerg Rieger. *Occupy Religion: Theology of the Multitude.* Lanham, MD: Rowman & Littlefield, 2012.

Lührmann, Dieter. "Gerechtigkeit III." In *Theologisches Handwörterbuch zum Alten Testament.* Edited by Ernst Jenni and Claus Westermann. Zürich: Theologischer Verlag, 1971.

Marshall, Christopher D. *Beyond Retribution: A New Testament Vision for Justice, Crime, and Punishment.* Auckland: Lime Grove House, 2001.

Masuzawa, Tomoko. *The Invention of World Religions: Or, How European Universalism Was Preserved in the Language of Pluralism.* Chicago: University of Chicago Press, 2005.

Raboteau, Albert J. *Slave Religion: The "Invisible Institution" in the Antebellum South.* New York: Oxford University Press, 1978.

Ramadan, Tariq. *Radical Reform: Islamic Ethics and Liberation.* New York: Oxford University Press, 2009.

Rieger, Joerg. *Christ and Empire: From Paul to Postcolonial Times.* Minneapolis: Fortress, 2007.

Rieger, Joerg, and Rosemarie Henkel-Rieger. *Unified We Are a Force: How Faith and Labor Can Overcome America's Inequalities.* St. Louis: Chalice, 2016.

Snarr, C. Melissa. *All You That Labor: Religion and Ethics in the Living Wage Movement.* New York: New York University Press, 2011.

"We Are the 1 Percent: We Stand with the 99 Percent." https://westandwiththe99percent.tumblr.com/.

Weber, Max. *The Protestant Ethic and the Spirit of Capitalism.* 2nd ed. Translated by Talcott Parsons. London: Allen & Unwin, 1976.

Zweig, Michael. *The Working Class Majority: America's Best Kept Secret.* London: IRL, 2000.

Section I

History of Class and Labor

2

Christianity and Socialism in China
Allies or Strange Bedfellows

Kwok Pui-lan

Introduction

In 2018, President Donald Trump initiated the trade war against China. He accused China of unfair trade practices, theft of intellectual property, and subsidizing of businesses by the government. After trade deal negotiations with China broke down in early May of 2019, Trump raised tariffs on $200 billion Chinese goods to 25 percent and threatened a technological cold war against Chinese tech companies.[1] Trump is concerned about the growing trade deficit with China, which has increased to $419 billion in 2018.[2] China has vowed to retaliate, and the escalation of trade friction between the world's two largest economies would affect world trade and government relationships.

Since its reform and liberalization in 1978, China has experienced phenomenal economic growth and lifted 800 million people out of

1. Lynch, "How the U.S.-China Trade War Became a Conflict."
2. Amadeo, "US Trade Deficit."

poverty. Chinese leaders called their economic system "socialism with Chinese characteristics," while pundits from outside have called this "state capitalism." The Beijing Consensus, or the Chinese economic model, has been hailed as an alternative to the Washington Consensus of market-friendly policies promoted by the International Monetary Fund, the World Bank, and the US Treasury. This Chinese model has been held up as a model of economic development for countries in the Global South.

The rise of China and its introduction of a market economy has changed our traditional views about socialism. It raises questions about the globalization of production, the plight of migrant workers, the concentration of wealth, and the future of organized labor. How should theologians and ethicists respond to the developments in China that will shape the politics and economics of the twenty-first century? What has been the experience of Chinese churches that have lived through momentous social changes? This chapter will focus on China as a case study, while drawing broader social and ethical implications.

Introduction of Marxist Thought to China

The year 2019 was the 100th anniversary of the May Fourth Movement in China. On May 4, 1919, students in Beijing took to the streets to protest against the Treaty of Versailles, agreed upon at the Paris Peace Conference to end World War I. The Allied Powers decided to transfer former German concessions in China's Shandong province to Japan, instead of returning them to China. Protests soon broke out in many cities, and demonstrators denounced Western imperialism and the Chinese government's weakness in protecting its territorial integrity. Merchants and workers in Shanghai and other cities went on strike in support of the students and boycotted Japanese goods. The May Fourth Movement criticized feudalistic and Confucian values and exalted Western ideas, especially science and democracy, to strengthen China in the face of foreign powers.

During this time, Chinese intellectuals introduced ideas such as liberalism, pragmatism, nationalism, anarchism, and socialism to China. One of the iconoclastic intellectual revolutionaries was Chen Duxiu (1879–1942), a professor of Peking University, who had started a monthly magazine *Xinqingnian* (New Youth) in 1915 to advocate for social reform. Li Dazhao (1889–1927) started a study group at the University and caught Chen's attention in 1919. *Xinqingnian* began publishing articles on Marxism and its philosophy and achieved wider readership because of the magazine's popularity. In 1921, Chen, Li, and other revolutionary leaders formed the Chinese Communist Party in Shanghai, and Chen was elected as its leader.

In the 1920s and 1930s, Chinese capitalists established light industries in the cities, which attracted a growing number of workers. For example, some rural women near Shanghai left their villages to work in the cotton mills in the city.[3] The working conditions were poor and workers did not have job security. These Chinese industries could not compete with foreign enterprises with more capital and better machinery. Chinese workers were exploited by the Chinese bourgeoisie, who in turn were oppressed by Western capitalists. Workers' protests broke out periodically and they demanded better working conditions and fairer compensation.[4] Some joined the Chinese Communist Party.

Following classic Marxist theory, Chen Duxiu saw the organization of the Chinese proletariat as key and made building the labor movement a priority, leading to the establishment of China's trade unions. His ideas conflicted with those of Mao Zedong, whose social survey in his native Hunan Province showed that the future of the Communist movement laid in organizing the peasants, who comprised the majority of the Chinese population.[5] As it turned out, Mao's strategy proved to be successful in the long run.

Radical intellectuals influenced by Marxist and liberal thoughts attacked religion as superstitious and singled out Christianity for its complicity with imperialism. In the 1920s, an anti-Christian movement broke out, attacking Christian missions as serving the interest of Western powers. Protesters wanted to curtail the influences of Christian mission schools, which were seen as undermining the native culture.[6] During a time when Chinese intellectuals harbored doubts about their Chinese heritage, Marxism was critical of Western imperialism despite coming from the West, and thus attracted the attention of radical intellectuals and activists.

3. Honig, *Sisters and Strangers*.
4. Tso, *Labor Movement in China*.
5. Mao, "Report on an Investigation."
6. Yip, *Religion, Nationalism, and Chinese Students*.

In the midst of rising anti-Christian sentiment, Chinese theologians began the process of indigenization to show that Christianity was relevant to the Chinese situation. An important leader was Wu Yaozong (1893–1979), a secretary of the YMCA, who argued that Christianity could not be concerned only with the salvation of souls. He wrote, "A true revival of the Church will come only when it has awakened to its social task and begins to tackle it fearlessly and sacrificially."[7] Wu saw that Jesus's personality could serve as a model and impetus for the social reconstruction of China. Inspired by Jesus's love and sacrifice on the cross, Wu emphasized pacifism and non-violence.[8]

In the 1930s, Wu became more critical of idealist Christianity and was radicalized. After Japan invaded China in 1937 and the future of China was at stake, Wu no longer thought that a spiritual reconstruction would be sufficient and believed that only a social revolution could save China. He saw that the agricultural sector was in a chaotic situation and that mining and industries were poorly developed. Workers were exploited and the people suffered from government corruption and high inflation. He became attracted to Marxism because Marxism provided critical tools to analyze the world's economic situation and because it advocated radical change, which China badly needed. He also changed his pacifist position and came to believe that the use of force would be acceptable during social revolution. He argued that although Jesus's Gospel emphasized peace, Jesus also taught about justice and confronted social evil, which ultimately led to his death. Wu's thinking on Marxism and social struggle anticipated Liberation Theology, which would emerge decades later.[9]

Wu was critical of the social teachings of Reinhold Niebuhr (1892–1971). In the 1920s, Niebuhr was attracted to pacifism and socialism and was sympathetic toward the working-class, especially the plight of auto workers in Detroit. In the 1930s, however, he changed his views and embraced a neo-orthodox Christian realist position, which emphasized the sinfulness of humanity, the competition of interests, and a balance of power. Niebuhr's Christian realism led him to criticize the pretense of all human institutions and the utopianism of socialism.[10] After World War

7. Wu, "China's Challenges to Christianity," 10.
8. Ng, *Jidujiao*, 80–81.
9. Ng, *Jidujiao*, 106.
10. Niebuhr, *Moral Man and Immoral Society*; *Interpretation of Christian Ethics*; and *Nature and Destiny of Man*, vol. 1.

II, Niebuhr supported American efforts to confront Soviet Communism and became an influential public thinker on foreign affairs during the Cold War era.

Wu pointed out that Niebuhr's emphasis on human depravity and the evil of human institutions, including Communism, led people to passively accept the status quo and support capitalism and imperialism.[11] China had been under the exploitation of capitalist powers, and Niebuhr's Christian realism spoke merely for American interests. After the People's Republic of China was established in 1949, Wu was instrumental in rallying Chinese Christian leaders to draft a Christian Manifesto to call upon the church to sever all ties to Western imperialism. He became a leader of the Three-Self Patriotic Movement of the Protestant Churches in China (TSPM), which advocated self-governance, self-support, self-propagation, and cutting ties with foreign missions.

The New China and Change of Production

In the 1950s, the new Chinese government initiated a series of social reforms to change the semi-feudal and semi-colonial country into a Communist society. It used class struggle as a strategy to take back power from the landlord class and capitalists. The means of production, including farms, factories, transportation, and communication, became either state-owned or collectively-owned. From 1950–1953, the land reform abolished landownership by the landlord class and transferred ownership to the peasants. In some places, the land reform was executed with more force than it called for, leading to the mistreatment and execution of landlords. In the process of collectivization, the peasants were organized into mutual aid teams. Later, these lower levels of cooperatives merged to form huge people's communes. Each commune was organized into progressively larger units: production teams, production brigades, and the commune itself. Collectivization brought a lot of problems and after the economic difficulties during the Great Leap Forward (1958–1962), the average size of the communes was reduced, private lots were returned to farmers, and wages were paid according to the work performed.

The Chinese industrial sector was severely damaged from the war with Japan and the civil war between the Nationalists and Communists. To promote industrial growth, the government brought in Soviet advisors

---

11. Ng, *Jidujiao*, 119.

and established large-scale capital-intensive Soviet-assisted projects. This led to an increase in the pace of industrialization and substantial growth in the gross domestic product.[12] Factory and service workers were organized into work units. Attention was paid to the redistribution of income and implementation of a set of egalitarian policies. For example, the wages of employees in the state sector were set nationally and did not vary with labor productivity. However, the Great Leap Forward undid many of the gains because widespread famine and poverty could not support industrial growth. Workers did not have incentives to increase productivity because there were not many material benefits to do so. The political turmoil during the Cultural Revolution (1966–1976) further stunted industrial growth, as workers had to participate in political campaigns and could not continue with their regular work.

Although the Chinese Constitution guarantees freedom of religious belief, the Communist government espouses atheism and has been skeptical of religion. Depending on the party line of the time, the government adopted different policies toward religion. At times, the government was antagonistic toward religion and suppressed religious activities. For example, foreign missionaries were expelled in the 1950s and Christian missions had to sever their ties to Christians outside of China. During the Cultural Revolution, churches were shut down and pastors were sent to work in farms or factories. But at other times, the policy toward religion was more tolerant and relaxed, as the leaders recognized that religion is a complex phenomenon and cannot be easily eradicated. Many religious believers are law-abiding citizens and contribute to society. In the post-Mao era, the government aimed to unite believers and non-believers for the common goal of building a modernized socialist country.[13]

Chinese Christian leaders responded to the Communist revolution and drastic social changes in diverse ways. For some of them, Communism and Christianity are incompatible since Communism is anti-religion and atheistic. At times, the Communist government has suppressed religion and exerted surveillance over religious people's behavior and activities. Others were appalled by the continuous class and social struggles, the use of violence, the disregard of human rights, and the havoc wreaked by the Cultural Revolution. Some of the leaders who refused to support the

12. Hirst, "A Brief History of China's Economic Growth."

13. For a discussion of the important document, "The Basic Standpoint" issued in 1982, see Ting, "The Church and the State," in his *God Is Love*, 562–75. See also Laliberté, "Contemporary Issues," 192–201.

government or join the TSPM, both the Protestant and Catholic, were imprisoned. An important leader was Wang Mingdao, the evangelical pastor of Christian Tabernacle in Beijing. Wang firmly believed in the separation of church and state and his church had always been independent of Western aid or connection. He saw the TSPM as a tool to bring churches under state control and refused to join. He was imprisoned for many years because of his stance against the government.[14]

Other Christian leaders saw that Christianity could function in a socialist society and worked with the government. For several decades, Bishop Ding Guangxun (K. H. Ting, 1915–2012) has influenced the development of the church in China. Ding worked as a YMCA student secretary and in the World Student Christian Federation in Geneva before he was consecrated an Anglican bishop in 1955. He became the principal of Nanjing Union Theological Seminary and lost his government positions during the Cultural Revolution. When the churches reopened in the late 1970s, Ding became the President of the China Christian Council and the head of the TSPM. He said that as Christianity spread, it adapted to local situations and "only a church with a Chinese selfhood could expect to gain its right to be heard by our fellow Chinese."[15]

Ding was influenced by Wu Yaozong, his predecessor as the leader of the TSPM. It was Wu who inspired Ding to develop his Christian faith and social commitments in new ways.[16] During the period of anticolonial struggles in Asia in the 1950s, Ding wrote that the church had to be concerned about human suffering and social justice. Working in the YMCA and serving as a pastor in Shanghai, Ding had first-hand experience of poverty and exploitation of the people by imperialism, capitalism, and feudalism. He later wrote that "what *is* new to many Chinese Christians is the awareness that people are not only sinners but also sinned against. The task of evangelism is not only to convince persons of their sin but to stand alongside those who are sinned against in our society."[17] Ding found inspiration in the person and teaching of Jesus. He said that Jesus did not simply show pity or condescension to the poor or give alms to the hungry, Jesus identified with the poor and those dehumanized by the unjust systems. Ding argued that the Communists are also concerned

14. Giles, "The Fall and Rise."
15. Ting, "A Wide Door," in Ting, *God Is Love*, 470.
16. Wickeri and Wickeri, "Introduction," x.
17. Ting, "The Sinned Against (1979)," 73.

about social injustice and evil, and Christians can work with them to build a better society.

Following Marx, many Communists regard religion as the opium of the people. But Ding noted that after the Cultural Revolution, party officials adopted a less dogmatic view and recognized the rootedness of religion in the mass of the people, its strong affinity to ethnic minorities, its long history and international connection, and the complexity of each religious tradition.[18] Many people in China believe that "religion encourages goodness" and its ethical dimensions play a positive and supplementary role in society.[19] Ding noted that many Christians have been selected as advanced or model workers and respected by their friends and co-workers. Religious institutions have undergone considerable reforms in socialist China, and religion is no longer considered to be the enemy of the people, but should be seen as an intrinsic part of the socialist cultural legacy.[20]

As the leader of the Chinese Protestant church, Ding wanted to build "Christianity with Chinese socialist characteristics."[21] According to the Communist Party, no religious group could take a contradictory stand against the Party. Christianity in Communist China had to balance between the political and religious demands. It had to work with the government on the one hand and carve out a space for the church to continue its religious activities under socialist rule on the other. Ding exhorted Christians to love the church and love the country at the same time. He noted that most religious people are patriotic, law-abiding, and supportive of the socialist system. But illegal and counter-revolutionary activities disguised as religion, which threaten the national interests and the lives of people, should be opposed.

Ding felt that the Chinese church needed theological reconstruction rooted in the Chinese soil and addressing the social, cultural, and political contexts. Given that class struggle and the Cultural Revolution tore the society apart, Ding emphasized the importance of reconciliation. "God is love" was an important theme of Ding's theology. Jesus shows us that love is the very nature of God, and this love includes both believers and non-believers. Christians understand God's great love and they

---

18. Ting, "A Wide Door," in Ting, *God Is Love*, 472.
19. Ting, "Religion and Socialism?" in Ting, *God Is Love*, 533.
20. Ting, "Religion and Socialism," in Ting, *God Is Love*, 538.
21. Ting, "Retrospect and Prospect," 25–39.

should love and reconcile with other people, including non-Christians. For Ding, loving our neighbors and even our enemies is the Gospel that Christians need to preach in China.[22] Ding also emphasized the concept of the "Cosmic Christ." He wrote that Christ "is not just the crucified one on the cross, the only image that has meaning to many Christians. He is the one who sustains the universe by his word of power. He is the primacy over all creation. He exists before all things, and all things are held together in him."[23] Ding saw creation as inseparable from redemption and Christ's love not only for those in the church but for the whole cosmos—God's creation. Thus, Chinese Christians should look at God and Christ in broader terms and not focus on the distinction between believers and non-believers and the spiritual and the worldly. The notion of the Cosmic Christ points to God's love for all humankind and the world and that God and humanity are reconciled in Jesus Christ. This message of love and reconciliation is important to build a harmonious society in which people would respect one another.

Class and Labor in Contemporary China

Under Deng Xiaoping's leadership in 1978, China began a process of reform and opening to the outside. Deng was a pragmatist and opposed Maoist egalitarianism. Mao's communes were abolished, but people who lived in communal lands were allowed to farm collectively if they wanted to. Farms were leased to families and they could decide what to grow and could sell their surplus, after giving a certain amount of produce to the state, at the markets. Productivity increased as emphasis was placed on peasant initiative and incentives.

The industrial and manufacturing sectors were also reformed. In addition to state-owned industries, China allowed the establishment of privately-owned small businesses and joint ventures with foreign investment. Thousands of privately-owned small businesses came into being, which employed millions of workers. The owners and managers of these small businesses wanted to increase profits by providing incentives for workers to become more productive.[24] In the 1980s and 1990s, further

22. Ng, "Global Christianity," 67.
23. Ting, "My View of God," in Ting, *God Is Love*, 40.
24. "Reforms under Deng Xiaoping." For the development of Chinese economy since Deng, see Cai and Lin, *Zhongguo jingji* .

reforms were introduced, including the privatizing and contracting-out of much state-owned industry and the elimination of price controls and protection policies and regulations. The market economy allowed businesses to produce goods according to market demand and to set prices accordingly. The private sector grew rapidly and was responsible for much of China's economic growth. In 2001, China joined the World Trade Organization, further integrating the Chinese economy into the globalized market.

By 2018, when China celebrated the fortieth anniversary of its reform, China had been transformed from a poor country to one having around an 18 percent share of the world's economy.[25] Due to reform and modernization, the gross domestic product increased to $13.4 trillion in 2018.[26] This growth was largely due to China's army of migrant workers, who moved from rural areas to look for work in the cities. In 2018, China had 288 million migrant workers, and the urban population exceeded the rural in 2011.[27] As China became a manufacturing powerhouse, goods "made in China" began to flood consumer markets all over the world.

Nevertheless, the phenomenal economic growth and drastic changes of society have caused many social problems. The introduction of the private sector and market economy has created an entrepreneurial capitalist class that has amassed great wealth. The gap between the rich and the poor has widened, and income inequality has increased. In 2017, the top 1 percent owned a third of the country's wealth. There was also a huge gap between incomes of people in urban and rural areas. Urban residents in 2016 had an average per capita income of $4,864, about 2.72 times higher than that of people in rural areas.[28] Because of this income disparity, many people left their villages to find work in the cities, making up half of the China's urban workforce and account for half of the country's gross domestic product. These workers have traditionally gone to Beijing, Shanghai, and Shenzhen and the coastal cities, but more are now going to the interior where new opportunities are opening up. They work for low pay, often under unfavorable conditions, in factories, mines, construction sites, and on railroads and roads.[29] Chinese migrant work-

25. Diplomacy & Beyond Team, "China Celebrates."
26. "China GDP."
27. Zhou, "China's Army"; Simpson, "China's Urban Population."
28. Leng, "China's Dirty Little Secret."
29. "Migration."

ers are also sent to work on Chinese companies' construction contracts and in other companies in African and other countries. In 2017, Chinese official sources reported that about 200,000 Chinese workers were working in Africa.[30] Going from place to place for work, Chinese migrant workers leave their families and children under the care of grandparents and older people in the villages. Some of these children feel isolated and uncared for by their parents and develop learning and social problems.

China's economic growth has brought education and employment opportunities for women, but they benefit less than men from these gains. In the 1980s, female participation in the labor force was high, averaging around 80 percent, but by 2018, female workforce participation had dropped to 68.6 percent, only slightly higher than in the United States (66.1 percent). The restructuring of state-owned enterprises in the 1990s had negative consequences for women. In order to achieve efficiency and productivity, the privatization process caused the layoffs of low-skilled—often female—workers. The income gap between urban male and female workers increased from 15 percent in 1990 to 22 percent in 2018.[31] Because of gender discrimination, women are less likely to be promoted to managerial positions, and some of the job postings include requirements such as "men only" or "men preferred."

Labor disputes, strikes, and protests have been on the rise in China. As China's economic growth has slowed down in recent years, many manufacturers and service-oriented companies have tried to pay their workers less and cut benefits. Strikes have increased from fewer than 200 in 2011 to 1,256 in 2017. As manufacturing jobs have moved to the middle of the country, labor strikes happened increasingly in the central provinces. Labor strife is not only affecting the traditional manufacturing sector, as white-collar workers and new industries such as ecommerce and green tech are also facing labor struggles. The Communist party is supposed to represent the interest of workers, but the government has treated these labor strikes and disputes as threats to law and order. Labor activists were arrested and demonstrators were beaten by the police.[32]

President Trump ran for office accusing China of stealing US jobs and vowed to bring them back. But these jobs are not coming back because workers are paid much less in China and Southeast Asia, and whole

30. "Data: Chinese Workers in Africa."
31. "Do Women in China."
32. Thomlinson, "China's Communist Party."

supply chains cannot be easily relocated. As a result, Trump's policy has not helped the working class and their families in the United States. His cutting of the corporate tax rate in 2017 from 35 percent to 21 percent has benefited business owners and shareholders, while just 6 percent of the tax savings were spent on workers.[33] While corporate executives and hedge-fund managers saw their compensations skyrocket, wages for average workers in 2018 were up by 1.2 percent, just $9.11 a week after adjusting for inflation. Millions of workers are working longer for lower wages. Average workers in the United States earn less today than they made 43 years ago after adjusting for inflation.[34] Since taking office, Trump has not made any effort to increase the minimum wage, which is currently $7.25 per hour. His administration has pulled back from its promises to protect workers' rights, safety, and economic welfare, seeking to limit the power of unions instead.[35]

While Trump is pitting US workers against Chinese workers, it is clear that they are both exploited by the transnational capitalist class who can shift capital, production, and labor across national borders. Trump seemingly wants to start a new Cold War and to contain China, but today's Chinese economy is far from a socialist one, having been so integrated into the neoliberal economy. Therefore, workers in different parts of the world must organize locally and globally to demand a more responsible and accountable global economic system. Global networks of labor movements can exchange information, support one another, and share strategies and tactics for change.

It is noteworthy that Christianity has not declined but flourished in socialist China. The number of Protestants has increased a hundred times since the founding of the People's Republic of China in 1949, from about 700,000 to possibly as many as 70,000,000 (some have given even higher numbers). Sociologist Fenggang Yang argues that the market transition in China has contributed to the revivals of religion. First, people want to achieve wealth by praying to gods or seeking supernatural intervention. Second, religion provides a collective identity in the loss of job security and social protection. Christianity, especially, offers group belonging, bonding, and charismatic churches emphasize spiritual healing. Third, the government has restored temples, churches, and mosques to attract

---

33. Cary and Holmes, "Workers Barely Benefitted."
34. Sanders, "Trump's Economy."
35. "Trump's War."

tourism and goodwill from overseas. In the market economy, churches and religious organizations have more financial resources to provide religious materials and services.[36] In the past, churches have focused on evangelism and religious activities and were not so involved in society. Today some of the larger churches with financial resources, have begun to offer social programs, including projects to help migrant workers.

As the number of Christians and churches increased in China, seminaries and Bible schools were opened or expanded to meet the needs for trained persons in ministry. Since the 1980s, theological education has followed a "pastoral model," with the aim to train leaders with practical skills to lead faith communities. From 1998, there has been a shift toward a "theological model" to educate leaders who are able to undertake theological reflection and research. Increased emphasis has been put on theological reconstruction and the development of Chinese Christian theology.[37] In the past several years, the focus has been on the Sinicization of Christianity, including the development of Sinicized theology. Chinese church leader Gao Feng stated that the Chinese church cannot depend on Western theology and must develop its own contextual theological formulation. He writes, "Construction of a system of theological thought suitable to the real situation of the Chinese church and conducive to the healthy development of the church is crucial."[38]

Chinese theologians and ethicists have discussed social issues as a result of rapid changes brought by modernization and economic development. Yang Donglong comments on church, economics, and society in the context of modernization. He says that the church encourages Christians to take an active part in the economy and the Bible encourages believers to work hard. But it is important to remember that Christians cannot serve both God and Mammon. Yang says Christians often have to make difficult and complex moral choices in the competitive market economy and warns that the pursuit of wealth and greed may lead to moral decline.[39] Lin Manhong notes that corruption has become an important issue in society. She argues that Confucian ethical resources, especially the concept of shame, can contribute to the task of anti-corruption. She also draws from Buddhism and Christian Liberation

---

36. Yang, "Market Economy," 214–17.
37. Chen, "Some Concepts," 16.
38. Gao, "Build Up the Chinese Protestant Church through Sinicization," 8.
39. Yang, "Theological and Cultural Reflections," 69–70.

Theology to suggest ways to overcome greed in a consumerist society.[40] While Chinese church leaders address certain issues of social justice, they do not want to touch on sensitive political issues, such as labor strikes and protests, especially in the past few years when the Chinese government has stepped up its surveillance on churches and religious activities.

In the United States, changing Sino-American relations and the nationalist and populist turn in politics challenge theologians to look at class, labor, economy, and faith in new ways. In 2017, a group of American theologians and scholars were enraged by Trump's Muslim ban, misogyny, racial bigotry, homophobia, and economic policies that benefit the rich. They issued the Boston Declaration in which they denounced the "false ideology of the corporate ruling class," the myth of American exceptionalism, and "economic policies that are grounded in an illusion of extreme individualism and favor the accumulation of wealth for a few to the detrimental of the many."[41] They pointed to the "Jesus Way," which affirms justice and dignity for all, protects the poor and vulnerable, and confronts evil wherever it exists. They confessed that churches and Christian groups have been often complicit in empire-building and American expansionism.

Theologian Kathryn Tanner has published *Christianity and the New Spirit of Capitalism*, in which she revisits Max Weber's work and offers a sustained analysis of contemporary capitalism and the ways Christian beliefs and value system can respond to it. Tanner argues that contemporary capitalism is finance-dominated, which is drastically different from the economic constellations during the rise of capitalism that Max Weber has described. Thus, there is a *new* spirit of capitalism, which she characterizes as magnifying the significance of the past for present, demand for total commitment of workers, total investment at the present and at every moment, management of future volatility, and emphasis on individual accountability and competition. Capitalism has a total demand for people's time, energy, and commitment and it has infused the private and public spheres of life, such that it can be seen as a quasi-religion. This work ethic is incompatible with Christian commitments, as God does not treat humans according to their achievements. Although Christians cannot dissociate themselves from this world, they can exploit the nodes

---

40. Lin, "A Confucian," 13–24.
41. "The Boston Declaration."

of vulnerabilities in the unjust system and work toward an alternative cooperative project.[42]

Tanner offers a *gestalt* of Christian beliefs and values, which can form the basis of a counter-narrative to capitalism's quasi-religious worldview: the Christian view of history, with a focus on God's redemptive action in Christ; commitment to God instead of to Mammon; God's abundant love instead of scarcity; confidence in the future because of God's grace and the hope for resurrected life; conversion and turning toward God; salvation is not contingent upon one's achievement; and a Christian way of being in the world that does not follow the logic of the work ethic of capitalism. While Tanner does not try to provide a blueprint of how an economic system that challenges capitalism would look like, I want to know more about how the Christian values and beliefs that she describes can be put to practice in a collective effort to undermine, if not undo, capitalism.

Other scholars have focused on the relationship between religion and social movements in the struggle for social and economic equity. As the fallout from neoliberal globalization has become so clear, there is renewed interest in some of the socialist ideals among millennials and radical politicians. Social ethicist Gary Dorrien traces the Christian and political roots of socialist movements in Europe, particularly in Britain and Germany, and argues for economic democracy and anti-imperial transnationalism. He surmises that "Christian socialism paved the way for all liberation theologies that makes the struggles of oppressed peoples the subject of redemption."[43] He is currently working on a book on the socialist movements in the United States. Theologian Joerg Rieger has been involved in labor and other social movements against domination and economic inequality. With labor organizer Rosemarie Henkel-Rieger, he has coauthored a book *Unified We Are a Force* on the connections between faith and work and offered advice on organizing people for collective bargaining power. In the book, the authors argue that the church must move from advocacy to deep solidarity. Advocacy often assumes that a privileged group is supporting an underprivileged group, and that work and labor are issues of special interest. In fact, the current economic status quo does not benefit the vast majority of people—the 99 percent. Even the middle class and the somewhat privileged can be a paycheck

---

42. Tanner, *Christianity and the New Spirit of Capitalism*.
43. Dorrien, *Social Democracy in the Making*, 3.

away from economic insecurity. Deep solidarity is possible when people become aware that their destinies are deeply connected, even though there are differences among them.[44] Deep solidarity, they say, "needs to rest on broad shoulders, drawing energy from all aspects of life, politics, economics, religion, and the realities of labor or work."[45] They cite Jesus as an example, for Jesus grew up as a carpenter—a construction worker—and throughout his ministry, he formed deep solidarity with working people, fishermen, and tax collectors and even reached out to some wealthy and prominent people. Jesus was committed to forming new communities and bringing out positive changes to society.[46]

Conclusion

Joerg Rieger has argued that theologians have paid more attention to race, gender, sexuality, and other identity issues and not enough to class and its intricate relation to religion.[47] The rise of China challenges us to rethink the intersection between class, labor, socialism, and Christianity. Christian leaders in China in the past have argued that Christianity is not incompatible with socialism and revised Marx's theory on religion. Today, China faces a new set of economic issues—widening gap between the rich and the poor, labor disputes, gender disparity, differences between urban and rural incomes, and the slowing down of economic growth. The ways China will address these issues will not only affect China, but the whole world. It is important to develop transnational and comparative analyses of class, labor, and faith in order to formulate a global religious ethic to address the needs of our time.

Bibliography

Amadeo, Kimberly. "US Trade Deficit with China and Why It's So High." *The Balance.* Feb. 23, 2020. https://www.thebalance.com/u-s-china-trade-deficit-causes-effects-and-solutions-3306277.

"The Boston Declaration Calls Christians to Repentance with Echoes of the Barmen Declaration." *Auburn Seminary* (blog). November 20, 2017. https://auburnseminary.org/voices/boston-declaration.

44. Rieger and Henkel-Rieger, *Unified We Are a Force*, 59–60.
45. Rieger and Henkel-Rieger, *Unified We Are a Force*, 3.
46. Rieger and Henkel-Rieger, *Unified We Are a Force*, 65–67.
47. Rieger, "Introduction," 1–26.

"A Brief History of China's Economic Growth." World Economic Forum. https://www.weforum.org/agenda/2015/07/brief-history-of-china-economic-growth/.

Cai, Fang, and Lin Yifu. *Zhongguo jingji* (Chinese economy). Singapore: McGraw-Hill Education, 2003.

Cary, Peter, and Allan Holmes. "Workers Barely Benefited from Trump's Sweeping Tax Cut, Investigation Shows." *The Guardian*, April 30, 2019, sec. US news. https://www.theguardian.com/us-news/2019/apr/30/trump-tax-cut-law-investigation-worker-benefits.

Chen, Yilu. "Some Concepts in Theological Education in China." *Chinese Theological Review* 17 (2003) 13–22.

"China GDP—Gross Domestic Product 2018." countryeconomy.com. https://countryeconomy.com/gdp/china?year=2018.

"Data: Chinese Workers in Africa." China Africa Research Initiative, Johns Hopkins School of Advanced International Studies. http://www.sais-cari.org/data-chinese-workers-in-africa.

Diplomacy & Beyond Team. "China Celebrates 40 Years of Reform and Opening Up." Diplomacy & Beyond, December 18, 2018. http://diplomacybeyond.com/articles/china-celebrates-40-years-of-reform-and-opening-up/.

"Do Women in China Face Greater Inequality than Women Elsewhere?" *ChinaPower Project* (blog). June 25, 2018. https://chinapower.csis.org/china-gender-inequality.

Dorrien, Gary J. *Social Democracy in the Making: Political and Religious Roots of European Socialism*. New Haven: Yale University Press, 2019.

Giles, Georgina. "The Fall and Rise of Wang Ming Dao." *Evangelical Times*, November 1999. https://www.evangelical-times.org/27192/the-fall-and-rise-of-wang-ming-dao.

Gao, Feng. "Build up the Chinese Protestant Church through Sinicization." *Chinese Theological Review* 28 (2017) 1–28.

Hirst, Tomas. "A Brief History of China's Economic Growth." *World Economic Forum*, July 30, 2015. https://www.weforum.org/agenda/2015/07/brief-history-of-china-economic-growth.

Honig, Emily. *Sisters and Strangers: Women in the Shanghai Cotton Mills, 1919–1949*. Stanford, CA: Stanford University Press, 1986.

Laliberté, André. "Contemporary Issues in State-Religion Relations." In *Chinese Religious Life*, edited by David A. Palmer, Glenn Shive, and Philip L. Wickeri, 192–208. New York: Oxford University Press, 2011.

Leng, Sidney. "China's Dirty Little Secret: Its Growing Wealth Gap." *South China Morning Post*, July 7, 2017. https://www.scmp.com/news/china/economy/article/2101775/chinas-rich-grabbing-bigger-slice-pie-ever.

Lin, Manhong. "A Confucian Ethical Understanding of the Positive Role of Shame in Anti-Corruption." *Chinese Theological Review* 22 (2010) 13–24.

Lynch, David J. "How the U.S.–China Trade War Became a Conflict over the Future of Tech." *Washington Post*, May 22, 2019. https://www.washingtonpost.com/business/economy/how-the-us-china-trade-war-became-a-conflict-over-the-future-of-tech/2019/05/22/18148d1c-7ccc-11e9-8ede-f4abf521ef17_story.html?noredirect=on&utm_term=.a8613dee74e6.

Mao, Tse-tung. "Report on an Investigation of the Peasant Movement in Hunan." https://www.marxists.org/reference/archive/mao/selected-works/volume-1/mswv1_2.htm.

"Migrant Workers in China." Facts and Details. http://factsanddetails.com/china/cat11/sub72/item150.html/.

Ng, Lee Ming. *Jidujiao yu Zhongguo shehui bianqian* (Christianity and Chinese social change). Hong Kong: Chinese Christian Literature Council, 1981.

Ng, Peter Tze Ming. "Global Christianity and Local Contexts: The Case of K. H. Ting and the Three-Self Church in China." *Exchange* 40.1 (January 1, 2011) 57–70. https://doi.org/10.1163/157254311X550731.

Niebuhr, Reinhold. *An Interpretation of Christian Ethics*. New York: Harper, 1935.

———. *Moral Man and Immoral Society: A Study in Ethics and Politics*. Louisville: Westminster John Knox, 2001.

———. *The Nature and Destiny of Man*. Vol. 1. New York: Scribner, 1949.

"Reforms under Deng Xiaoping." http://www.fsmitha.com/h2/ch32prc.html.

Rieger, Joerg. "Introduction." In *Religion, Theology, and Class: Fresh Engagements after Long Silence*, edited by Joerg Rieger, 1–26. New York: Palgrave Macmillan, 2013.

———, and Rosemarie Henkel-Rieger. *Unified We Are a Force: How Faith and Labor Can Overcome America's Inequalities*. St. Louis: Chalice, 2016.

Sanders, Bernie. "Trump's Economy Is Great for Billionaires, not for Working People." *The Guardian*, January 16, 2019, sec. US news. https://www.theguardian.com/us-news/2019/jan/16/trump-economy-billionaires-working-people.

Simpson, Peter. "China's Urban Population Exceeds Rural for First Time Ever." *The Telegraph*, January 17, 2012, sec. World. https://www.telegraph.co.uk/news/worldnews/asia/china/9020486/Chinas-urban-population-exceeds-rural-for-first-time-ever.html/.

Tanner, Kathryn. *Christianity and the New Spirit of Capitalism*. New Haven: Yale University Press, 2019.

Thomlinson, Harvey. "China's Communist Party Is Abandoning Workers." *The New York Times*, April 2, 2018, sec. Opinion. https://www.nytimes.com/2018/04/02/opinion/china-communist-party-workers-strikes.html/.

Ting, K. H. *God Is Love: Collected Writings of Bishop K. H. Ting*. Colorado Springs, CO: Cook, 2004.

———. "Retrospect and Prospect." *International Review of Mission* 70, no. 278 (April 1981) 25–42.

———. "The Sinned Against (1979)." In *No Longer Strangers: Selected Writings of Bishop K. H. Ting*, edited by Raymond L. Whitehead, 72–74. Maryknoll, NY: Orbis, 1989.

"Trump's War on Worker Rights." New York Times, June 3, 2019. https://www.nytimes.com/2019/06/03/opinion/trump-worker-safety-osha.html/.

Tso, S. K. Sheldon. *The Labor Movement in China*. 1928. Reprint, Westport, CT: Hyerion, 1981.

Wickeri, Janice, and Philip Wickeri. "Introduction." In *A Chinese Contribution to Ecumenical Theology: Selected Writings of Bishop K. H. Ting*, edited by Janice Wickeri and Philip Wickeri, vii–xii. Geneva: World Council of Churches Publications, 2002.

Wu, Y. T. "China's Challenges to Christianity." *Chinese Recorder* 65 (1934) 7–11.

Yang, Donglong. "Theological and Cultural Reflections on the Relationship between Church and Society in China." *Chinese Theological Review* 17 (2003) 64–75.

Yang, Fenggang. "Market Economy and the Revival of Religions." In *Chinese Religious Life*, edited by David A. Palmer, Glenn Shive, and Philip L. Wickeri, 209–26. New York: Oxford University Press, 2011.

Yip, Ka-che. *Religion, Nationalism, and Chinese Students: The Anti-Christian Movement of 1922–1927*. Bellingham: Center for East Asian Studies, Western Washington University, 1980.

Zhou, Cissy. "China's Army of Migrant Workers Is Becoming Older and Less Mobile, New Government Data Shows." *South China Morning Post*, May 1, 2019, https://www.scmp.com/economy/china-economy/article/3008285/chinas-army-migrant-workers-becoming-older-and-less-mobile.

3

The God That Never Failed

Black Christian Marxism as Prophetic Call to Action and Hope

Juan M. Floyd-Thomas

Introduction

THE YEAR 2019 MARKED several anniversaries that speak directly to my specific research interests and areas of expertise pertaining to race, class, and economic justice. First and foremost, 2019 represented 400 years since the earliest Africans were brought by force and sold into bondage as human chattel as a last-ditch effort to salvage what historian Edmund Morgan termed "the Jamestown fiasco" in 1619.[1] It is with this auspicious yet ignominious event that colonial American society and eventually this nation began its long, twisted experience with the "peculiar institution" of American slavery. As observer to this historic occurrence, John Rolfe described the appearance of enslaved Africans in the Virginia colony in a rather nondescript fashion: "About the last of August came in a dutch man of warre [sic] that sold us twenty Negars."[2] Although the historical record follows Rolfe's comment, the rising influx of enslaved Africans into

---

1. Morgan, *American Slavery*, 71–91.
2. Arber, *Travels and Works*, 541; Jordan, *White over Black*, 73.

the struggling colony coincided with the burgeoning financial success of Jamestown's tobacco cash crop.³ When this nascent system of enslavement was introduced to Jamestown in 1619, there was no official definition of "slave" in English law. However, by the end of the seventeenth century, this state of affairs had changed so radically due to legal measures approved by the Virginia House of Burgesses—the governing body that was democratically elected by the white male colonists who were entitled and enfranchised within that society—that Africans and their American-born heirs were considered enslaved for life (*durante vita*) not only as a *de facto* issue but ultimately a *de jure* reality. As African conversion to Christianity became more prevalent from the mid-seventeenth to the early eighteenth century, legal and religious authorities of the era grappled with the problem of whether it was wrong to enslave fellow Christians. However, as history reveals, the primacy of maximizing the profitability of the emergent slave economy in colonial America superseded any prospect that Christian baptism had any emancipatory (much less salvific) power in the worldly fate of the enslaved Africans and their American-born descendants. As many scholars of race and racism in the U.S. context have argued, 1619 represents the persistent and pernicious roots of "America's original sin" that defines our society's investment in systematic and systemic modes of oppression that still haunts us to this very day.⁴

Secondly, and more germane to the matter at hand, 2019 also represented the fiftieth anniversary of the Black Manifesto, a boldly prophetic document intended to address the structural and spiritual injustices spawned by the genesis of the slave system several centuries earlier. This revolutionary document, infused with the religious commitments to social justice and revolutionary Marxist critique that permeated a great deal of civil rights activism during the 1960s, sparked a landmark debate about the nexus of race, religion, and reparations. Written largely by former Student Nonviolent Coordinating Committee (SNCC) activist James Forman in conjunction with Mark Hamlin and John Watson, leading organizers of the League of Revolutionary Black Workers, this statement was endorsed by the National Black Economic Development Conference

---

3. Morgan, *American Slavery*, 71–130; Wood, *Slavery in Colonial America*, 3–8.

4. Although countless African American scholars, clergy, journalists, artist, political leaders, and activists have espoused and advanced this concept of racism as "America's original sin" for generations, this idea has been popularized by white antiracist scholarship such as Myrdal, *An American Dilemma*, and Wallis, *America's Original Sin*.

(NBEDC) on April 26, 1969, in Detroit, Michigan. James Forman was a member of SNCC as it transitioned from its King-influenced Christian nonviolence to its Black Power phase, where it was gravitating towards a greater infusion of Marxist-Leninist-Maoist thought. This placed him in a similar political and ideological orbit as the Black Panthers and the League of Revolutionary Black Workers, in the hope of seeing Black laborers as crucial to the "workers' vanguard"—hence their collaborative work in the NBEDC, which led to the Manifesto. The critical backlash and contemporaneous attacks against the Manifesto in its heyday by many critics both in church and society (regardless of race), largely ascribed Marxist influences to the document and its advocates. This sort of anti-radical attack served as a major stumbling block regarding any mass movement seeking wealth redistribution in the U.S. since the Gilded Age. In quick fashion, the activists from the League of Revolutionary Black Workers took over the more liberal conference proceedings. According to historian Robin D. G. Kelley, they succeeded in shifting the vision of the NBEDC by "creating what was essentially a black socialist agenda" because of the Marxist-Leninist-Maoist commitments of the Black workers.[5] Moreover, Forman and the authors of the Black Manifesto agreed that May 4, 1969, would be the date for the start of an active campaign of disrupting religious institutions to advance their cause in honor of the May Fourth Movement in Beijing fifty years earlier.[6] On the gathering's second evening, Forman announced to the participants that "We must begin seizing power wherever we are, and we must say to the planners of this conference that you are no longer in charge ... The conference is now the property of the people who are assembled here ... We demand $500 million for reparations" to African Americans. Forman further warned those gathered that day "if the white Christians and Jews are not willing to meet our demands through peace and good will, then we declare war and we are prepared to fight by whatever means necessary."[7] It was in this spirit that Forman stood at the pulpit in the middle of Sunday worship services at the renowned Riverside Church on May 4, 1969, and read this lengthy demand for reparations to the congregation. Forman's presentation of the Black Manifesto from the pulpit of Riverside Church on that fateful Sunday centered on an insurgent reparations demand from white

5. Kelley, *Freedom Dreams*, 121.
6. A wonderful volume that highlights this history is Ho and Mullen, *Afro Asia*.
7. Forman, *Making of Black Revolutionaries*, 545; "Black Manifesto"; Lechtreck, "We Are Demanding," 41.

mainline religious denominations as an economic redress for chattel slavery.

This chapter explores the origins and evolution of the Black Manifesto as the first full-fledged prophetic appeal for financial restitution for African American enslavement from religious institutions in the nation's history. In addition to this chapter's focus on how and why the Black Manifesto linked religion, racism, and reparations during its heyday in the late 1960s and early 1970s, it also contextualizes the Manifesto within the *longue durée* of the reparations debate from the end of the U.S. Civil War to its current resurgence in public life and political discourse. Of particular interest in this chapter is serious consideration of how prophetic Black Christian tradition and Black Marxism worked together to redefine the Church's role and responsibility in the ongoing struggles against institutional racism, religious hypocrisy, and structural poverty. Thus, the result of this interplay represents the development of an organic political theology wherein Black Christian eschatological beliefs in a better world to come joined together with Marxist conceptions of the political economy that presaged the prospects for an integrated race-class analysis through the prism of the hidden history of Black labor radicalism and religious belief.

Building a Revolutionary Movement: The Origins and Evolution of the Black Manifesto

Reflecting its genesis at the tail end of the 1960s within the sociopolitical crucible defined largely, in the words of the late theologian James Cone, by the confluence of "Black Theology and Black Power," the Black Manifesto called on white religious institutions across the theological and denominational spectrum to pay reparations for the historic ravages of Black chattel slavery in the U.S. as well as the ensuing structural oppression that still impacted people of African descent contemporaneously. As Robin Kelley contends, "Half a billion dollars is a paltry sum... but Forman and fellow drafters of the Black Manifesto considered their request seed money to build a new revolutionary movement and to strengthen black political and economic institutions."[8] Within this legendary statement, the authors of the manifesto outline a visionary programmatic agenda for how this money would be used to redress the systematic and systemic

---

8. Kelley, *Freedom Dreams*, 121.

forms of oppression that plagued Black women, men, and children as a resulting legacy of centuries regarding both enslavement and segregation. As an attempt to remedy this crisis constructively, the NBEDC sought to establish a fund that would underwrite various projects intended to benefit Blacks, including the establishment of: a southern land bank; major printing and publishing companies in Detroit, Atlanta, and Los Angeles; four television networks based in Detroit, Chicago, Cleveland, and Washington, DC; a research center; a training center; and a national Black Labor Strike and Defense Fund. Moreover, the Manifesto indicted white religious organizations for their historic complicity in white supremacy in America while also calling on Blacks to bring any and all pressure that they deemed necessary in order to force churches and synagogues to comply to their demands.

Forman ostensibly represented the NBEDC, itself an outgrowth of the ecumenical Interreligious Foundation for Community Organization (IFCO), which had approved the Manifesto only a few weeks earlier yet moved forward with an irrepressible degree of holy boldness. The Interreligious Foundation for Community Organization (IFCO) was an interfaith group established in late 1966 in the wake of nationwide insurrections in numerous U.S. cities with the goal of seeking remedies to the problem of urban poverty in America.[9] The IFCO concentrated its various funding projects and related efforts at confronting what the National Council of Churches (NCC) termed in 1967 as "the crisis in the nation."[10] In vivid, often inflammatory rhetoric even by the standards of 1960s radicalism, the Manifesto demanded $500 million dollars "from the Christian white churches and the Jewish synagogues," while also detailing in grand fashion how it was to be spent on a range of revolutionary programs and services for the Black community. Even more, the IFCO

---

9. The IFCO was compromised of denominational bodies such as the American Baptist Convention, the American Jewish Committee, the Lutheran Church in America, the National Catholic Conference Committees, the Presbyterian Church USA, the Protestant Episcopal Church, the United Church of Christ, the United Methodist Church, "Investment Committee for Ghetto Community Development" of the National Council of Churches (NCC) and other missionary societies brought together to pool their funds and resources in an *ad hoc* fashion to ameliorate the ravages of high unemployment and meager economic opportunities prevalent in impoverished urban neighborhoods.

10. "Administrative History," IFCO Records Finding Guide; "Attendance at Board Meeting," IFCO Records Finding Guid; "Report of Investment Committee for Community Development of the National Council of Churches," IFCO Records Finding Guide.

planned to use money raised by the Manifesto for a number of projects, including the funding of Black Star Publications, a Detroit-based Black owned and operated publishing house to which James Forman was connected.

Many American religious historians have frequently interpreted the circumstances surrounding the Black Manifesto as a shining symbol of the ongoing fragmentation of the religious establishment in the U.S. in the late 1960s and 1970s, especially regarding the Protestant mainline churches. Mounting schisms over the proper role of churches and larger ecclesiastical institutions, most notably the NCC, in civil rights activism as well as increasing advocacy for feminism and antiwar protests against the Vietnam War in the broader society grew increasingly heated and contentious throughout the 1960s. Yet the rising cries for "Black Power" and the advent of Black liberation theology from both within and from outside of religious institutions pushed religious leaders to reconsider their proper place in debates over race and civil rights, even as anti-war activists challenged the church to clarify or rethink its position on the Vietnam War. In many ways the Black Manifesto mirrored the bold declarations of Rev. Dr. Martin Luther King Jr.'s fabled "Beyond Vietnam" sermon from Riverside Church in April 1967 in which he illuminated that the two issues of his time, civil rights and Vietnam, were hardly distinct. However, in an ironic development, some supporters of the Black Manifesto actually criticized the NCC for giving too much attention to Vietnam War. Nor were they the only issues that the establishment had to address, as the Sixties offered more than its share of challenges to traditions of religious authority, moral conventions, and the general relationship between religion, culture, and politics. The Black Manifesto, then, often appears as one significant debate amidst an endless series of other, related debates, a symbol of the infighting that ultimately led to the decline of mainline Protestant establishment.

Lauded as a preeminent bastion of theological liberalism, progressive social thought, and radical activism, Riverside Church was deemed the most appropriate site for this pronouncement by Forman and his colleagues because of the church's proximity to Harlem's Black community as well as its connections with the Rockefeller family. Despite the notable philanthropic acts of the Rockefellers throughout much of the late nineteenth and early twentieth centuries, it was still equally fresh in the memories of many activists that the family's grand patriarch, John D. Rockefeller, was also widely recognized by the Manifesto's authors as one of the nation's most infamous robber barons. To their credit, some predominantly white churches expressed some sympathy with the aims of the Black Manifesto, but their response was essentially to increase aid they already allocated to new or existing programs of their own denominations rather than providing money for the reparations fund as prescribed by the Manifesto's authors. In the wake of Forman's pronouncement from the pulpit, the movement raised roughly half a million dollars that day, with an estimated $200,000 coming from Riverside Church alone via an annual fund for the disadvantaged that became known as "the Riverside Fund for Social Justice."[11]

In the wake of the Black Manifesto's debut, the impact of fiery language and the level of increasingly audacious activism it sparked for both religious and irreligious activists alike was matched only by the heated discussions within and among religious groups over what was the Manifesto's original intent and how the church and society were supposed to respond to it. Robin Kelley notes, "Forman . . . felt that Christianity had been a source of oppression; by teaching passivity and acceptance of the dominant order, he argued, Christianity had kept black people from embracing revolution."[12] Even though many religious leaders and organizations dismissed the Manifesto's demands without reservation, many others saw the document and the activism it generated as speaking directly to a pernicious as well as persistent complicity in the vast web of racist structures and strictures at the core of America's mainline religious institutions. Therefore, it can be argued that the disruptions and demonstrations spurred by the Manifesto intersected with the longer, broader liberation struggles mounted by progressive activists and prophetic religious groups who sought to compel their denominations, institutions, and leadership to engage with and confront the key issues of the era. As a result of these internecine conflicts, the swirling controversies prompted by the Manifesto were feverishly debated in church and denominational board meetings, seminary classrooms, religious publications, and numerous other settings. Whether by choice or by force, many of America's largest religious organizations were forced to issue statements addressing the demands of Black Manifesto as credible and reasonable.

When asked bluntly whether he believed the Black Manifesto could succeed during a September 5, 1969 interview, NBEDC vice-chairman

11. Lubasch, "Pastor at Riverside," 1–2; Paris, et al., *Riverside Church*, 89; Lechtreck, "We Are Demanding," 49.

12. Kelley, *Freedom Dreams*, 122.

Muhammed Kenyatta rebuffed that loaded question by explaining in a forthright fashion why he believed "the Black Manifesto cannot fail" by drawing a distinction between religious conviction and political action.

> My viewpoint is that . . . the Black Manifesto cannot fail because it speaks to historical matter of fact and it speaks to the real needs of Black people. It speaks to historical matter of fact that Black people had suffered economic exploitation, that slave labor of black people was a source of capital for the development of America, and that Black people after slavery were further exploited economically. Thus, we have back capital—back pay—owed to us collectively by the institutions of this country.

As Kenyatta further elaborates,

> Our historical basis is sound. More important, perhaps . . . is the fact that our programs and our analysis [speaks] to the needs of the Black community and Black people—rich and poor, clergy, secular people, young and old—are beginning to move around the Manifesto. It's becoming a national mass movement. When I say that we can't fail, it's because I think the black community cannot and will not fail in its struggle for liberation, of which we are a part, a significant part but only a part.

The interviewer then poses what is admittedly a "possibly cynical question" by asking "do you feel there's going to be that much moral change within the Church?" "No . . . I have been largely disabused of that notion," Kenyatta states flatly but then admits:

> what we have found is this, though, and this is real, that there are individuals in the Church, especially Black people, Black clergymen, in the Church who are serious about their ethics, who are serious about their morality. And morality, ethics, religious convictions, faith in God, belief in brotherhood, transcendent ethics has been a motive force behind individuals and small groups of people. But what we have found is the only way we can deal effectively with the Church is to take . . . that moral force, organize it and move politically.

To demonstrate his case in point, he cites the fact that the Black Episcopalian clergy recently had to "go further than preaching and praying" to their white counterparts in the denomination and had to actually "organize a union of Black clergy and laity."[13]

13. "Muhammed Kenyatta, Community Organizer."

Furthermore, this action was an attempt to exhort African Americans nationwide to follow Forman's example and do what he had done, namely to disrupt religious services across the country in support of the Manifesto's appeals. And so many did. For example, Forman went before the National Committee of Black Churchmen (NCBC) in Atlanta and read his list of demands on May 7, 1969. It should be noted that there were numerous NCBC members who were present in Detroit at the NCBC planning sessions that helped give rise to the Manifesto in the first place. Shortly thereafter, the organization issued a statement of support: "There is no question that the American religious establishment, along with almost every other institution in the society was the conscious beneficiary of the enforced labor of one of the most inhumane forms of chattel slavery the world has ever known."[14] J. Metz Rollins, the executive director of NCBC, and the board of directors immediately called for the creation of "Black caucuses" within predominantly white mainline denominations as well as asked for historically African American denominations to develop unified strategies deemed necessary to facilitate the distribution of funds if the reparations were ever paid.[15] Moreover, there was an interracial group of students who were inspired by Forman and the NBEDC and proceeded to occupy the offices of New York's fabled Union Theological Seminary roughly a week later. Likewise, similar occupations of various other denominational offices followed suit. Union eventually donated start-up funds of $500,000 for Black-owned economic enterprises in Harlem, $100,000 to NBEDC, and ultimately pledged to raise $1 million for future economic projects in Harlem.[16] What's more, Riverside Church's relatively new pastor, Rev. Ernest Campbell, not only supported the Manifesto by allowing Forman and others access to the pulpit and facilitated funding for the growing initiative but also delivered his own sermons and even a book, *The Christian Manifesto*, in which he strenuously called on churches nationwide to become more deeply committed to confronting social problems.[17]

---

14. "Statement," IFCO Records.
15. "Statement," IFCO Records.
16. "Message," IFCO Records; Lechtreck, "We Are Demanding," 51.
17. Paris et al., *Riverside Church*, 88–89; Lechtreck, "We Are Demanding," 48–50; Campbell, *Christian Manifesto*.

"The Most Serious Crisis":
Backlash against the Black Manifesto

This is not to suggest that public reaction to the Black Manifesto was either unanimous or uncritical in nature. Numerous copies of the Black Manifesto were printed and either distributed to ordained and lay religious leaders or read aloud to congregations of churches both large and small, often interrupting Sunday worship services unapologetically. Initially there were numerous whites who wanted to disregard the whole discussion of reparations altogether, dismissing Forman as a lone figure with few supporters for his radical demands within the Black community.[18] The editorial board of Harlem's *Amsterdam News* was largely unwelcoming to Forman's tactics and generally dismissive of the Manifesto on the whole. In fact, opposition and criticism to the growing fervor surrounding the Black Manifesto became more frequent in various sectors of the Black community. It should be noted many of the foremost Black organizations, most notably the National Association for the Advancement of Colored People (NAACP) and the National Baptist Convention (NBC), quickly formulated a contradictory position towards the Black Manifesto. Rev. Dr. Joseph H. Jackson, the conservative president of the National Baptist Convention U.S.A., compared the document to Marx and Engel's *Communist Manifesto*. As an outspoken foe of Dr. Martin Luther King Jr. as well as Black Power advocates, Jackson never identified with the Manifesto's programs and methods.[19] In a letter dated July 2, 1969 to Rev. Frank Wilson, a good friend and longtime Presbyterian Church official, renowned theologian Howard Thurman ridiculed Forman's demand for reparations from churches, claiming "who am I to compete with the prophet of the 21st Century, Foreman [sic]?" Later, Thurman jokingly remarks to Wilson that Forman's "cohorts invaded [the Presbyterian Church's] headquarters while [Forman] himself was 'manifestoing' on the floor of the General Assembly.[20] Previously occupying great prominence in the Civil Rights Movement more than a decade earlier, both the Black Press, the Black Church, and civil rights organizations effectively distanced themselves from the Black Manifesto's radical agenda and yet urged that any money generated by the call for

18. Harvey, "White Protestants," 125–50.
19. Lecky and Wright, *Black Manifesto*, 4.
20. "Letter to Rev. Frank Wilson" in *Papers of Howard Washington Thurman*, 202–203.

reparations summarily be given to their respective coffers for related purposes instead. By mid-May 1969, both the FBI and the US Department of Justice had begun targeted federal investigations into the NBEDC.[21]

While the roughly two-month period of church-based efforts by Forman was met with wildly kaleidoscopic responses, the main setback the Manifesto encountered could be somewhat blithely summarized as "death by a thousand caucuses." Many mainline religious denominations—most particularly Protestant groups—earnestly admitted their complicity in and benefits from the historic enslavement and contemporary exploitation of African Americans and offered some sort of reparations but not all the money that was originally sought in the Manifesto. More often than not, however, they directed those funds into hands other than those of Forman and the NBEDC. As a keenly critical observer of events surrounding the Manifesto, religious scholar and prominent Black Presbyterian minister Gayraud S. Wilmore offers a pretty scathing critique of the entire situation indicating that the Black Manifesto represents "the most serious crisis in the American religious establishment since the bitter polemics and antagonisms, which divided it prior to the Civil War."[22] One of the first critical failures Wilmore notes is Forman's inability to negotiate directly with white denominations, dealing with Black caucuses as intermediaries instead. This shortcoming, he argues, revealed Forman's "lack of knowledge and experience in dealing with white church structures."[23] Oddly enough, this scenario replicated the kind of segregation and racial subordination the Manifesto was intended to halt. Moreover, Wilmore notes that Forman's lack of finesse in dealing with the racialized hierarchies of the mainline denominations was compounded by deeply ingrained problems inherent to these church bodies across racial lines. On the one hand, the mainline churches reflected what Wilmore calls "unreconstructed conservatism and a dismal failure of creative imagination" that "are to be blamed for the depressing performance" in response to the Manifesto's demands.[24] On the other hand, the brewing controversy around the Manifesto's faltering implementation also illustrated that there was a deep-seated "naivete and vulnerability

---

21. "Black Manifesto."
22. "Gayraud Wilmore" IFCO Records.
23. Wilmore, *Black Religion*, 240.
24. Wilmore, *Black Religion*, 241.

of black clergy when they are in competition for scarce resources—the lingering divisive effects of welfare mentality... within the NCBC."[25]

While this interpretation appears to be a perfectly reasonable and a useful understanding of the Black Manifesto's ultimate fate in American culture and history, I would suggest that the conventional wisdom of this historical approach remains somewhat skewed. More often than not, the normative historic treatment of the Black Manifesto leans towards reinforcing an overall narrative of the mainline church's decline. As Trevor Burrows, explains:

> scholars have primarily focused on top-level responses to the Manifesto, especially from the leaders of religious institutions, and have largely slighted two other interrelated aspects of the story: first, the nature of the Manifesto itself and its religious (or non-religious) elements; and second, the grassroots efforts of activists across the nation who took up Forman's suggestions to pressure churches and synagogues to act on the Manifesto's demands.[26]

Taking this latter question quite seriously, I present this brief story in order to suggest there are alternate possibilities for understanding how Forman and his supporters crafted the Manifesto as a prophetic call to action and hope to the Church. The vitally necessary yet clearly unfulfilled work of the Manifesto's authors and adherents to compel religious leaders and institutions to envision reparations is a meaningful first step towards racial reconciliation in the U.S.

"A Simple Matter of Justice": The Race, Religion, and the Reparations Debate

Without question, Forman and the NBEDC were not the first or only proponents of reparations for Black descendants of chattel slavery.[27] Even in the heyday of America's Gilded Age, a formerly enslaved African American woman named Callie House founded the National Ex-Slave

25. Wilmore, *Black Religion*, 241.

26. Burrows, "'Black Manifesto' in Twentieth-Century American Religious History."

27. Coates, "The Case for Reparations." Also for more details about the issue of reparations, see Lecky and Wright, *Black Manifesto*; Schuchter, *Reparations*; Robinson, *The Debt*; Winbush, *Should America Pay?*; Marable, *Great Wells*, 223–54; Berry, *My Face Is Black*; Kelley, *Freedom Dreams*, 110–34; Walters, *Price of Racial Reconciliation*.

Mutual Relief, Bounty, and Pension Association (MRB&PA) in 1898, which historian Mary Frances Berry has called "one of the largest grassroots movements in African American history." Decades later, Queen Mother Moore, a renowned activist in Harlem, established the Reparations Committee of Descendants of United States Slaves in 1955; she was able to mobilize a modest campaign that kept the movement alive for several decades.

In 1963, Dr. Martin Luther King Jr. recommended a "Bill of Rights for the Disadvantaged" for all American regardless of backgrounds in his book *Why We Can't Wait*. Within his proposed Bill of Rights, however, Dr. King made a clarion call for reparations for both the victimization and exploitation of enslaved forebears and present-day degradations. During the same period as he assumed the leadership of the Southern civil rights struggle, Dr. King had made the moral argument that:

> Few people consider the fact that, in addition to being enslaved for two centuries, the Negro was during all of those years robbed of wages of [his / her] toil. No amount of gold could provide adequate compensation for the exploitation and humiliation of the Negro in America down through the centuries. Not all the wealth of this affluent society could meet the bill. Yet a price can be placed on the unpaid wages. The ancient common law has always provided a remedy for the appropriation of the labor of one human being by another. This law should be made to apply for the American Negroes.[28]

Moreover, King even suggested the redress should be programmatic in nature, noting that this proposed compensation would be cheaper than reimbursing African Americans for 200 years of unpaid wages and the interest which has accrued. In order to address this historic injustice, King summarily advocated:

> The payment should be in the form of a massive program, by the government, of special compensatory measures which could be regarded as a settlement in accordance with accepted practices of common law ... The moral justification for special measures for Negroes is rooted in the robberies inherent in the institution of slavery ... It is a simple matter of justice.[29]

---

28. King, *Why We Can't Wait*, 128–30.
29. King, *Why We Can't Wait*, 128–29.

In addition to being somewhat surprising to find that Dr. King had advocated such a "radical" plan as reparations several years before Forman and the NBEDC devised the Black Manifesto, it is equally worthwhile to recognize that King felt the ultimate effects of receiving long awaited reparations would have a tremendous impact on the inherent dignity and self-esteem of the intended beneficiaries: "The most profound alteration would not reside so much in the specific grants as in the basic psychological and motivational transformation of the Negro."[30] King argued that such a measure to bolster the collective psyche of African Americans would bring about a marked decline in many social ills—i.e. dysfunctional families, school drop-outs, homelessness, high crime rates, etc. Even though one can only speculate if Dr. King's call for reparations would have succeeded had he survived, it leads one to wonder what this might have meant for the shape of reparations to come. When comparing the divergent paradigms promoted by King and Forman respectively, what kinds of programs are worthwhile to consider in terms of what would happen if we went beyond government programs and worked on transforming the structural nature of the US political economy by constantly keeping reparations front of mind?

I crafted the title and trajectory of this chapter around two rather obscure texts, one being sacred and the other quite sacred. On the one hand, the perspective of the activist Muhammad Kenyatta about his hope and belief—no matter how short-lived or unfulfilled—that the Black Manifesto would not fail reminded me of the passage from the Hebrew scripture Joshua 21:45 that "Not one word of all the good promises that the LORD had made to the house of Israel had failed; all came to pass." On the other hand, the title of this piece is a direct homage to the classic 1949 volume *The God That Failed*, whose numerous contributors including most notably for my purposes the renowned Black writer Richard Wright, spoke about their respective experiences of disillusionment with and ultimate abandonment of communism but also how their departures never served to rekindle their previously abandoned religious faith. As a result, even though they were writers who were nestled in the heart of the mid-twentieth century, they predicted many of the fears, feelings, and frustrations about both political economy and personal spirituality that have become the stock in trade of the post-everything millennial generation. Straddling between these twin concerns, it is the complex lesson

30. King, *Why We Can't Wait*, 128.

and legacy of Black Christian Marxism that has proclaimed a God that has never failed. Though facing a society, culture, political economy, and even a church that has conspired to demonize, devalue, and destroy Black humanity for more than half a millennium, I argue elsewhere that Black Christian Marxism has emerged and evolved as a hermeneutic and praxis roughly a century and a half ago that bore witness to the radical and reckless belief that divine justice and social justice—much like Blackness and humanity—are not and have never been mutually exclusive concerns.[31]

Pertaining to the issue of class and labor, I assert that reparations must be central to our work towards achieving economic justice. The fact that we, as a church, society, and culture have had such persistent problems acknowledging the rights of "free" labor is likely because we still have not properly reconciled the widespread damage done and debt owed to "enslaved" laborers and their descendants. The question of reparations for chattel slavery can be viewed in many ways but the most logical, meaningful argument in my perspective is to frame it in terms of restitution/redress of wage theft by employers (in this case, all institutions who had a fiduciary responsibility to the "workers" and benefitted from the literal as well as figurative fruit of the workers' labor). Arguably, this logic of what owners owe laborers is the groundwork of all capital-labor disputes in the recent modern era. To me, the most straightforward manner to address this matter is in terms of wage theft. Wage theft is when employees are denied salary, compensation, or related benefits to which they are entitled by law. Whether on an individual or collective basis, this sort of violation invariably often places liability upon the employer or the party that is responsible for paying the employees. In most cases of wage-theft, attorneys, labor unions or *ad hoc* coalitions have lobbied for back pay on behalf of workers, a process which is lawful, necessary, and good. The interesting question here, however, is how to address this issue when the responsible party is the entire American society? Taken one step further, how do the descendants and defendants of the enslaved demand recompense from the U.S., a nation that has prospered so wildly in both historical and contemporary terms from stolen labor, lucre, land, and lives, when it refuses to acknowledge the vast wealth produced by this epic theft much less atone for such a historic feat of larceny? For the overall reparation debate, this has loosely been misconstrued as simply handing Black people some lump sum of money as "back pay" in order

---

31. Floyd-Thomas, "Seeing Red in the Black Church."

to resolve the matter, thereby forgoing any deeper critique of exploitation and undervaluing of work that continues today. This scenario might repair injustices of the past but fail address injustices of the present, as whatever is given will quickly be taken away again.

Therefore, as I see it, if we fail to fix this most historic problem of structural poverty and economic injustice to working people (at least in the American context even though reparation potentially has transnational repercussions), all others will be equally inconclusive. What the critics, skeptics, and cynics need to understand is that reparations for slavery are neither a generous gift, charitable donation, nor kind favor for Black people, but rather the redress of the most extreme and egregious instance of wage theft in modern world history. Oddly enough, many labor activists and social justice advocates will denounce employers who force their workers to toil "like slaves" or have living on "slave wages" (clearly an oxymoron). Chattel slavery is more than a metaphorical reference but rather was a metaphysical reality for millions of people with lasting repercussions that impact their descendants even now.

Any honest appraisal of history reveals that abolitionism, somehow, eventually cleared the path for the triumph of wage labor. The struggle to end slavery forced its opponents to specify the difference between the illegitimate sale and economic exploitation of a human being and the "legitimate" sale of one's labor power in a wage-based economy. In the 1840s, Frederick Douglass condemned his Baltimore master for robbing him of his weekly wages and he said that his new life as a free man began the first day he received his earned wages while working on the docks of New Bedford. The fact that Douglass derived such memorable pride from not only earning but keeping the wages for an honest day's work—no matter how strenuous the exertion or meager the earnings—clearly dramatized the stark difference between slavery and free labor.[32] Said another way, it is barely surprising that Frederick Douglass would pronounce a heartfelt defense of wage labor in the mid-nineteenth century, just as the crisis over slavery was approaching its climax in the U.S. As historian James Oakes contends, "If capitalism and slavery had been joined at the hip for centuries, so were capitalism and antislavery… If it was wrong to treat humans as commodities, some reformers asked, was it also wrong to treat labor power as a commodity?"[33] The paradox of this convergence of

---

32. Douglas, *Narrative of the Life*, 102–6.
33. Oakes, "Slavery Is Theft."

antislavery and the early labor movement in the mid-nineteenth century was that chattel slavery legitimized capitalism and anti-capitalism at the same time. Yet there has been a Marxist tradition amongst Black radical intellectuals and activists from the Gilded Age to present who have been intent upon rethinking capitalism as an economic system in light of Marx's prescient assertion in *Das Kapital* that "labour cannot emancipate itself in white skin where in the black it is branded."[34]

The beauty of the Black Manifesto was the way in which it helped to extend and expand the issue of reparations as both a monetary and moral concern for modern American society. Moreover, when one engages in any assessment of modern political economy, ranging from the most lovingly capitalist or scathingly Marxist in nature, there is one emergent truth: injustice is the most blatant form of economic inefficiency as well as human inequality imaginable. For instance, despite the obscene levels of wealth generated during many centuries of the Transatlantic Slave Trade and chattel slavery in the Americas, the extent to which the widespread expropriation of human labor and lives for monetary gain by such regimes of enslavement was far costlier than the human imagination can grasp. Theologian M. Shawn Copeland elaborates that "as a nation, we understand ourselves in terms of freedom, but we have been unable to grapple with our depriving [African Americans] of freedom in the name of white prosperity and with our tolerance of legalized racial segregation and discrimination."[35] As I once saw emblazoned on a T-shirt by a white man who was most definitely not an antiracist ally, "If I knew that it was gonna cause all this trouble, I would've picked the cotton myself!" When one looks at the structural nature of our segregated public realm, the economic dimension of Jim and Jane Crow racism created a state of affairs throughout much of the U.S. wherein American culture and society not only undervalued the capacity and contribution of its Black citizenry but also undermined its own ability as a nation to make even greater strides towards scientific innovations and intellectual progress. Even in contemporary terms, the continued legacy of this sort of disparity between the rapid escalation of accumulation of monetary capital and the escalating divestment in human capital has been hugely daunting when we realize that it was far more profitable to lock millions of Black women, men,

---

34. Marx, *Capital*, 329.
35. Copeland, "Black Theology."

and children into privatized prisons than to lift them up through robust investments in public education.

Unfortunately, the world currently finds itself in a completely different reality than it was half a century ago. Despite the putative end of the church's "most segregated hour," people of all demographic backgrounds are arguably welcome in our present era to attend white mainline congregations yet many of those churches remain half full while facing budget deficits, "white flight" to the suburbs, shrinking staff sizes and social services, and generally struggling for social relevance and even survival. Unlike five decades earlier, a majority of churches are no longer the wealthy financial institutions they used to be and thus, even if they are wholeheartedly committed to reparations as an act of social justice, they are no longer in an economically viable position to support such a move. Meanwhile, to the matter of reparations for chattel slavery at the heart of this essay, I feel deeply encouraged by the fact that the past few years have witnessed an exponential growth in reactions and responses to Ta-Nehisi Coates's provocative essay, "A Case for Reparations," published in the June 2014 issue of *The Atlantic*. To put the influential impact of the shift in this debate into stark relief, I would raise the example of the shifting stance of the Democratic Party in the U.S. on this issue. In 2008 (the last time the Democrats had a relatively large field of contenders for the party's presidential nomination), there was only one out of eight candidates who wholeheartedly supported reparations and his name was not Barack Obama but rather Dennis Kucinich, former US Congressman from Ohio. Compare that with right now when, in a current field of 24 contenders vying for the 2020 Democratic presidential nomination, eight have openly embraced the idea of exploring reparations in earnest. That is quite a sea change.

Simply put, the idea of reparations is not a new concept, but it is one witnessing a significant resurgence in political urgency. Most notably, members of the Congressional Black Caucus have introduced H.R.40—a bill seeking to establish a commission that would study reparations—since the late 1980s. Just prior to a June 2019 Congressional hearing on this bill (the first hearing held since 2007), Senate Majority Leader Mitch McConnell spoke out against any discussion about reparations for slavery, saying he did not think "reparations for something that happened 150 years ago, for whom none of us currently living are responsible, is a good idea." The following day, Ta-Nehisi Coates was invited to testify at the House hearing to passionately argue in favor of the topic of reparations and decided to use his five-minute opening statement to renounce the Republican Senator's argument that reparations are not a "good idea." While Coates observed that the contemporary call for reparations is crucial in order to prompt America to take steps toward restorative justice on behalf of the Black community writ large, he recognized that for someone like McConnell "it is tempting to divorce this modern campaign of terror, of plunder, from enslavement, but the logic of enslavement, of white supremacy respects no such borders. And the god of bondage was lustful and begat many heirs: coup d'etats and convict leasing, vagrancy laws and debt peonage, redlining and racist G.I. bills, poll taxes and state-sponsored terrorism."[36] Meanwhile, on the complete opposite side of the political spectrum, FOX News primetime and conservative host Laura Ingraham during her Thursday, June 20, 2019 podcast offered her opinions on the ongoing debate over reparations for descendants of the enslaved by proclaiming there are no "do-overs" after a "conquest."[37] Nevertheless, on a personal as well as professional basis, I am grateful that there is currently a potential prophetic moment where, unlike just a few years ago, the reparations debate has moved from a laughing matter to a legitimate topic once again.

It has been extremely useful to acknowledge the Black Manifesto as an appropriately proper starting point for considering various aspects of the modern reparations debate. Whereas polemical essayists, political pundits, and presidential candidates are finally giving reparations some thoughtful consideration, the lukewarm reception that greets this concept in many of our religious institutions is the worst take imaginable. Most churches, synagogues, temples, and other faith-based institutions have embraced the conventional wisdom that the only remedy for transgenerational structural poverty and systemic oppression rooted in past as well as present modes of white supremacist exploitation is to create job outreach centers, soup kitchens, share closets, homeless shelters, after-school programs, and charitable aid funds intended to help the needy pay their bills. While these are all very nice and admirable endeavors in order to help impoverished people in the midst of their dire straits, ironically that is precisely the problem: such holy and anointed half-measures ensure that the poor will stay in their wretched state in perpetuity. Even though it can certainly be argued that all the aforementioned activities

36. Aguilera, "Author Ta-Nehisi Coates."
37. Mazza, "Laura Ingraham Slams."

constitute varying forms of "reparations"—apology, acts of contrition and repentance, Christian love (agape), restitution, and charity—as I contend here, all of these efforts pale in comparison to the brave and bold new social order that the Black Manifesto attempted to bring into existence.

Furthermore, what most people fail to realize is that, for most of modern history, Black people across the African diaspora have been set completely outside of the class structure within civil society and political economy. Since being designated historically as profitable property as well as a tradable commodity at the height of chattel slavery in North America, African Americans have been perennially defined as a classless non-people within most white Western literature and discourse. Regardless of whether addressed in academic, artistic, or public policy, the clear identification of Black women, men, and children by race within contemporary global order meant we had NO class in terms of political consciousness or personal agency but not classless based on social condition or socioeconomic context.

By this token, the nexus of class and labor developed not just as a political and economic matter but also as an embodied issue, one that ought to pay attention to race, gender, religion, nationality, sexuality, and other factors both in isolation and in various combinations. In a fashion akin to the Marxist notion of false consciousness, whiteness in America—regardless of income—became a marker of power and privilege in and of itself and remains so. Conversely, Blackness has become a permanent marker of inferiority in and of itself, regardless of the economic or cultural capital one possesses. While being cognizant that the conflation of race, class, and power, it is necessary to note that whiteness does not ostensibly place all white people as elite members of the ruling class just as much as all nonwhite people are not automatically defined as subservient or subhuman. Towards this end, James Cone speaks of a redemptive conversion in which white people can express sympathy and seek solidarity with subjugated people of color if they choose to "destroy their whiteness by becoming members of an oppressed community"[38]

But please do not confuse my racial analysis for not understanding the role of class and how it is linked to racialized power. Yet, in order to understand this analysis, one must look at WHY Black people are SO disproportionately poor and there is just one answer: We are the descendants

---

38. Cone and Hordern, "Dialogue on Black Theology," 1080; Cone, *Black Theology of Liberation*, 102–3; and Cone, *God of the Oppressed*, 222. See also McGee, "Against (White) Redemption."

of the invaded, enslaved, the segregated, the colonized, and the exploited. Even if our ancestors were not all of the above, at least one of these describes their plight. Ever since Reconstruction, numerous public policy measures, charitable initiatives, and universal social programs intended to lift Black people out of structural, transgenerational poverty are crucial to our future and I support them, money alone cannot and will not bring about equality. They still do not deal with the fact that rampant housing discrimination and health care disparities means Black people can have more money but still not move into higher-resourced neighborhoods or enjoy greater, healthier longevity. Or that black people can go to college but still suffer higher unemployment than white high school grads. Or the lack of transgenerational wealth that means Black people have the income to buy a home but not a sufficient credit score to qualify for a mortgage. Moreover, this lack of wealth that means even middle-class Black people are just one personal calamity or financial mishap away from poverty. Lest we forget, a contemporary world order still rooted in white supremacy and defined by patriarchy and class privilege has no intention to deal with the extraction of wealth from Black bodies simply because it is fair and right to do so. In this regard, many of the most ardent critics in the reparations debate describe those Black women, men, and children who are descendants of the enslaved as categorically being part of what historian Michael Katz has described as the "undeserving poor."[39] Let me add this final point for emphasis: I was born as part of the FIRST generation of Black people in the history of the Black Atlantic for whom it was not LEGAL to discriminate against us in housing, social services, employment, public accommodations, and education. Currently I am in my late 40s and I can easily say there's no white equivalent to my situation. That we know this but then say race-specific remedies are not practical and are unfair says everything we need to know about the seriousness about addressing racial inequality.

Conclusion

In the half century since the advent of the Black Manifesto, we have witnessed a great many ways in which the church has retreated from the challenging mandate to pursue economic justice in our time. During the intervening half century, we have seen not only a turning away from such

---

39. Katz, *The Undeserving Poor*.

revolutionary rhetoric and utopian imagination in most of our church sanctuaries and theological schools but this move was also accompanied by the swift and steady emergence of the "prosperity gospel" in the sacred sphere as well as neoliberalism in the secular sphere. To put an even finer point on this criticism, the mere fact that the existence and evolution of the Black Manifesto are new, previously unknown facts to many contemporary readers is suggestive of the truly disturbing extent that normative thought and praxis in the academy, church, and society have internalized the exploitative logic of capital to the exclusion of any radical alternative, especially if it originates from faithful people of color. In 1969 it was suggested by *The Christian Century*'s Albert Vorspan that the Black Manifesto may have saved the Church as a whole from becoming irrelevant.[40] In her examination of the African American reparations' debate *longue duree*, historian Mary Frances Berry suggests that, even though it was "lambasted by most whites" when it debuted, it kept the movement alive.[41] More recently, historian Elaine Allen Lechtreck notes, "The Black Manifesto can be understood as an expression of rebellion rooted in the despair of a people who had given up hope of 'integrating' into the mainstream socioeconomic systems and structures in the United States."[42]

To this end, this exploration of historic as well as contemporary examples of the Black Christian-Marxist perspective must be reinvigorated by those striving for worldwide aspirations for racial equality, radical democracy, and economic justice. Emphasizing the need to merge divine faith with conscious human action in the transition to a new social order, the presentation will demonstrate that the influence and embrace of Marxist ideology among numerous African American preachers, theologians, and religious scholars over more than a century has been a greatly overlooked facet of Black Christianity. Even more, the Manifesto's calls for reparations were so forceful that the statement's resonance with a greater quest for economic justice even encouraged other marginalized racial ethnic minority groups such Latinx peoples and Native Americans who appealed to mainline churches for financial support if not outright reparations.

More than fifty years after the Black Manifesto's debut, it is important to recognize how it transformed the interplay of race, religion, and

---

40. Vorspan, "How James Forman," 1042–43.
41. Berry, *My Face Is Black*, 239.
42. Lechtreck, "We Are Demanding," 40.

reparations. The debates that were provoked by the Manifesto's demand for reparations challenged mainline Christian and Jewish denominations to view themselves differently as sacred institutions in a secular world. In many ways, this Black prophetic statement emerged as a "holy writ" that challenged the clergy and laity of the nation's religious organizations to reassess their societal as well as spiritual priorities in order to reinterpret their core principles. When Rev. Calvin B. Marshall III, pastor of Varick Memorial AMEZ Church in Brooklyn, New York, became NBEDC chairman in 1970, he was asked, "Why did [the NBEDC] single out the church?" Without a moment's delay, Marshall replied "Because the Church is the only institution claiming to be in the business of salvation, resurrection, and the giving and restoring of life . . . General Motors has never made that kind of claim."[43] Whereas one might contend that Marshall's claim could be interpreted as letting CEOs and corporate America "off the hook" for their history of racial subordination and economic exploitation, nothing could be further from the truth. Instead, advocates of the Manifesto were holding accountable white Christian leaders and mainline churches to their own declared moral standards despite silent complicity with profitability rather than prophetic action. In light of Marshall's comments, the Manifesto during its height was making a prophetic hue and cry that the Church should reorient itself in keeping with its broad-based mission: feeding the hungry; sheltering the homeless; offering hospitality to strangers and refugees; fostering peace among adversaries; providing educational and employment opportunities for the disadvantaged; giving compassion to the bereaved; and advocacy on behalf of the disinherited regardless of race, ethnicity, gender, sexuality, and nationality.

Bibliography

Aguilera, Jasmine. "Author Ta-Nehisi Coates Criticized Mitch McConnell for Saying Slavery's Effects Were in the Past." *Time*, June 19, 2019. https://time.com/5610151/ta-nehisi-coates-criticized-mcconnell-reparations/.

Berry, Mary Frances. *My Face Is Black Is True: Callie House and the Struggle for Ex-Slave Reparations.* New York: Knopf, 2005.

"Black Manifesto | Encyclopedia.Com." https://www.encyclopedia.com/history/biographies/historians-us-biographies/black-manifesto/.

---

43. Johnson, "Blacks Press Reparations Demands."

Johnson, Thomas A. "Blacks Press Demands for Reparations." *New York Times*, June 10, 1970. http://timesmachine.nytimes.com/timesmachine/1970/06/10/81843686.html/.

Burrows, Trevor. "The 'Black Manifesto' in Twentieth-Century American Religious History." *Religion in American History*, Aug. 5, 2014 (blog). https://usreligion.blogspot.com/2014/08/the-black-manifesto-in-twentieth.html.

Campbell, Ernest T. *Christian Manifesto*. New York: Harper & Row, 1970.

Coates, Ta-Nehisi. "The Case for Reparations." *The Atlantic*, June 2014. https://www.theatlantic.com/magazine/archive/2014/06/the-case-for-reparations/361631/.

Copeland, M. Shawn (Mary Shawn). "Black Theology and a Legacy of Oppression." *America Magazine*, June 24, 2014. https://www.americamagazine.org/faith/2014/06/24/black-theology-and-legacy-oppression/.

Douglass, Frederick. *Narrative of the Life of Frederick Douglass: An American Slave*. Cambridge, MA: Belknap, 1967.

Floyd-Thomas, Juan M. "Seeing Red in the Black Church: Marxist Thought and African American Christianity." *Journal of Race, Ethnicity, and Religion* 1.12 (2010) 46.

Forman, J. "The Black Manifesto." *Africa Today* 16.4 (1969) 21–24.

Forman, James. *The Making of Black Revolutionaries*. Washington, DC: Open Hand, 1985.

Ho, Fred Wei-han, and Bill Mullen, eds. *Afro Asia: Revolutionary Political and Cultural Connections between African Americans and Asian Americans*. Durham: Duke University Press, 2008.

Jordan, Winthrop D. *White over Black: American Attitudes toward the Negro, 1550–1812*. Chapel Hill: Published for the Institute of Early American History and Culture at Williamsburg, VA, by the University of North Carolina Press, 1968.

Katz, Michael B. *The Undeserving Poor: America's Enduring Confrontation with Poverty*. Oxford: Oxford University Press, 2013.

Kelley, Robin D. G. *Freedom Dreams: The Black Radical Imagination*. Boston: Beacon, 2002.

King, Martin Luther. *Why We Can't Wait*. New York: New American Library, 1964.

Lechtreck, Elaine Allen. "'We Are Demanding $500 Million For Reparations': The Black Manifesto, Mainline Religious Denominations and Black Economic Development." *Journal of African American History* 97.1–2 (2012) 39–71.

Lecky, Robert S. *Black Manifesto: Religion, Racism, and Reparations*. New York: Sheed & Ward, 1969.

Lubasch, Arnold H. "Pastor at Riverside Pledges a Fund for the Poor." *The New York Times*, May 11, 1969, sec. Archives. https://www.nytimes.com/1969/05/11/archives/pastor-at-riverside-pledges-a-fund-for-the-poor.html/.

Marable, Manning. *The Great Wells of Democracy: The Meaning of Race in American Life*. New York: Basic Civitas, 2002.

Marx, Karl. *Capital*. Moscow: Foreign Language Publishing House, 1957.

Mazza, Ed. "Laura Ingraham Slams 'Preposterous' Reparations Calls: 'No Do-Overs. That's It.'" *Huffington Post*, June 21, 2019. https://www.huffpost.com/entry/laura-ingraham-reparations_n_5d0c569be4b0a394186008c4.

McGee, Timothy. "Against (White) Redemption: James Cone and the Christological Disruption of Racial Discourse and White Solidarity." *Political Theology* 18.7 (2017) 542–59.

Morgan, Edmund S. *American Slavery, American Freedom: The Ordeal of Colonial Virginia*. New York: Norton, 1975.

"Muhammed Kenyatta, Community Organizer. The Church Awakens: African Americans and the Struggle for Justice." September 4, 1969. https://www.episcopalarchives.org/church-awakens/items/show/321.

Myrdal, Gunnar. *An American Dilemma: The Negro Problem and Modern Democracy*. New Brunswick, NJ: Transaction, 1996.

Oakes, James. "Slavery Is Theft." *Jacobin*, August 13, 2015. https://jacobinmag.com/2015/08/slavery-abolition-lincoln-oakes-property/.

Paris, Peter J., John W. Cook, and James Hudnut-Beumler, eds. *The History of the Riverside Church in the City of New York*. Religion, Race, and Ethnicity. New York: New York University Press, 2004.

Robinson, Randall. *The Debt: What America Owes to Blacks*. New York: Dutton, 2000.

Schuchter, Arnold. *Reparations: The Black Manifesto and Its Challenge to White America*. Philadelphia: Lippincott, 1970.

Smith, John. *Travels and Works of Captain John Smith*. Edinburgh: Grant, 1910.

Vorspan, Albert. "How James Forman Lost His Cool but Saved Religion in 1969: A Modern Bible Story." *Christian Century* 86.32 (August 6, 1969) 1042.

Wallis, Jim. *America's Original Sin: Racism, White Privilege, and the Bridge to a New America*. Grand Rapids: Brazos, 2016.

Walters, Ronald W. *The Price of Racial Reconciliation*. Ann Arbor: University of Michigan Press, 2008.

Wilmore, Gayraud S. *Black Religion and Black Radicalism: An Interpretation of the Religious History of African Americans*. Maryknoll, NY: Orbis, 1998.

Winbush, Raymond A., ed. *Should America Pay? Slavery and the Raging Debate on Reparations*. New York: Amistad, 2003.

Wood, Betty. *Slavery in Colonial America, 1619–1776*. Lanham, MD: Rowman & Littlefield, 2005.

4

With Our Hands We Build Machines, With Our Hearts We Build the Future

Religion, Labor, and Class Consciousness

Marcus Trammell

The Great Depression and the Remaking of a Family

In the late 1930s, at the depths of the Great Depression, my great-grandparents migrated from southern Indiana to Michigan where my great-grandfather would eventually find work in General Motor's Oldsmobile Assembly plant in Lansing. This was just a few years after the United Auto Workers union won recognition to negotiate with the automaker in the now famous sit-down strikes. A number of economic and labor factors profoundly effected my family: the economic depression of the 1930s, the surge of labor activism in the region, and the rise of New Deal politics under the leadership of President Franklin Roosevelt and Michigan Governor Frank Murphy. Within one generation my family rose from desperate financial circumstances to seeing three of their four children receive college educations and obtain professional employment. Their youngest daughter would marry an autoworker and enjoy what could be called a stable working-class life. Their two sons would obtain graduate degrees, one would be elected to the Michigan House of Representatives as a Democrat for a term and the other would balance both work as a state civil servant and being a prominent pastor and leader of the United Pentecostal Church. One of their daughters would earn a bachelor's degree in the 1950s, well before it was common in American society and all but unheard of in their socially conservative Pentecostal religious sect.

The Great Depression dislodged my great-grandparents from their rural community in southern Indiana where their ancestors (who were of predominately immigrant German stock) had settled nearly a hundred years before and move them into both a new economic and social reality in the twentieth century. In Indiana they sustained themselves as subsistence farmers and semi-skilled laborers and would for a time achieve a level of social and economic stability, allowing my great-grandfather to purchase his first automobile for $500 dollars cash and build a small home with the help of a government-backed loan for his growing family of five. But in 1932, when the economic depression finally slowed and eventually dried up his work as a foreman at a local stone quarry, he would lose the home he built—almost entirely with his own hands—and the family would find itself existing on intermittent earnings from day labor and the charity of their neighbors. These desperate conditions forced them on an economic migration North in search of consistent industrial work. It would also propel them on a religious migration—from nominal religious involvement—into the emerging Pentecostal movement, along with thousands of others, who like them, were seeking solace for the anger and distress that arose from seeing their modest economic fortunes suddenly collapse.

The American economic collapse in the third decade of the twentieth century spurred them on a geographic, religious, social, and political migration. They left agrarian lives in the middle South and relocated to an industrial urban life in the northern states. There they would encounter a unique mix of labor union activism and New Deal liberal political ideology, fused with a Christian social gospel that would apply the teachings of Jesus to the social and economic problems of their era. At the same time, they would expand their own personal religious commitments in the Pentecostal movement, founding a church in the capital city of Lansing just blocks from the Oldsmobile plant. This was a small but vibrant congregation that consisted mostly of industrial workers and wage laborers. The economic deprivation they experienced during the 1930s would unite their religious beliefs and their class consciousness into a liberal political identity often at odds with the more conservative and reactionary political identities of other leaders in the emerging Pentecostal movement. They would instill in their children a commitment to democratic political ideals and a reverence for the New Deal programs that had changed their lives and offered a modicum of security to the struggling working-class to which they belonged. They also recognized the role labor unions had played in securing for them consistent and gainful employment. Their experience as a part of the aggressively pro-civil rights United Auto Workers union (UAW) under the leadership of Walter Reuther, along with their experience as members of the multi-racial Pentecostals Assemblies of the World (PAW), made them firm supporters of civil rights for black and brown Americans well before the movement gained national appeal. Even before the turbulent years of the 1960s, their support of the civil rights movement was vocal and often in conflict with others in their religious community. This commitment carried on in their children, and as late as the 1970s a family member recalls boycotting certain fruits in solidarity with the United Farm Workers Union, which would join the AFL-CIO in 1972 and gain the support of the UAW in its efforts to negotiate on behalf of exploited Hispanic migrant workers in California and the American South. Their story was similar to millions of other old stock white European Americans whose class consciousness would be developed through their economic and social migration northward where it would be influenced by the policies of the New Deal and the progressive politics of the United Auto Workers. They were not unique but rare, especially among the leadership of the almost entirely white United Pentecostal Church in which they would become members in the 1940s after first joining the predominately black Pentecostal Assemblies of the World. Their experiences with African American Pentecostal believers, support for the New Deal politics of Franklin and Eleanor Roosevelt, my great-grandfather's membership in the UAW, and their steadfast belief in the value of education arguably helped to blunt the effects of the more conservative, reactionary political and social beliefs common amongst their peers in the Pentecostal Church. And this would profoundly influence me three-generations later in my work as a community and labor organizer and my choice to study religion and social movements to try and understand the paradoxes of the religious and social experiences that defined my family story.

In this chapter I attempt to unpack the social, religious, political, and class context in which my family history was formed and how it was influenced by both rudimentary religious impulses and the social gospel theology preached by labor organizations that sought to fuse class and religious identities. I argue that labor unions, and specifically the UAW, were both directly and indirectly responsible for their ability to form integrated religious and class consciousness that allowed them to support collectivist political policies like the New Deal. Labor unions are a crucial factor in helping my family understand that the quality of their religious commitment was bound up in the plight of their neighbors, both white, black, and Hispanic. Although most others in their Pentecostal sect gravitated to nativist, racist, and reactionary political ideologies, or preached resignation and isolation in response to political class struggle, they felt they had a Christian duty to the poor and marginalized that extended to their political identity. Where did this expression of their faith come from? How did they hold in tension the predominant political ideology of the Pentecostal movement, which favored the status quo, with their own progressive political values? Where did they get the vision to expand their personally-oriented faith to one that felt an obligation to stand for the common good for all people? To be sure they had their problems: they struggled just as we do with how to respond in the face of life's challenges and conflicts. They embodied their share of contradictions and human shortcomings but despite all, they left a courageous legacy of choosing a life of solidarity with the poor and oppressed. They also persisted in resisting the racist and xenophobic currents that sought to divide the country by undermining the New Deal economic reforms of the era that included expanded labor rights. They maintained a progressive political identity more in line with the membership of their denomination than it was with the other pastors and leaders alongside whom they served.

Visions of the Disinherited

Robert Mapes Anderson, examining Pentecostalism in the context of class struggle, argues that Pentecostalism was primarily a response to the massive social change taking place in the late nineteenth and early twentieth century. In that period, he observes, "the old norms of belief, morality, manners and behavior were collapsing and … all social institutions were compelled to adjust to that fact." For Pentecostals, the way in which mainstream religious denominations accommodated to this social change was unacceptable and they sought to separate themselves from the society. "It was ... the need to bring order to the chaos of their lives that led so many into the Pentecostal fold. What these converts expected was a clear set of directions through the social maze."[1] Pentecostal religion emphasized personal salvation and the moral obligation to avoid sin by separating from the world, shunning the broader culture, and choosing instead a religious identity based on the belief they had an exclusive understanding of the truth of the Bible, which would allow only those who shared their specific understanding to be saved. The point here is to emphasize just how dramatic the difference was between religious groupings, not just between Catholics and mainline Protestants as well as African American Protestants, but even within the evangelical sects of white Protestantism, where Pentecostals represented the most fractured groups. The movement was marred by the extreme individualism of its leaders, and it splintered into hundreds of different organizations all claiming their own exclusive religious truth and rejecting the salvation of others who were in almost all other ways exactly like them. Anderson, quoting Howard Goss, the first superintendent of the United Pentecostal Church and a friend of my family, comments "a preacher, who did not dig up some new slant on Scripture, or get some new revelation to his own heart ever so often...was considered slow, stupid, and unspiritual."[2]

My family was part of a religious sect that exhibited some of the most extreme religious sectarianism at work in American Christianity. These traditions often fostered a status-quo attitude towards political matters, advocating political indifference and a scriptural interpretation demanding subservience to political authority, while favoring arcane and protracted religious debates. Anderson asserts that although Pentecostals often denounced cultural and political elites and the corrupt social norms of the time, their response was to preach that political and social problems would only be solved by the return of Christ, thus engendering apathy and resignation in response to social and political issues.[3]

Anderson further notes that the preachers in this movement often denounced labor unions and other political solutions, teaching submission to authority and the acceptance of the status quo, and focusing

---

1. Anderson, *Vision of the Disinherited*, 153.
2. Anderson, *Vision of the Disinherited*, 155.
3. Anderson, *Vision of the Disinherited*, 201.

members hopes on the life to come. This includes the denouncing of labor unions not only as useless but on many occasions as demonic.[4] Nevertheless, Anderson continues, union organizers often found members of Pentecostal churches easier to recruit than members of established denominations and he references studies that assert it may have been their class identification that made this possible.[5] His conclusion is that early Pentecostalism has to be understood as a part of a long-term and wide spread protest of the social consequences of modern industrial capitalism.[6] He concludes that if their impulses had been channeled in the proper place they would have been social reformers, but because of their class position and lack of education they did not have the resources to comprehend—much less combat—the larger social and economic structures they were trapped within. Consequently, they turned to ecstatic experience and meaning making through religion, with the result that most Pentecostal leaders taught acceptance the political status quo.[7]

The Making of Working-Class Religion

Historian Matthew Pehl gives us a frame in which to understand the intersection of religion, labor, and New Deal politics in the region by examining the labor struggles of twentieth-century century Detroit. Pehl acknowledges that from the beginning the tradition of intellectual analysis of class and capitalism, there has been a strong suspicion of religion and its role as a perceived consolation prize for those on the underside of capitalism. This is one interpretation of the conclusion offered by Karl Marx in his now famous critique that religion was "the sigh of the oppressed . . . the opium of the people."[8] In this tradition, religion is seen as a comfort for life's sorrows, which fails to offer political or historical solutions to the exploitation inherent in the capitalist economy. Pehl notes that scholars still mostly see American religious movements as a moderating influence on political radicalism, providing status-quo

---

4. Anderson, *Vision of the Disinherited*, 214.

5. Anderson, *Vision of the Disinherited*, 211. Anderson makes it clear that it was members as distinct from pastors or other leaders who were most often, for their own survival in a fractured movement, deeply committed to individualism and reluctant to embrace collectivist ideas. See page 224.

6. Anderson, *Vision of the Disinherited*, 223.

7. Anderson, *Vision of the Disinherited*, 212, 221.

8. Pehl, *Making of Working-Class Religion*, 2.

solutions to the problems that emerged with the predominant American social and economic order. He acknowledges the difficulty of trying to sort out the influence of religion in the lives of workers in Detroit in the early twentieth century and he accepts that religion was often used as a tool for control or as a moderating influence on the working class. But Pehl also argues that there was a unique and influential "working-class religion," which developed in the industrial plants of Detroit and that supported the cause of the workers. There was a worker-oriented theology, comprised of stories and biblical interpretations that challenged the exploitative labor practices of the industrial owners, which put God and scripture on the side of the worker. Pehl writes, "if scholars have long persisted in viewing religion as a tool for exploitation (at worst) or a consolation prize for history's losers (at best), another scholarly tradition has insisted on religion's radical potential for inspiring social and political movement."[9] And Pehl orients his scholarship of working-class religion in Detroit in this tradition. His work traces the unique and intersecting histories of mainline Protestants, Catholics, as well as African American and White Evangelical Protestants in post-World War I Detroit. The picture that he paints is a unique and powerful image of the converging streams of religious expression with working-class struggle.

Detroit was not only the quintessential American "blue-collar" city, it was also one of the most important creative and tumultuous religious centers in the United States. In the early 1900s, Detroit was the place of the first pastorate for a young Reinhold Niebuhr, who would later emerge as one of America's most renowned theologians. Early in his career, Niebuhr would establish his reputation as a social gospeler by opposing industrialist Henry Ford. Detroit was also the home of Father Charles Coughlin, the Catholic radio priest whose populist Catholicism would catapult him to national influence in matters of politics and religion. It was, furthermore, the place from where the Nation of Islam would emerge, and it was the center of activity for several early fundamentalist preachers who had migrated from the South along with the thousands of workers in search of work in the northern industrial plants. In addition, Detroit was also the home to several African American clergy who would rise to national prominence for both their religious and political leadership, such as the Rev. Dr. C.L. Franklin, a Baptist pastor and father of singer Aretha Franklin. Detroit's Roman Catholic bishop, John Cardinal

---

9. Pehl, *Making of Working-Class Religion*, 3.

Dearden, helped make Detroit the epicenter of experimentation as the Roman Catholic church sought to implement the changes that the Second Vatican Council had proposed. Detroit, in the early twentieth century was without question a place of not only unprecedented industrial development, labor, and political activism,[10]

Pehl argues that the fuel for these developments was the growth of a seemingly permanent underclass of wage laborers (like the members of my own family) who existed on the fringes of society and whose economic struggles became the central moral challenge of the time. The question of what to do about the conditions of industrial labor became the most pressing social, moral, and political question.[11] It was during this time, under the strain of the Great Depression, that the relationship between workers' political consciousness and their religious culture began to shift. Also, from 1937–1939, Frank Murphy, a progressive Roman Catholic, would attain political success as Governor of Michigan by appealing to working-class voters using religious language. At the very same time, the UAW would spread rapidly within Detroit's industrial plants, establishing Detroit as the quintessential union town. Pehl, writing about this transformative period, states that the UAW

> initiated a new relationship between working-class religion and the labor movement. Union leaders acutely recognized the deep nature of working-class religiosity and endeavored to minimize any tensions between religious and class identities. More, the union aggressively claims the social gospel for the working class and recasts the entire labor movement through the prism of religious consciousness. The remaking of working-class religious consciousness, then, was deeply implicated in the rise of the New Deal Order.[12]

Murphy as a devout Roman Catholic, in response to Pope Leo XIII's famous labor encyclical, *Rerum Novarum,* appealed to industrial workers by claiming empathically that "a government's whole reason for existence

---

10. Pehl, *Making of Working-Class Religion*, 7–8. Some unique mainline Protestant religious organizations emerged in Detroit, like the People's Institute for Applied Religion, led by Presbyterian Claude Williams (a Vanderbilt alumnus) and focused on the struggles of working people of all races and ethnicities. The ecumenical agencies that emerged during this time, such as the Detroit Industrial Mission, sought to reimagine urban religion in response to the challenges of the new industrial age.

11. Pehl, *Making of Working-Class Religion*, 57.

12. Pehl, *Making of Working-Class Religion*, 57.

was to promote the common good and, especially, to defend the rights of working people."[13] It was in this context that religious expression fused with working class labor struggle to create what Pehl has termed "working class religion," a religious movement cultivated and led by workers and labor leaders. In contrast, most of the local clergy would continue to deny the existence of a problem and would emphasize only the individual's responsibility to work.[14]

Historian Heath Carter, studying the same period in metropolitan Chicago, has argued that the rise of the Social Gospel movement was "union made." Its propagation was more often in the union hall than the church sanctuary.[15] Few clergy played substantial roles; rather, as Pehl argues, it was "UAW leaders and members themselves who invented a working-class religion." It was the "plant preachers" who disseminated new interpretations of scriptures that gave workers a new way to fuse their religious and political identities.[16] Pehl writes, "At its most ambitious, the UAW argued that membership and support of a union constituted a basic part of religious commitment." It was an expression of duty to all workers, an unselfish act, a moral obligation to their fellow workers. Seeking an individualistic path to economic security was considered selfish and shortsighted. This transformation cut across religious lines, from immigrant Roman Catholics to African Americans and also to white Evangelicals, whose religion was often seen as the most staunchly conservative, emphasizing personal responsibility and respect for authority in the workplace. Even white Evangelicals (the broad category into which that my great-grandfather would have been lumped) whose religious sentiments were often felt to be the most corrupted, began to develop a new relationship between their political and religious consciousness. Pehl writes,

> To many [white Evangelicals], that appeal of the CIO became a revival movement. Largely because of their deep sense of common folk equality, [white Evangelicals] embraced the cause of union labor with religious fervor . . .[17]

13. Pehl, *Making of Working-Class Religion*, 69.
14. Pehl, *Making of Working-Class Religion*, 9.
15. Carter, *Union Made*, chapters 4–7.
16. Pehl, *Making of Working-Class Religion*, 74.
17. The UAW was a part of the Congress of Industrial Organizations and was often supported and directed in its organizing efforts by CIO leadership and in conjunction with CIO campaigns across industrial unions, like the United Mine Workers and the

Consequently, many white Evangelicals emerged as key leaders in the UAW during this period.[18] New idioms of work and religion emerged, and they embedded themselves deeply within the democratic ideals of the period. This coming together of class identity and religious tradition became the very heart of the democratic experiment during the era of the New Deal.

The UAW and The New Deal

What is noteworthy about my family is that they, along with others, would hold together paradoxical belief systems, finding deep identity in the Pentecostal church with its individualistic, experiential, and apocalyptic theology that often more easily aligned with a conservative political frame. My family and others would come to be strong supporters of the Roosevelts and the New Deal, and they were vocal in their support for the UAW, which would fervently embrace liberal policies and leaders like Walter Reuther and New Deal Michigan governors like Frank Murphy and G. Mennen Williams. And they would expressly connect their religious faith to the need for civil rights for African Americans. No doubt, the depths of their own economic deprivation during the Great Depression had a profound effect on the formation of their political views, their support for the New Deal, and their early involvement in a predominantly African American Pentecostal organization helped to shape their view on civil rights. But there is also no denying the role of the UAW as a force in their political formation, supported by their location in its most powerful region. The role of the UAW in promoting New Deal politics and civil rights created a dynamic in mid-twentieth century Michigan that would bring together a formidable coalition of black and white working-class Americans, whose religious beliefs were often transformed beyond their traditional parochialism into a more progressive and communally diverse expression. It is hard to say what would have become of my family if they would not have migrated to the region, beyond their basic economic survival. Would they have still developed their commitment to liberal politics and civil rights? Without the influence of labor organizations like the UAW and political leaders like Governors

---

United Steel Workers, whose products were necessary in the production of automobiles. Pehl, *Making of Working-Class Religion*, 143.

18. Pehl, *Making of Working-Class Religion*, 143.

Murphy and Williams and President Roosevelt, things might have turned out differently. The members of my family were in many ways products of their time and place and could have chosen a more tribal and bigoted politics.

Their political identity was clearly sparked by their profound economic hardship in the 1930s; their primary response was to work out these emotions through religious means. But they were also somehow able to connect their simple religious faith to an understanding of Christian ideals that included political solutions like the New Deal and civil rights reforms. Even while waiting on the imminent return of Christ, they challenged the political status quo of the time, which led them into a firm commitment for civil rights for African Americans, for fairness for Mexican migrant workers, and even expanding in their minds the right of women to work and gain an education. Many others in their own religious communities held very different views.

The collection of the Walter Ruether Library at Wayne State University contains a striking poster, bearing modernist depiction of three faces, black, brown and white, with the caption: "With Our Hands We Build Machines With Our Hearts We Build The Future." Little information about this poster is available, and it even lacks a specific date of its printing. There is another that depicts two hands conducting a shell game stating, "It's the old shell game . . . YOU CAN'T WIN WHICHEVER YOU CHOOSE—YOU'RE SURE TO LOSE." The shells are labeled Racial Hate, Religious Hate, and Hate the Foreigner. The images illustrate the deliberate methods the UAW used to confront bigotry and to cast a more inclusive vision for its diverse membership. Reuther and his allies understood that religious, ethnic, and racial bigotry were powerful forces that had long been used to stifle collective action to address labor and economic inequities, and so they expressly connected the union cause with the cause of civil rights. And for a time, this aligning of union ideology with civil rights and moral teaching was successful. It helped to build a strong labor movement, a thriving middle class, and set the United States on course as a pioneer of civil and human rights. But soon enough that distinction was lost. And now we find ourselves confronted with some of the same insidious forces of racial, religious, and ethnic hate, focused on dividing American society against itself and in service of an economic ideology focused on the flourishing of a few at the cost of the many. What remains of the labor movement in the United States seems trapped in a cycle of reactionary activities, focused on holding on to whatever is left from their heydays at the middle of the twentieth century, having at times abandoned their beliefs in labor rights as a part of a broad struggle for human rights for an ideology that serves a more narrow interest. Many religious communities as well have lost touch with their commitments to organized labor and economic justice. But there is a possibility that things could be different. Reuniting the concerns of what it means to labor in our modern economy with religious belief could offer us a new path to face the challenges of our own time.

The Forces We Face

The significance of this exploration is underscored by the current religious and political dynamics of the United States, on the eve of a presidential election year that will undoubtedly serve for many as a measure of the direction of this nation and the world. The breakdown of the New Deal economic order, that had such a profoundly positive effect on the economic and social fortunes of my family is evident. The growing economic inequity not seen since before the Great Depression and coupled with the angry reactionary political populism manifested by the administration of Donald Trump provides some evidence that something is profoundly wrong with the economic order. Even more troubling is the support from so called conservative Christians, including millions of American Pentecostals who ironically see in Donald Trump the last hope for America to return to "godly" government. American Pentecostals, including the clergy and members of the United Pentecostal Church to which my family belongs, are now a long way from the disinterest in political affairs that early Pentecostals taught and have now been brought squarely inside the Christian fundamentalist political crusade to return America to its "Christian roots" and reconnect it to "God's favor." This belief exists alongside an apocalyptic vision that the rapture of the church is soon to come and to be followed by the battle of Armageddon and the destruction of the earth. In this mindset, America is a wayward nation once blessed by God but now is in decline because of its rejection of Christian values, particularly the heterosexual male dominated patriarchy often colloquially referred to as family values. The vision of God's favored nation in decline in dire need of a savior dovetails neatly, if not strangely, with the rhetoric and character of Donald Trump. And the rightwing extremists who preach a political gospel of restoring America to greatness by denigrating immigrants and eradicating "godless socialist" policies—that infringe on the freedom hardworking God-fearing Americas in service of lazy freeloaders who often are pictured as black and brown and or foreign natives—have found their most ardent supporters among the fundamentalist "Christian" faithful. The cause is clear and includes restoring traditional values by rolling back reproductive rights for women and civil rights for minorities in an effort to reassert the dominance of "Christian" hetero-patriarchal values. Economic elites have deliberately inflamed the anxieties of white "Christian" Americans, using them as an opportunity to propagate neoliberal economic theory focused on financial policies of austerity to undermine government's role in the economy and promote a religion of laissez-faire "free" market capitalism, with its omniscient power to rightly order the economic affairs of humanity without the intervention of the state.[19] This is coupled with the well-financed libertarian political ideas of billionaire Charles Koch and his extensive web of ideological organizations, which promote a radical notion of individual freedom and property rights that supersede any social responsibility for the well-being of others. These political ideas, which are not new, are made all the more concerning as they are bolstered by the deliberate inflaming of old racial, religious, and ethnic resentments. They effectively undermine important class coalitions between white, black, and brown Americans that for a period in the second half of the twentieth century seemed to be charting a course of racial and economic improvement for an expanding group of Americans and offering the possibility of a more egalitarian society.

Can Faith and Labor Overcome?

Joerg Rieger and Rosemarie Henkel-Rieger present a vision of "deep solidarity," a radical reordering that asks us to look at what unites us rather what divides us, without ignoring or abandoning our differences. Offering fresh interpretations of passages in the Bible, much like adherents of the Social Gospel did in the New Deal era, they ask us to think about the Hebrew Scriptures, the writings of Paul, and the words of Jesus in new ways and consider what else might be possible. Rieger and Henkel-Rieger suggest that our misconceptions of God lead us into the trap of the supremacy of top-down power and alienate us from one another.

19. Kruse, *One Nation under God*.

"What if religion were not primarily about pious ideals but about work, community, and solidarity, alternative power that flows from the bottom up rather than the top down, and a new way of life?"[20] The implication is that how one sees religion and God shapes how one will understand political power and how it defines community. As a result, reimagining our concepts of God and our interpretation of the Bible can contribute to the formation of a new social order. Rieger and Henkel-Rieger go on to write, "if working people have some influence over their work, as they do in some places, chances are their voices will also carry some weight in their communities and that they will gain some influence in matters of politics."[21]

In our current age, is there a way to bring together the profound anxiety people feel in their economic lives with a religious expression that believes that their faith requires them to work for something better in this world? How are commitments formed to reject racial, religious, and ethnic bigotry in favor of a material analysis of the economic system and to demand of it a higher order of being for all people? Would this be in line with the deeply communal aspirations of the Hebrews, the early Christians, and the working-class religion of my grandparents? The current state of affairs, at least from the perspective of the United States examined at close range, offers us what seems to be negative proof. But this could just as easily have been the conclusion a century ago, when some of these very same forces were at work.

Nevertheless, as history shows, there were brief alignments of religious and material values whose consequences would have lasting impact and still offer us hope today. The reality of organizations such as the UAW and religious communities that straddled the events of the mid-twentieth century were invariably messy, discordant, and often steeped in petty disagreements and contradictions. Yet through all of this, new economic and social opportunities were achieved. These achievements continue to nourish a small sense of hope and optimism for our own time, a hope that a better future is possible. Still it is only realistic to acknowledge that the challenge of our time includes not only deep class struggle and the ongoing struggle for economic and civil rights for black and brown Americans but also a deeper engagement than what was attempted in the twentieth century, one that strikes at the heart of the patriarchal

---

20. Rieger and Henkel-Rieger, *Unified We Are a Force*, 15.
21. Rieger and Henkel-Rieger, *Unified We Are a Force*, 19.

white-supremacist culture that is so deeply enmeshed in American and Christian identity. Can the forces of liberation at work in the Jewish and Christian scriptures overcome the forces of heteropatriarchal dominance and control at work not only in our current cultural situation but in the scriptures themselves? Can religion help us build a better future or is it one of the most stubborn and persistent obstacles? The answer to me continues to be elusive, and only a seemingly unsatisfiable need to wrestle with the inherent contradictions of my experience and history is clear at this point.

For the past decade I have worked as an organizer for several national labor organizations including the UAW and the AFL-CIO. I've spent that time attempting to assist people solve their economic and social problems through collective action. I have knocked on thousands of doors, convened meetings in community centers, union halls, and church buildings. All in an effort to help people find ways to improve their lives and the lives of their neighbors. It's in these experiences that I've seen people embody the more clearly measurable part of what Jesus called the greatest commandment. Love God with all your heart, but also equally to love your neighbor as yourself. This commandment, if taken in the context of Jesus's other teachings on who is one's neighbor, presents a radically collective notion of personal salvation. At the center of the struggles for fairness and equality we often find coalitions of people brought together by their faith and by the organizations and techniques forged in years of labor and social struggle. No matter how deeply flawed these institutions are, they remain vitally important to progress in our society. From my experience of working with thousands of people across the country, unions remain the most effective force for transcending the white-supremacist heteropatriarchal reactionary politics that has existed in our country from the beginning, and of which the current US president is just a flagrant expression.

In the final days of the 2016 election I found myself in a UAW hall in suburban Detroit listening to a gospel choir sing and sway on a Sunday afternoon as a diverse group of autoworkers filed past, picking up precinct packets for their fellow members. In this line African-American men and women mingled with white men and women and with people of several other ethnicities. The crowd without a doubt represented a wide range of religious beliefs among other forms of social grouping and identity, all brought together around shared economic values. This was likely one of the more diverse gatherings in the region that Sunday—church and football included. The UAW is much smaller now than it was a half century ago, currently mired in legal trouble, often hobbled with disfunction, its commitment to religious values, social justice and racial equality much less pronounced than it was nearly a century ago. Nevertheless, it still provides a vision of how class consciousness that embraces the inherent value of all human life can build a more inclusive world. The hope for a better world and the possibility of transcending our current social challenges seems to me today less likely to be found in a church sanctuary or even a union hall, but it will undoubtedly include the best agreed-upon values that both of these traditions hold. These values include a profound love and concern for fellow human beings, which include their economic wellbeing. That is what I learned from the lives of my grandparents Herbert and Eleanor Starr and their children, and I will do my best to pass it on to another generation.

Bibliography

Anderson, Robert Mapes. *Vision of the Disinherited: The Making of American Pentecostalism*. New York: Oxford University Press, 1979.

Carter, Heath W. *Union Made: Working People and the Rise of Social Christianity in Chicago*. New York: Oxford University Press, 2015.

Kruse, Kevin Michael. *One Nation under God: How Corporate America Invented Christian America*. New York: Basic Books, 2015.

Pehl, Matthew. *The Making of Working-Class Religion*. The Working Class in America. Urbana: University of Illinois Press, 2016.

Rieger, Joerg, and Rosemarie Henkel-Rieger. *Unified We Are a Force: How Faith and Labor Can Overcome America's Inequalities*. St. Louis: Chalice, 2016.

Section II

Reading Bible, Reading Class

5

People's Money, Women's Precarious Life, and Empire

JIN YOUNG CHOI

Introduction

LUISE SCHOTTROFF SAYS, "FOR too long we have had all these exegetical strategies of making invisible the gospel of the poor. It is time to put an end to this."[1] The traditional interpretation of Mark 12:38–44, which focuses on the widow's offering as a paradigm for individual piety or true discipleship, is a prime example of suffocating the gospel of the poor. By idealizing the poor, this kind of interpretation perpetuates the status quo.[2]

Alternatively, the poor widow's act can be viewed negatively because it exposes the exploitation of the poor by the Jerusalem Temple and its authorities. In this interpretation, Jesus grieves at the poor widow's offering as the result of her being misled by the religious authorities, and thus she is depicted as a victim.[3] This interpretation pays attention to the political-economic system that abused individuals in the lowest class of the society but fails not only to address complex relations of economy

1. Baptist, Damico, and Theoharis, "Responses of the Poor to Empire," 171.
2. Ste. Croix, *Class Struggle*, 439.
3. Wright, "Widow's Mites: Praise or Lament?," 256.

and particularly issues of labor but also to take into account that the poor are not merely victims.

Both traditional and liberationist or revisionist interpretations can make the poor invisible. Instead, I read the story of the poor widow through the lens of her precarious life in the Roman imperial context, as well as in the context of Mark's narrative, in which Jesus appears to be concerned with economic transactions against or around the multitude (*ochlos*).[4] By transecting the Roman Empire, Mark's narrative world, and the current globalized world of neoliberal capitalism, this new reading leads us to attend to the precariousness of the un(der)employed and the impoverished, particularly women, among the population.

Roman Imperial Political Economy

Rome's Social Structure, Economy, and Class

Mark writes the story of Jesus after the Jewish War against Rome (66–70 CE), probably from a location in northern Palestine or southern Syria. Galilee was a Roman client kingdom in Jesus's time, and the Roman imperial power had already engulfed Judea as a tributary province.[5] Mark must have had a sense of how production, social relations, and political institutions were organized in Roman-occupied Palestine.

The early empire was the climax of Roman political history, as Rome pursued its greatest geographical expansion and the integration of the provinces into the Roman social system. The hierarchical order of the social structure and integration of provincials were promoted not only by coercive means of military conquest but also by the imperial cult and the ideology of *Pax Romana*.[6] In particular, Rome used the unification of local elites in order to assimilate the wider strata of the population to the empire.[7]

Seated at the apex of the Roman hierarchical social structure, the emperor—*pater patriae*—embodied humanity and ruled over the world. No more than one percent of the population—the imperial aristocratic elites—possessed wealth, power, and prestige; by contrast, the masses

---

4. The Greek word *ochlos* is rendered differently such as "multitude" (RSV), "crowd" (NRSV), and "people" (KJV).

5. Ste. Croix, *Class Struggle*, 430.

6. Crossan, "Roman Imperial Theology," 59–74.

7. Alföldy, *Social History of Rome*, 95.

divided between city-dwellers and country-dwellers lived in wretched conditions.[8] The most oppressed social class consisted of the poverty-stricken sections of the rural population, particularly free peasants. According to Géza Alföldy, while the legal status of the peasants in Judea was "free," their living conditions were much worse than those of the slaves on the estates or plantations.[9]

The elites gained wealth and power both by possessing land and by controlling unfree labor in the forms of tenancy and chattel slavery.[10] This resulted in the tremendous social and economic inequality between Rome's elites and the rural population. In addition to the exploitation of manual labor of peasant farmers and artisans, imperial and local elites also imposed heavy tributes and taxes over the production, distribution, and consumption of goods.[11] If peasants resisted paying taxes imposed in the name of Rome, Rome supported aggressive retribution that also led to debt bondage. Debt bondage was pandemic. The incredibly oppressive burdens resulted in forcing the majority of population into poverty or slavery. Some managed to live at or near a subsistence level. The survival of people living below subsistence level, such as "some farm families, unattached widows, orphans, beggars, disabled, unskilled day laborers, prisoners," was threatened.[12]

---

8. The lower strata of the population were also divided according to the different legal status of free-born, freedpeople, and slaves. Alföldy, *Social History of Rome*, 147.

9. The peasant population included small tenants, landless peasants living on estates, and other peasants living outside the estates. With the small number of independent farm owners, the majority of the rural population was landless peasants and day- or seasonal laborers. Alföldy, *Social History of Rome*, 145–46.

10. According to Carter, Rome's elites owned most of its land and consumed about 65 percent of its production at the expense of masses. Patronage networks and alliances between Rome and the elites in the provinces promoted the elite's interests and fortified the status quo. Carter, *Roman Empire*, 3–4; Ste. Croix, *Class Struggle*, 31–33.

11. "Taxes and rents were usually paid in goods, so a peasant farmer or fisherman literally handed over to elites an estimated 20 to 40 percent of the catch, crop, or herd." Carter, *Roman Empire*, 3, 9.

12. Although Friesen's "poverty scale" applies to urban population for Pauline studies, those people in the lowest, "below subsistence," level (PS7) are often mentioned in the Gospels. Friesen, "Poverty in Pauline Studies," 341; Powell, *Introducing the New Testament*, 41–42.

Empire, the Temple, and Galilean Jews

Thus, most Judeans and Galileans made up the lowest strata of the entire Roman society, without hardly any benefits from the privileges that city-dwellers enjoyed.[13] Regarded as "born for slavery," "inferior," and "learned to be slaves" by the empire, Judeans were also controlled through their local elites and the institution of the Temple.[14] As the Roman governor appointed the chief priest, high-priestly families governed temple operations in cooperation with the Roman authorities. The Temple, the center for Jewish religion and of national identity, also functioned as "part slaughterhouse in offering sacrifices, part warehouse in storing supplies, and part bank with storage chambers for wealth."[15]

The labor force was concentrated in the Temple. While Josephus's estimate might have been exaggerated, he reported that over 18,000 *technitai* were engaged in completing the Second Temple in 64 BC, just before the outbreak of the Jewish War.[16] These workers were free craftsmen, who worked for daily wages or for daily bread, but according to Josephus they received less if they had done only one hour's work (cf. Matt 20:1–15). These laborers might have come from the countryside of Judea, Galilee, or even farther regions reaching into Jerusalem, but when the construction work was finished, they returned to the status of unemployment and no payment.[17]

Domination and Resistance of Peasants in Galilee

The local elites who collaborated with Rome not only precipitated strained conditions of labor, unemployment, and poverty in and around Jerusalem but also imposed the burden of Roman rule on peasants in

---

13. Mark, just like other Gospel authors, calls towns or villages that Jesus visited *"poleis"* (e.g., 6:56). However, those towns, including Capernaum, were not cities (1:21, 45). Even calling Jerusalem a city is not accurate (11:19), although it functioned as "the administrative capital of Judea, of the *ethnos* (the 'nation') of the Jews." Tcherikover, "Was Jerusalem a 'Polis'?," 61–78, cited in Ste. Corix, *Class Struggle*, 428.

14. Josephus, *Jewish War* 6.37–42; and Cicero, *De Provinciis Consularibus* 5:10, quoted by Carter, *Roman Empire*, 10.

15. Carter, *Roman Empire*, 66–67.

16. Josephus, *Jewish Antiquities* 20.219; Ste. Corix, *Class Struggle*, 192. Note that Jesus is identified as a *tekton* (craftsman, Mark 6:3), which refers to anyone who works with his hands in hard material like a builder or stoneworker (not only a carpenter).

17. Ste. Corix, *Class Struggle*, 192.

rural areas. The severe oppression of the Jewish population in Palestine caused the Jewish revolt against Rome in 66–70 CE. The peasant insurgents attempted not only to obtain freedom from imperial rule but also to abolish the rule of their own landowners and priestly aristocracy.[18]

But the cost of such resistance was inconceivably high. Towns in Galilee and Judea, as well as Jerusalem and the Temple, were destroyed. The land was appropriated as Roman military bases. Many people were scattered or sold into slavery. Josephus postulates that the number of those who perished during the siege was 1,100,000. They included not only the citizens of Jerusalem but also those who came up from all the country for the feast of Unleavened Bread and were blockaded by the army. Josephus illustrated this when he said, "the entire nation was now shut up by fate as in a prison."[19] Two thousand dead bodies, variously destroyed by the Romans, by their own hands, by one another, and by famine and illness, were found. 97,000 people became captive and enslaved during the entire war. Josephus continues to describe: "They left only the populace (*demotikous*), and sold the rest of the multitude (*ton alton ochlon*), with their wives and children, and every one of them at a very low price, and that because such as were sold were very many, and the buyers were few."[20] And many others fled to other areas. Judea fell under Roman provincial administration. While each free Jew above twenty years of age was required to pay the temple tax even after the destruction of the Temple, the *fiscus Iudaicus* (Jewish tax) was imposed upon *all* Jews, including women, children, and slaves, to be sent to the temple of Jupiter in Rome.[21]

The Judeans who were able to flee and scatter lived as a defeated people in the diaspora. They could no longer resist Rome but had to become compliant, assimilated, and submissive. This was the situation in which Mark wrote his Gospel, recollecting the traumatic memories of violence done by the empire to Galileans and Judeans. New Testament scholars have used James C. Scott's concept of "hidden transcripts" to describe the concealed or disguised forms of resistance or "nonviolent acts of protest" of early Christians.[22] Carter argues this hidden script "affirms

18. Alföldy, *Social History of Rome*, 156.
19. Josephus, *Jewish War*, 6.9.3–4.
20. Josephus, *Jewish War*, 6.8.2.
21. Kunsthistorisches Museum Wien, "The Consequences of the Jewish War."
22. Carter, *Roman Empire*, 12; Horsley, *Hidden Transcripts*.

the peasant's dignity as one who refuses to be completely subjected. It attests a much larger web of protest against and dissents from the elite's societal order and version of reality."[23]

In his field studies of the uprooting of the Algerian peasantry in the midst of a caste society ripped by capitalist expansion and a brutal war of national liberation, Pierre Bourdieu made a similar observation. Although "the peasant world in Algeria experienced particularly deep overthrow, as a result of major land laws, confiscations, and more recently war and resettlement" and thus they are victims of colonialism, but they are also actors.[24] Bourdieu sees agency in their "acute memory of the expropriations and despoliations" of which they were victim.[25] While I do not intend to transform the poor widow in Mark's story from a victim to an agent, I nonetheless attend to the act of the poor widow among the *ochlos*, and Jesus watching among the peasants, in the midst of revolution or in the aftermath of war.

Watching Where the Poor's Money Goes

The *Ochlos*'s Money and the Widow's Two *Lepta*

Interpreters focus only on the widow's "two copper coins" and never give attention to the "money" put into the temple treasury by the multitude (Mark 12:41; cf. 6:8; Matt 10:9). This tendency is reflected in Luke's account of this story, which completely omits the scene of the *ochlos* putting down money. Luke only describes that Jesus sees the rich people putting their "gift" (*dōron*) into the treasury and a poor widow putting in two copper coins (Luke 21:1, 4).

In contrast, Mark highlights that the story is not about gifts offered to the treasury, but the people's money put into it. Also, Mark contrasts the "many" rich people who put in large sums with the one poor widow putting in the two copper coins out of her poverty, which is all she has—literally, all her living (*bios*). Furthermore, Mark stresses the temple treasury (*gazophylakion*) into which the multitude and the poor widow cast money, and *against* which Jesus is sitting. These three subjects—the multitude, rich/poor, and the Temple—are all important throughout Mark's narrative.

---

23. Carter, *Roman Empire*, 12.
24. Bourdieu, *Political Interventions*, 16.
25. Bourdieu, *Political Interventions*, 16.

Korean Minjung theologian Ahn Byung-Mu argues that the multitude (*ochlos*) do not play merely a background role as the audience of Jesus in Mark's story, but as the subject who transmit the Jesus tradition in the form of story. The *ochlos* are *minjung* (the "masses"). According to Ahn, while the *ochlos* are alienated from the ruling elites and from the communities, they do not constitute an identifiable economic class.[26] They include day laborers, but most of them are those who are physically unable to work or are socially stigmatized, such as the sick, the possessed, sinners, tax collectors, and prostitutes. Then, what does Mark want to communicate to the reader about money of the *ochlos* brought to the temple treasury?

Economic Transactions in Empire, Temple-State, and Patriarchy

Before the story of the poor widow, there is a block of so-called "controversy stories," which scholars view as christological debates with religious leaders.[27] I argue that these controversies do not arise around theological issues but present Jesus's objections to the political economy of the temple-state, the empire, and patriarchy. I choose only a few among the stories that are most explicit in describing Jesus as countering the predominant political economic institutions and practices.

After entering Jerusalem, Jesus first drives out those who buy and sell the animals in the Temple. Such transactions are not only necessary for sacrifices but also require money-changers to exchange Jewish or Tyrian coins to Greek or Roman coinage, with fees (11:15–19).[28] Jesus overturns their tables and the seats of those selling sacrificial pigeons. His acts should not be interpreted as abrogating his own religious institution and cult, but rather as protesting the Temple's monopoly in its commercial trade, which has functioned to exploit the peasants. He "shuts down" the operations of the Temple, critiquing it as the "den of robbers" (v. 16).[29] The motivation of his actions is further illustrated when Jesus sits down opposite (*katevanti*) the treasury, watching the *ochlos* casting money into

26. Ahn, "Jesus and the Minjung," 142, 150.

27. They are controversies with Jesus's opponents regarding the authority of Jesus (11:27–33); the parable of the vineyard (12:1–12); taxes to Caesar (12:13–17); the resurrection (12:18–27); the great commandment (12:28–34); the messiah and the son of David (12:35–38). There is another block of controversy stories in Mark 2:1—3:6.

28. Donahue and Harrington, *Mark*, 327.

29. Chance, "Cursing of the Temple," 271.

it (12:41).³⁰ This posture countering the treasury is repeated when Jesus sits on the Mount of Olives opposite (*katenanti*) the Temple and depicts apocalyptic events that include the destruction of the Temple (13:3).

Jesus's counter stance signifies his critique of both the ruling class and imperial politics. The money of the peasants, day laborers, and the poor who do not even have day wages has been stocked in the Temple. Second Maccabees describes, "the treasury in Jerusalem was full of untold sums of money, the amount of the funds could not be reckoned, did not belong to the account of the sacrifices, there were some deposits belonging to widows and orphans" (3:6, 10). While there were portions of money that should be distributed to widows, our story depicts the *poor* widow putting two copper coins into the treasury. While sitting opposite it, Jesus is watching how money is put in the treasury.

In interpreting this story, Tat-siong Benny Liew takes notice of the *lepta*, minted first during the Maccabean period. By using the transliteration of the two copper coins—*lepta* in Greek—into *kodrantēs* in Latin, Mark not only communicates the monetary value, but also reminds the audience of the Temple rededicated as a symbol for national independence at the end of the Maccabean revolt against the Seleucid Empire (167–164 BCE). Thus, the action of the poor widow can be viewed as an act of resistance in the entangled structures of imperial and local political economies.³¹

In the controversy with some Pharisees and Herodians about taxes to Caesar, Jesus's critique of imperial political economy becomes more explicit. They test him by asking whether it is lawful to pay imperial tax (*kēnsos*, "census" tax) to Caesar (12:14). Jesus asks them to bring a *denarius*, a top-currency in the Roman Empire, which he does not carry with him.³² It is the daily wage paid to a worker in first-century Palestine (Matt 20:2). When the local elites use the coinage that bears the image (*eikōn*) and title (*epigraphē*) of the emperor to pay that daily wage and in

---

30. Like most readers of Mark, Luke is not interested in Jesus's oppositional posture and gaze and omits them (Luke 21:1).

31. However, this is not Liew's conclusion. I will discuss his argument later in this chapter. Liew, "Lost in Translation?," 102–17.

32. This dominant type of monetization was stimulated by military expansion, urbanization, taxation, provincial exploitation, and exchanges in the ownership of the land. While this unified currency facilitated the collection of taxes and the flow of coins between Rome and the provinces, old coinages, such as bronze coins, continued to be used and produced in local economies. Von Reden, "Money and Finance," 275.

the economy overall, they inscribe the people's subordination to Caesar's sovereignty (Mark 12:16).[33]

In the transaction of paying tax, the people are obligated to *give* back (*apodidōmi*) to Caesar the things that are Caesar's—not only the Roman coinage but also themselves. Then, what are the things that are God's that must be given back to God? Scholars only highlight that it is a "theological debate about who really rules" and/or a "subversive message," but we can go beyond arguing about God's sovereignty over Rome's.[34] While Rome has sovereignty over land, sea, labor, and production, Jesus exposes the oppressive nature of economic transaction in the form of taxation by reorienting the question of whether or not to pay imperial tax into a statement about participating in God's economy. Before we discuss the economic transactions Jesus advocates—which are exclusively focused on *giving* to the poor—we need to examine the political economy of patriarchal systems.

The family or house is the basic unit of imperial politics in which the emperor is revered as the *pater patriae*. Thus, patriarchy is a fundamental social system of the imperial social structure in which women are completely dependent on the *pater familias*. For Jewish women, while a minor daughter, wife, and levirate widow were "legally controlled by the man who owns the sole right to use or profit from her biological function: her father, husband, or brother-in-law as the case may be," an adult unmarried daughter, divorcee, and regular widow were relatively independent in legal terms.[35]

We have two types of widows in the Gospel of Mark. One is the poor widow in our story, and the other is the levirate widow found in another controversy story in which Jesus debates about the resurrection with the Sadducees based in Jerusalem (12:18–27). What is at issue is not a theological doctrine about resurrection, but the patriarchal system maintained by marriage, particularly levirate marriage. The levirate widow's role is to secure family and its inheritance and wealth through posteriority. "The levirate law protecting and perpetuating the patriarchal structures of the 'house' was of utmost importance."[36] An independent widow's economic condition was not better than that of a levirate

33. Donahue and Harrington, *Mark*, 345.
34. Donahue and Harrington, *Mark*, 346; Carter, *Roman Empire*, 12.
35. Nathanson, "Toward a Multicultural Ecumenical History," 281.
36. The question for the Sadducees is who she would "belong to" in the afterlife. Myers, *Binding the Strong Man*, 315.

widow. As women's labor is limited to the domestic sphere and reproduction (e.g., 1:30–31), a widow's house (*oikia*) is scarce of provisions and protection.³⁷ Single women or mothers struggle to survive and are vulnerable to alienation, abuse, and exploitation (e.g., 5:24–34; 7:24–30). As in his argument against the patriarchal system enforced by levirate marriage, Jesus critiques the "houses" of widows as insecure because they are devoured by other male elites, whether they are scribes or doctors.³⁸

Economic Transactions for the Poor

Jesus consistently challenges political economies of the Temple, the empire, and patriarchy. Under the controls of those systems, the poor, and particularly women among the *ochlos,* suffer most. Jesus is concerned with economic transactions for the poor. When Jesus feels a need to feed a great multitude (*ochlos*) in the wilderness, his disciples suggest sending "them away so that they may go into the surrounding country and villages and *buy* something for themselves to eat" (6:36).³⁹ Jesus orders, however, "You *give* them something to eat." Then they respond that they need "two hundred *denarii*" to *buy* bread to feed the *ochlos* (v. 37). How should the Roman coinage be used? Not to expand empire and subjugate peoples but to restore the displaced who are without bread for the day.⁴⁰ Jesus orders the rich man to *sell* whatever he has to *give* the poor (10:21).⁴¹ Later when Jesus's final days approach, a woman intrudes in the house of Simon the leper in Bethany to anoint Jesus with the expensive ointment (14:3–9).

---

37. In contrast to the manumission of male slaves, women of child-bearing age are retained because of their reproductive capacity. Scheidell, "Slavery," 93. "The Mishnah, Talmuds, and Midrash envisioned women's roles as generally confined to the domestic and private sphere, focusing on such activities as food preparation, child care, and weaving." Nathanson, "Toward a Multicultural Ecumenical History," 282. Garnsey and Saller contend that families and patterns of reproduction are closely linked with the broader conditions of the economy, the state, and war. Garnsey and Saller, *Roman Empire,* 171.

38. Carter argues that Jesus's creation of fictive kinship among his followers and his upholding of the kinship values of peasant households provides an alternative to elite imperial practices (10:29–30). Carter, *Roman Empire,* 52.

39. I emphasize the words that indicate economic transactions in this and following citations from the Gospel of Mark.

40. Michel Clévenot makes similar observations in *Materialist Approaches to the Bible,* 78.

41. Compare "whatever he [the rich man] has" (*hosa echeis*) to the poor widow's act of putting in "everything she had" (*panta hosa eichen,* 12:44).

Some of the men show indignation because the ointment amounts to "more than three hundred *denarii*," and the money could have been *given* to the poor. That amount could have fed more than five thousand *ochlos* once more. Yet, Jesus could not feed the poor forever.

In the Galilean subsistence economy, there are those who cannot get enough daily bread for survival. The prevalent perception of the poor (*ptōchoi*) in ancient Greco-Roman society is more than what the English word "poor" conveys. A more appropriate rendering for *ptōchos* is "beggar."[42] Jesus eats with beggars (the poor), prostitutes, and tax collectors (Mark 2:13–17), and provides the displaced with food and the sick with health care. Knowing that their lives are dependent on God who can *give* them their daily bread free of charge (Matt 9:9–13; Luke 11:3), however, Jesus also is critical of the exploitative systems of the temple-state and the empire, which perpetuate poverty of the *ochlos*: "For you always have the poor with you" (Mark 14:7). Jesus wishes to eradicate the exploitive political systems, but he also knows that poverty will not be eliminated even through revolutions. He believes that his death will bring a new social order, so the anonymous woman's symbolic act of burial is significant at the moment: "but you will not always have me" (v. 7).[43] Among the poor, Jesus's close attention is drawn to the poor widow. Watching the widow's two copper coins put into the treasury, Jesus perceives her destitute living condition.

Throwing Money into the Memory of Deep Overthrow

If we do not read the widow's offering of two *leptas* as either an exemplary self-sacrifice or her victimhood, what alternative readings reveal her agency? Such a reading may highlight the widow's action and choice. Seong Hee Kim argues that the widow recognizes "the portent of the destruction of the temple" and "the clash of two kingdoms and the dawning

---

42. A representative of *ptōchoi* in the New Testament is Lazarus. His title *ptōchos* is translated into "beggar" (Luke 16:20, 22). In Greek comedy *Plutus* ("Wealth") written by Aristophanes, the goddess *Penia* is the personification of poverty. She strongly objects to being identified as the sister of *Ptōcheia* (beggary), and also distinguishes the life (*bios*) of her poor man (*penēs*) who lives thriftily and is never negligent in his work from the life of beggar (*ptōchou... bios*) who never possesses anything. Whereas the former does not have excess but has enough to live on like a day laborer, the latter is simply a beggar (lines 548–54). Also, see Ste. Corix, *Class Struggle*, 431.

43. See Choi, "Absent Body," 351–60.

of the new era through Jesus."⁴⁴ Through the action of throwing out all she has—"everything which belonged to the worldly empire," she "radically chooses to live on the side of the kingdom of God in front of Jesus" and urges him to continue on his suffering journey.⁴⁵ Yet, this feminist interpretation is not quite different from the traditional interpretation in that the widow voluntarily sacrifices herself—and her life—to help the male Messiah accomplish his mission.

Liew also approaches the widow's agency by employing the concept of subaltern. While the widow's act might be viewed as "a political statement against imperialism and about her agency with her gift" even in silence, Liew implies the widow's agency as "her choice not to inform."⁴⁶ When a subaltern woman like the poor widow is not given her voice as in Mark, we have to admit our "inability to know the other" and that her act of resistance remains unrecognizable. Amy-Jill Levin suggests a similar conclusion: "But in Mark's narrative, causes of poverty go unaddressed; the widow's fate especially goes unnoticed, given the predicted destruction of the temple—a temple in whose system she participates; and the widow's own interior thoughts go unnoted. She requires a political response."⁴⁷

I do not know if she even "chooses" not to inform, nor if she "requires" a response, but her silent action invites us to be present at her "acute memory of the expropriations and despoliations."⁴⁸ In solidarity, Jesus not only preserves the collective memory of how the labor and money of the *ochlos* were exploited by imperial and local ruling classes; he also observes the singular act of the poor widow. The memory traces back to the Jewish War, again. When the Romans burnt down the temple treasury, which rich people had built for themselves, the quantity of money and treasures stacked there amounted to "the entire riches of the Jews." Josephus depicts, "The soldiers also came to... whither the women and children, and a great mixed multitude of the people (*ochlos*), fled, in number about six thousand."⁴⁹ Mark's Jesus foretells the destruction of

44. Kim, "Rupturing the Empire."
45. Kim, "Rupturing the Empire."
46. Liew, "Lost in Translation," 110.
47. Levin, "This Poor Widow," 193.
48. Bourdieu, *Political Interventions*, 16.
49. Josephus *Jewish War* 6:282–83. Roman officials such as Sabinus (4 BCE), Pilate, and Florus (1 CE) frequently looted the wealth in the temple treasury. Carter, *Roman Empire*, 67.

the Temple and how people will flee (13:14). Likewise, all of his disciples are going to flee when he is arrested and tortured by Roman soldiers (14:50, 52; 16:8).

If Mark was written during or after the war, what do the act of the poor widow and Jesus's remarks that she put everything she had—her *bios*—signify? It can be viewed as a social commentary that depicts the fate of those women. Yet, she stands up, not fleeing, and performs what is going to happen to her nation, her temple, her people, and her life. She knows that her two copper coins would not add anything to all the riches of the Jews stored in the treasury. However, her two copper coins represent the money of the *ochlos*, among which she is the poorest and the most vulnerable. For the reader, throwing her precarious life into the intense memory of deep overthrow of the war grows into a standstill. "You will always have the poor with you."

Precariousness of Globalized and Gendered Labor

Being Thrown into the Surplus Population—Precariousness

Mark does not sufficiently speak about labor of the peasants, partly because those with whom Jesus interacted were mainly unemployed or jobless. However, this point speaks to the conditions of their *labor* and life. I find Karl Marx' theory of the reserve army of labor helpful to see that reality. In his monumental work, *Capital*, Marx argues that "general law of capitalist accumulation" caused general conditions of precariousness of the working class, that is, the proletariat. Precariousness is intensified by the consistent threat of being thrown into the "surplus population" of the unemployed and underemployed.[50]

Among this reserve army of labor, the first group is the *floating* population consisting of children, young women, and migrant laborers, who are most easily exploitable in the situation in which the application of machinery increases and the labor process is extensively strained. The second group, the *latent* surplus population, mostly comes from the

---

50. While Engels called this population an "unemployed reserve army of labor," Marx fully developed its theory. Marx, *Capital*, 762–870. Recently the notion of precariousness as a general condition of working class life has been rediscovered in terms of "subproletariat," "precariat," and "precarity." Bourdieu, *Acts of Resistance*, 83; Standing, *Precariot*; Butler, *Precarious Life*. See Jonna and Foster, "Marx's Theory," 25.

self-supporting segments of the agricultural population and thus functions as "a vast source of potential labor for capitalist industry."[51]

The third group of the reserve army—the *stagnant* population, which provides the most precarious form of wage labor—draws our attention, as we see irregular day laborers in the Gospels. With a minimum of working time, they often commute "long distances to get to work and back, long hours for a minimum of wages [or less than the minimum wage], and absolutely no safeguards, promoting sicknesses, disease, and want."[52] Women and young girls, who are "freshly exploitable" and "disposable," are the most significant labor force in the forms of domestic industry or "outwork" (subcontracting attached to the factory system).[53]

The stagnant population is easily deserted into the last and "lowest sediment" of the relative surplus population with *pauperized* workers. They include the mutilated and the sickly, vagabonds and criminals, the widows and prostitutes, and orphans and pauper children. Pauperism is like "the hospital of the active labor-army."[54]

Iris Marion Young's comparison between exploitation and marginalization further elaborates not only types of oppressions caused by labor conditions but also aspects that Marxist theory of exploitation, which focuses solely on class, does not address.[55] While exploitation occurs "through a systemic process of the transfer of the results of the labor of one social group to benefit another," marginals are people "the system of labor cannot or will not use" and thus seem similar to the pauperized group of the reserve army of labor.[56] Neither exploitation nor marginal-

51. Jonna and Foster, "Marx's Theory," 26–27.

52. Jonna and Foster, "Marx's Theory," 27–28; Marx, *Capital*, 865.

53. In this form of labor, "worker's power of resistance declines with their dispersal." Marx, *Capital*, 825, 863–65.

54. Jonna and Foster, "Marx's Theory," 31.

55. I appreciate Joerg Rieger, who helped me pay attention to the difference between exploitation and marginalization, as economically caused oppressions, according to Iris Marion Young's five faces of oppression. There are three other categories: powerlessness, cultural imperialism, and violence. Young contends that not only class but also other factors such as gender, sexuality, and race cause different types of oppression. For example, women's domestic labor is transferred to benefit men in the structure of the patriarchal family. It leads women to depend on the state's support, and henceforth, creates a new system of exploitation, which is called public patriarchy. Young, *Justice and the Politics of Difference*, 39–65.

56. Marginalization causes not only material deprivation or poverty but also dependency so that people such as the poor, women, children, and persons with mental illness are excluded from equal citizenship rights and denied their agency. Young, *Justice and the Politics of Difference*.

ization can be resolved by redistribution of benefits (e.g., shelter or food) because these oppressions are generated by the structural relations and institutionalized practices that continually re-create systems of unequal distribution and perpetual dependence.

However, in the poor widow we see that the distinction between exploitation and marginalization is not obvious. The poor widow is among the pauperized whose labor cannot be used, while being still exploited when she appears to put her two *leptas—bios* into the temple treasury. The exploitations that the hemorrhaging woman and the levirate widow experience occur in gender specific forms in which the female body or her sexuality is used for the economic interests of patriarchal systems. Although in first-century Roman Palestine the mode of production was not defined by intensity and division of labor, Mark's Jesus clearly saw the precariousness of the *ochlos*—particularly, precariousness of women—as produced by the dominant political economic systems.

Globalized and Gendered Precarious Work

Marx's theory of the reserve army of labor further helps understand the precariousness of the *ochlos* in terms of increasingly globalized precarious work. Even in Marx's time, capitalism was a global system of production and thus the precariousness of working class was "an international phenomenon," affecting the colonized regions profoundly.[57] However, by the late 1970s with the emergence of neoliberalism, capital began to restructure the process of global economy through the deregulation of national economies and the control of international finances. In this process, transnational corporations have taken advantage by using cheaper labor in the periphery to the extent that about 70 percent of world production occurred in the Global South by 2008.[58] Despite the difference in the mode of production, Roman political economy shared the features of globalization as the "intensification of international economic and political integration," which created the enormous gulf between a handful of economic elites and the majority of the multitude.[59] The life of the *ochlos*

57. Jonna and Foster, "Marx's Theory," 30.

58. "An enormous growth of part-time, temporary, and contingent work, as well as greater unemployment/underemployment generally, constituted the new, more perilous structural condition of the international labor market." Jonna and Foster, "Marx's Theory," 34.

59. Fudge and Owens, *Precarious Work*, 4.

in the colonized peripheries such as villages in Galilee and Judea was more precarious than those in Roman and Greek cities.

The precariousness of the reserve army of labor in today's neoliberal capitalism is not fundamentally different from Mark's time, but the spread of information-based systems and technologies created a new economy defined by "flexibility" in the labor market and in employment relations. These changes not only amplify precariousness but also increase precarious work as a gendered phenomenon.[60] While social reproduction is predominantly organized through households and by a gendered division of labor, flexibility in the labor market demands unskilled, irregular, and cheaper labor of women. The widows' houses are not devoured by the scribes but by neoliberal capitalism.

Concluding Remarks

Jesus's watching the collective act of the *ochlos* contributing money leads us to observe where the money came from—how their labor was controlled and exploited by imperial and local institutions and elites. The singular act of the poor widow in the midst of the socio-political turmoil tells more than what Jesus says about her on the surface level of the narrative. Rather than using Jesus's words in a way that idealizes the poor and thus perpetuates precarious conditions of the poor, we look attentively to histories and realities of the *ochlos* and poor women through Jesus's gaze at the poor widow's silent act of throwing herself into painful memories of patriarchy, economic exploitation, war, and colonialism. Across the times—Mark's time (Roman political economy), Marx's time (industrial capitalism), and our time (neoliberal capitalism), poor women have been the most marginalized and vulnerable of the lowest class of society. The widow's precariousness in terms of colonialism, patriarchy, class, and gender challenges us to see what is going on with the money and labor of the *ochlos-minjung* and poor women. As Jesus says, the poor are with us.

Bibliography

Ahn, Byung-Mu. "Jesus and the Minjung in the Gospel of Mark." In *Minjung Theology: People as the Subjects of History*, edited by Kim Yong Bock, 138–52. Singapore: CTCCCA, 1981.

---

60. Fudge and Owens, *Precarious Work*.

Alföldy, Géza. *The Social History of Rome.* Translated by David Braund and Frank Pollock. Baltimore: Johns Hopkins University Press, 1985.

Aristophanes. *Plutus.* Edited by Michael T. Quinn, London: Clive, 1890. https://babel.hathitrust.org/cgi/pt?id=uc2.ark:/13960/t74t6j220&view=1up&seq=7.

Baptist, Willie, Noelle Damico, and Liz Theoharis. "Responses of the Poor to Empire, Then and Now." *Union Seminary Quarterly Review* 59 (2005) 162–71.

Bourdieu, Pierre. *Acts of Resistance.* Translated by Richard Nice. New York: New Press, 1999.

———. *Political Interventions: Social Science and Political Action.* Translated by David Fernbach. London: Verso, 2008.

Butler, Judith. *Precarious Life: The Powers of Mourning and Violence.* London: Verso, 2006.

Carter, Warren. *The Roman Empire and the New Testament.* Nashville: Abingdon, 2006.

Chance, J. Bradley. "The Cursing of the Temple and the Tearing of the Veil in the Gospel of Mark." *Biblical Interpretation* 15 (2007) 268–91.

Choi, Jin Young. "The Absent Body and Postcolonial Melancholy (Mk 14:3–9)." In *T&T Clark Handbook to Asian American Biblical Hermeneutics,* edited by Uriah Kim and Seung Ai Yang, 351–60. New York: T&T Clark, 2019.

Clévenot, Michel. *Materialist Approaches to the Bible.* Translated by William J. Nottingham. Maryknoll, NY: Orbis,1985.

Crossan, John Dominic. "Roman Imperial Theology." In *In the Shadow of Empire: Reclaiming the Bible as a History of Faithful Resistance,* edited by Richard Horsley, 59–74. Louisville: Westminster John Knox, 2008.

Donahue, John, and Daniel Harrington. *The Gospel of Mark.* Sacra Pagina 2. Collegeville, MN: Liturgical, 2002.

Friesen, Steven J. "Poverty in Pauline Studies: Beyond the So-called New Consensus." *Journal for the Study of the New Testament* 26 (2004) 323–61.

Fudge, Judy, and Rosemary Owens, eds. *Precarious Work, Women, and the New Economy: The Challenge to Legal Norms.* Oxford: Hart, 2006.

Garnsey, Peter M., and Richard Saller, eds. *The Roman Empire: Economy, Society and Culture.* 2nd ed. London: Bloomsbury, 2014.

Horsley, Richard A., ed. *Hidden Transcripts and the Arts of Resistance: Applying the Work of James C. Scott to Jesus and Paul.* Semeia Studies 48. Atlanta: Society of Biblical Literature, 2004.

Jonna, R. Jamil, and J. Bellamy Foster. "Marx's Theory of Working-Class Precariousness— and Its Relevance Today." *Alternate Routes: A Journal of Critical Social Research* 27 (2016) 21–45.

Josephus. *The Jewish War, Volume III: Books 5–7.* Translated by H. St. J. Thackeray. Loeb Classical Library 210. Cambridge: Harvard University Press, 1928.

———. *Jewish Antiquities, Volume IX: Book 20.* Translated by Louis H. Feldman. Loeb Classical Library 456. Cambridge: Harvard University Press, 1965.

Kim, Seong Hee. "Rupturing the Empire: Reading the Poor Widow as a Postcolonial Female Subject (Mark 12:41–44)." *lectio difficilior* 1 (2006). http://lectio.unibe.ch/06_1/kim_rupturing.htm.

Kunst Historisches Museum Wien. "The Consequences of the Jewish War." http://www.muenze-und-macht.at/showcases/showcase14?language=en.

Levin, Amy-Jill. "This Poor Widow . . . (Mark 12:43): From Donation to Diatribe." In *A Most Reliable Witness: Essays in Honor of Ross Shepard Kraemer,* edited by Susan

Ashbrook Harvey, Nathaniel DesRosiers, Shira L. Lander, Jacqueline Z. Pastis, and Daniel Ullucci, 183–94. Brown Judaic Studies 358. Providence: Brown Judaic Studies, 2015.

Liew, Tat-siong Benny. "Lost in Translation? Tracing Linguistic and Economic Transactions in Three Texts." In *Planetary Loves: Spivak, Postcoloniality, and Theology*, edited by Stephen D. Moore and Mayra Rivera, 102–17. New York: Fordham University Press, 2010.

Marx, Karl. *Capital: A Critique of Political Economy.* Vol. 1. Translated by Ben Fowkes. London: Penguin, 1976.

Myers, Ched. *Binding the Strong Man: A Political Reading of Mark's Story of Jesus.* Twentieth anniversary ed. Maryknoll, NY: Orbis, 2008.

Nathanson, Barbara H. Geller. "Toward a Multicultural Ecumenical History of Women in the First Century/ies C.E." In *Searching the Scripture: A Feminist Introduction.* Vol. 1, *A Feminist Introduction*, edited by Elisabeth Schüssler Fiorenza, 272–89. New York: Crossroad, 1993.

Powell, Mark Allan. *Introducing the New Testament: A Historical, Literary, and Theological Survey.* Grand Rapids: Baker Academic, 2009.

Scheidell, Walter. "Slavery." In *The Cambridge Companion to the Roman Economy*, edited by Walter Scheidel, 89–113. Cambridge: Cambridge University Press, 2012.

Standing, Guy. *The Precariat: The New Dangerous Class.* New York: Bloomsbury Academic, 2016.

Ste. Croix, G. E. M. *The Class Struggle in the Ancient Greek World: From the Archaic Age to the Arab Conquests.* Ithaca, NY: Cornell University Press, 1981.

Tcherikover, V. A. "Was Jerusalem a 'Polis'?" *Israel Exploration Journal* 14 (1964) 61–78.

Von Reden, Sitta. "Money and Finance." In *The Cambridge Companion to the Roman Economy*, edited by Walter Scheidel, 266–86. Cambridge: Cambridge University Press, 2012.

Wright, Addison G. "The Widow's Mites: Praise or Lament?—A Matter of Context." *Catholic Biblical Quarterly* 44 (1982) 256–65.

Young, Iris Marion. *Justice and the Politics of Difference.* Princeton: Princeton University Press, 1990.

6

A Trans-textual and Trans-sectoral Gender-economic Reading of the Rape of Tamar (2 Sam 13) and the Expropriation of Naboth's Land (1 Kgs 21)

GERALD O. WEST

Introduction

"CONTEXTUAL BIBLE STUDY" IS a form of praxis in which the Ujamaa Centre for Community Development and Research re-reads an already present (and significant) Bible with and within particular organized communities of the poor and marginalized, recognizing that theological change is required for sustained-systemic social change in contexts where the Bible is a sacred site.[1] Typically, the Ujamaa Centre is invited by a community-based or faith-based group to work with them on a particular contextually generated concern. In each case there is some recognition that the contextual concern has a theological component, which is why the group invites the Ujamaa Centre to work with it. In each case the group has its own local resources and makes use of a range of other available resources from its community-based networks. The collaborative contribution of the Ujamaa Centre, through Contextual Bible

---

1. There is extensive literature on the Ujamaa Centre's "Contextual Bible Study"; for an overview see: West, "Reading the Bible with the Marginalized."

Study (CBS) processes, is only one set of resources among others. But, if it is true, as we argue it is, that without theological change there can be no sustained social systemic change in communities where the Bible is a significant-sacred text, then CBS is a significant resource.[2]

This essay documents and reflects on two independent CBS, our ongoing work on the story of the rape of Tamar (with a focus, first, on a CBS on violence against women, and, second, on a companion CBS on redemptive masculinities), and a more recent CBS on the intersections between class, land, and gender in the story of the expropriation of Naboth's family land. In each case it has been community-based initiatives that have generated these CBS.

Reflection on the practice of CBS is part of our praxis within the Ujamaa Centre, so it is not unusual for us to reflect on a particular CBS, to analyze its affects, effects, its outcomes, and its impacts (over time).[3] Such reflection is central to the kinds of theoretical and methodological conceptual contributions we have made over the past thirty years. What has prompted the particular trans-textual reflections of this essay is actual community-based work on two different CBS.

I use "trans-textual" (with the hyphen) in a deliberate manner. Gérard Genette, for example, uses the term "transtextuality" as a superordinate term, including within its domain other relational forms, such as "intertextuality."[4] I use the term differently, where "trans" is understood as "to cross over" and "to transgress." I also include a third component, potentially constructed by these two components, "to trans-form" or "to trans-act." My usage emphasizes the reader's role as agent in setting up engagements between biblical texts; I am not claiming "intertextual" historical relationships of dependency (though this does not stop me from wondering . . .).[5] The two texts discussed here are brought into dialogue because of the emancipatory potential we as readers see in crossing over, back-and-forth, between them, even if this requires transgressing the boundaries biblical scholarship constructs between them.

In each of the sections that constitute this essay I reflect on how an intentional trans-textual reading foregrounds the often neglected

2. West, "Contextual Bible Study."

3. Affect theory offers additional analytical resources for reflecting on this aspect of our work; see for example: Kotrosits, "How Things Feel."

4. Genette, *The Architext*, 83–84.

5. This is another slippery term that requires careful clarification in how it is used in particular cases; see for example: Allen, *Intertextuality*.

dimension of class within biblical texts. What makes class analysis particularly significant for our work within South African contexts is that Dutch and British colonialism and White Afrikaner apartheid (as a form of settler-colonialism) construct race as class.[6] Racial distinctions are class distinctions.

Trans-gressing/Trans-forming Scholar/"Non-scholar"

Our praxiological preference as the Ujamaa Centre is that we offer a CBS at the request of or summons by a local organized community. This is how the 2 Samuel 13 "Tamar" CBS emerged in 1996, and how its companion version on "Redemptive Masculinities" was envisaged in 2007.[7] Similarly, this was how both an earlier version of the 1 Kings 21 CBS came about (constructed in 2003), as well the more recent version discussed here.[8]

Community summons is the first trans-textual moment. What generated the trans-actions across these texts were not scholarly concerns (about, for example, Deuteronomistic redactions or intertextual resonances), but community-based concerns about gender and land injustices.[9] The work of CBS is collaborative work, with CBS structuring through its processes an interpretive alliance between what I prefer to refer to as "ordinary readers" and socially engaged biblical scholars.[10] South Africans are wary of "non"-language, so Teresa Okure's term "non-scholar" has not been readily adopted, but it does capture rather well an important contribution of CBS to the interpretive alliance.[11] The particular resources of biblical studies identify and focus on the detail of biblical texts. Though only one of the constituent features of CBS processes, textual detail not ordinarily accessible to "ordinary non-scholar readers" is a distinctive feature of CBS.[12]

---

6. Terreblanche, *History of Inequality in South Africa*.

7. West and Zondi-Mabizela, "The Bible Story"; West, "Deploying the Literary Detail," 307–8.

8. West and Ndlazi, "Leadership and land," 177–81. See also the community-based website: http://www.churchland.org.za/wp-content/uploads/2012/07/BibleStudy1.pdf

9. There does not seem to have been scholarly interest in reading these two texts as related texts.

10. West, "Reading the Bible."

11. Okure, "Feminist interpretation in Africa," 77.

12. See again, for example: West, "Interested Readers."

Collaborative interpretation between scholar and non-scholar (or the trained reader and the ordinary reader of the Bible) has, like so much of South African reality, been marked by race and/as class. Biblical scholars have historically been, in the majority, White, and middle-class.[13] Ordinary readers of the Bible have historically been, in the majority, Black and working-class. CBS collaboration recognizes, but deconstructs–transgresses and trans-forms, the historically sectoral (scholar/non-scholar) and class/racial (White/Black) realities of biblical interpretation in South Africa.[14]

Transgressing/Trans-forming Sectionality/Sectorality

Because biblical studies generates potentially useful textual detail for the construction of CBS, I trawl "biblical studies" for such (subversive) detail.[15] In the case of 1 Kings 21 (the story of Naboth's vineyard) the work of South African Makosazana Nzimande provided additional detail for our ongoing CBS work on this biblical text. While trawling, I came across Nzimande's work on this text in her (U.S.-based) doctoral dissertation (2005), and invited her to write a summary version of her argument as an essay for a collection on African biblical interpretation so that it would be more readily available to an African audience.[16]

In constructing our earlier version of the 1 Kings 21 CBS, working with the Church Land Program and the Rural Network in 2003, Nzimande's work was not yet available.[17] Our CBS then took the following form:[18]

1. What is this text about?

2. Who are the characters and what do we know about them?

3. Why does Ahab want Naboth's vineyard?

---

13. Masenya and Ramantswana, "Anything New"; Tshehla, "Africa, Where Art Thou?"

14. Maluleke and Nadar, "Alien Fraudsters."

15. Vaage, *Subversive Scriptures*.

16. Nzimande, "Postcolonial Biblical"; and Nzimande, "Reconfiguring Jezebel."

17. We drew on a range of other African biblical scholarship, especially: Farisani, "Land in the Old Testament."

18. The line-spacing between groups of questions indicates both how we group questions for report-back from small groups and how questions are grouped in textual and contextual clusters.

4. Why does Naboth want to keep his vineyard?

5. What strategies are used to take Naboth's vineyard from him?

6. What role do race and class and ethnicity play in this story?

7. Why and how have people in your community lost their land?

8. Why is this land your land?

9. What strategies are there to regain your land?

10. What will be your plan of action?

[Or, if the community is struggling to retain its land:]

7. Why is this land your land?

8. What strategies are being used to take away your land?

9. What resources are there for you to retain your land?

10. What will be your plan of action?

Even in this earlier version, our commitment to an "inter-sectional" or "inter-sectoral/trans-sectoral" analysis is clear. Though "intersectionality" has made a significant conceptual contribution within biblical studies, we prefer the more Marxist notion of "sectoral," indicating as it does the fundamental presence of the economic and an implied ideological commitment to marginalized economic sectors.[19] Among the many intersectional/inter-sectoral features of life, race and/as class must be included. We constructed a CBS that would facilitate re-readings of biblical text and contemporary context that would recognize the inter-sectoral/trans-sectoral realities of "race, class, and ethnicity," transgressing and potentially trans-forming their boundaries.

The CBS on 1 Kings 21 was constructed, as each CBS is, for a particular community struggle.[20] We are clear about the particularities of each community struggle as we work with a local community within their local struggle through the See-Judge-Act process (which provides the shape to each and every CBS).[21] Together, led by the local community, we "see" the contextual reality of the local struggle from the particular perspective of the marginalized sector/s with whom we are working. We

---

19. Schüssler Fiorenza, "Between Movement and Academy," 9–12.

20. West and Ndlazi, "Leadership and Land."

21. We have reflected at length on the See-Judge-Act process as it is used within the Ujamaa Centre; for a recent example see: West, "Contextual Bible Study."

then reflect on how we might use a biblical text to "judge" that reality—a text that constructs an ideo-theologically "prophetic" systemic-structural resonance and so resources for an analysis ("judging") of that reality. A CBS is designed to focus on the See-Judge dimensions of the process, but deliberately constructs (safe and sacred) space for local community-based action planning (Act) in order to mobilize, organize, and address the structural injustices identified through the See-Judge moments of the process.

What Nzimande's work on 1 Kings 21 offered us when we returned to 1 Kings 21 some years later in order to construct a CBS with another local community was an overtly inter/trans-sectoral hermeneutic. The Ujamaa Centre was invited by Abahlali baseMjondolo, the shack-dwellers movement in South Africa, together with other formations of unemployed youth we have been working with, coordinated by my colleague Sithembiso Zwane over the past three years.[22] The coalition of Abahlali and unemployed youth from the Pietermaritzburg area invited us to facilitate a "Contextual Bible Study" on "Our Kairos Moment: Unemployment, Land, and Gender" (on Wednesday 7th November 2018). Being tasked with constructing a CBS for this workshop, we turned to Nzimande's postcolonial feminist liberationist interpretation of 1 Kings 21:1–16.[23]

She uses the metaphor of "imbokodo" (grinding stone), a site of rural African women's work, in order to overtly intersect/transect race, class, gender, and culture.[24] She draws deeply on the trajectories of the three overlapping phases of South African Black Theology within which she stands, and inaugurates a fourth phase in which class is a distinctive feature not only within an analysis of apartheid but also of "traditional" indigenous African culture and community.[25] Like Itumeleng Mosala, whose class-laden analysis she takes up, Nzimande sets out to establish lines of connection between the economic systems of contemporary struggles and the economic struggles of "the oppressed and exploited in the text."[26] In so doing she also takes up Mosala's challenge of under-

22. http://abahlali.org/. See also West, *Stolen Bible*, 545–55.

23. Nzimande, "Reconfiguring Jezebel."

24. "Wathint' abafazi, wathint' imbokodo" (You strike a woman, you strike a grinding stone).

25. For an analysis of these four phases see: West, *Stolen Bible*, 318–62.

26. Mosala, *Biblical Hermeneutics and Black Theology*; Nzimande, "Reconfiguring Jezebel," 230.

standing what is required hermeneutically to use the Bible to get the land back.[27]

Nzimande's contribution to the post-apartheid land restitution project is to bring her South African context into dialogue with kindred struggles "over stolen lands" in the biblical text.[28] Her first interpretive move follows Mosala, using historical-critical resources to locate the biblical text (1 Kgs 21:1–16) historically. But her next move is not a Marxist materialist sociological analysis of this period; instead, she draws on feminist literary analysis in order to provide a detailed characterization of the leading female character (queen Jezebel). The sociological contribution, using postcolonial theory, comes in her next move, where she locates the text within its imperial setting (Phoenician imperialism), giving attention to both the literary-narrative imperial setting and the socio-historical imperial setting of the biblical text. She follows Mosala's economic emphasis in her final textual interpretive move, which is to delineate the class relations within this imperial context (including Jezebel as part of a royal household).[29]

She then brings this text and her set of (imbokodo) inter/trans-sectoral interpretive resources into dialogue with an inter/trans-sectoral analysis of the South African context, recovering the identity and agency of African queen-mothers in their governance of African land. The postcolonial recovery of African culture and/as religion as envisaged by South African Black Theology is apparent here. But, innovatively, she does not conclude her work with this religio-cultural recovery. She pushes the boundaries of (African) feminist postcolonial criticism to include matters of class, recovering the "voices" of "those at the receiving end of the Queens' and Queen Mothers' policies."[30] She uses her imbokodo hermeneutics "to read with sensitivity towards the marginalized and dispossessed,"[31] the South African equivalents of Naboth's wife, recognizing that "the beneficiaries" of indigenous elites, including indigenous queens and queen-mothers, "are themselves and their sons, rather than

---

27. Mosala, *Biblical Hermeneutics and Black Theology*, 153.
28. Nzimande, "Reconfiguring Jezebel," 234.
29. Nzimande, "Reconfiguring Jezebel," 234–37.
30. Nzimande, "Reconfiguring Jezebel," 243.
31. Nzimande, "Reconfiguring Jezebel," 243.

the general grassroots populace they are expected to represent by virtue of their royal privileges."[32]

Summoned by a local community struggle, shaped by the realities of unemployed South African youth, and resourced afresh by Nzimande's inter/trans-sectoral work on 1 Kings 21, we constructed and facilitated the following CBS:

1. Listen to a dramatic reading of 1 Kgs 21:1–16.

    What is this text about?

2. Who are the characters in this story and what do we know about them? Draw a picture of their relationships.

3. What are the strategies and systems that those in power (Ahab and Jezebel) use to take Naboth's land?

4. What indications does the story give about why there is no solidarity between Jezebel and Naboth's wife as women?[33]

5. What strategies are used by the powerful in South Africa (both in the private and public sector) to control land and other economic resources?

6. Read 1 Kgs 21:17–20.

    How does God respond to this injustice?

    How does the prophet Elijah respond to this injustice?

7. How should the churches respond?

    How should the churches collaborate with the unemployed and landless?

    What actions can we take to challenge the churches to work in solidarity with the unemployed and landless?

The participants, most of whom are unemployed youth, devoted more than seven hours to this CBS, refusing to conclude the process until they felt it was complete[34] We will report on this participation in another

---

32. Nzimande, "Reconfiguring Jezebel," 243, 246–48.

33. We prioritize literary-narrative questions, recognizing that such questions provide an egalitarian, but still "critical" in the biblical studies sense, entry to the detail of a biblical text. For a fuller discussion see: West, "Reading the Bible with the marginalized: the value/s of contextual Bible reading.

34. We will report on this participation in another publication, for the focus of this essay is different. This essay has a deliberately trans-textual focus.

publication, for the focus of this essay is different. This essay has a deliberately trans-textual focus.So I will move in the next section to trans-textual reflections between 1 Kings 21 and 2 Samuel 13.

Trans-textual Engagement: Hetero-patriarchy and/as Econo-patriarchy (2 Sam 13:4 and 1 Kgs 21:5)[35]

> Jonadab said to him, "For what reason are you thus depressed, O son of the king, morning after morning? Will you not tell me?"
> But Jezebel his wife came to him and said to him, "How is it that your spirit is so sullen that you are not eating food?"

Jonadab's question, represented in direct speech, to Amnon has been a significant literary detail of the text in both our "Tamar" CBS and our "Redemptive Masculinities" CBS. In the "Tamar" CBS it signals the potential for the activation of hetero-patriarchy. Jonadab is attentive to the disposition of another male, his cousin Amnon. Jonadab's question demonstrates not only the familial but also the fraternal bond between men. Jonadab is the first of the many men in this story to play a part in the rape of Tamar. Indeed, CBS participants have noted, each and every man in this story is complicit in the rape of Tamar. In the "Redemptive Masculinities" CBS the role of Jonadab was even more significant, for in this CBS we discern a literary pause between v. 2 and vv. 3–4, between the inactivity of Amnon and the active instigation of Jonadab.[36] For the "Redemptive Masculinities" CBS it was important to recognize both *that* Amnon *becomes* a rapist and *how* he *becomes* a rapist. Amnon, in this version of the CBS, allows his "love" (*aheb*, v. 1) to become obsessive and sick (*chalah*, v. 2). Yet he remains inactive (v. 2). It is Jonadab's question in v. 4 that deploys hetero-patriarchy by invoking Amnon's hetero-patriarchal power as "son of the king." Surely, Jonadab's question implies, the eldest son of the king should not be "depressed" (*dal*) in such an enduring manner, "morning after morning," for he has power. By reminding Amnon of his hetero-patriarchal power, Jonadab activates the networks of hetero-patriarchal complicity across socio-economic sectors, including

---

35. Beverley Haddad and I have sought to find a phrase that would reflect aspects of "patriarchy and/as economic power." We have coined the term "econo-patriarchy," riffing off the more familiar "hetero-patriarchy."

36. West, "Interested Readers."

even Amnon's male servant (*naar*, v. 17). Hetero-patriarchy in this case co-opts across class distinctions.

The focus in 1 Kings 21, participants argued, is on the activation of patriarchal power networks for economic exploitation. Participants, through their discussion of Question 4, were disturbed by the lack of solidarity between Jezebel and Naboth's wife. "Wathint' abafazi, wathint' imbokodo" (You strike a woman, you strike a grinding stone) is a familiar refrain, echoing though "African time,"[37] since the 9th of August 1956, when over 20,000 South African women of different races and/as classes marched to the Union Buildings, singing this resistance song "Wathint' Abafazi, Wathint' Imbokodo," to protest the apartheid "Pass" laws.[38] Such "Pass" laws requried "non-Europeans" to carry "Passes."[39] Where was the solidarity among these biblical sisters, the CBS participants wondered? What shocked participants was not only that Jezebel had exploited her sister, but how she had carefully employed patriarchal power (vv. 8–10), writing letters "in Ahab's name" and sealing them "with his seal" and sending them to his fraternal networks of other powerful men (v. 8). Instead of using her educational privilege (as one of the Persian elite) in solidarity with other women, Jezebel chose to use her education to exploit her sister, Naboth's wife. Participants were also appalled by the content of the letters, in which Jezebel in her guise as patriarch "captured" the religious and legal systems of ancient Israel for her own family's economic gain (vv. 9–10).[40] The econo-patriarchy of "the men of his city" (v. 11) was employed by a woman.

What the participants did not hear in this text was the trans-textual call to 2 Samuel 13. Though many of the participants would have participated in a CBS on 2 Samuel 13, the interrogative resonance of 2 Samuel 13:4 and 1 Kings 21:25 was a detail that I noticed because of the many times I have read these texts. Jonadab's question echoed, trans-textually, with Jezebel's questions to Ahab. Like Jonadab, Jezebel is attentive to the

---

37. As Achille Mbembe reminds us, African time is not simple linear time, but entangled time: Mbembe, *On the Postcolony*, 16.

38. "SAHA—South African History Archive—You Strike the Women, You Strike the Rock!" http://www.saha.org.za/women/national_womens_day.htm/.

39. "Pass Laws in South Africa 1800–1994 | South African History Online." https://www.sahistory.org.za/article/pass-laws-south-africa-1800-1994/.

40. The discourse of "state capture" is prevalent in South Africa at this time, as we recognize to what extent political elites have plundered state resources for personal economic gain; see: https://www.sastatecapture.org.za/.

"sullen" (*sar*) disposition of a patriarchy (v. 4) that does not get what it wants. Like Jonadab she asks a question prompted by a similar performance of patriarchy, twice (v. 5 and v. 7a). Eager to participate in econo-patriarchy because of the benefits it would bring to her household (v. 7), it is Jezebel who employs econo-patriarchal power.

Having heard this trans-textual resonance, I shared it with the 1 Kings 21 CBS participants. They concurred. Patriarchy, whether hetero-patriarchy or econo-patriarchy could be employed by both men and women.

The trans-textual reverberations did not end here for me. What, I wondered, were the econo-patriarchal dimensions of Jonadab's invocation of hetero-patriarchal power? Besides his own self-interest, insinuating himself at the very center of monarchic power (which he does again later in the story, vv. 32–35), a trans-textual engagement asserts that hetero-patriarchal power is always also econo-patriarchal power. These two young men, Amnon and Jonadab, are among the very small emerging generation of elites constructed through the monarchic city-temple-state system.

If we make another trans-textual move, reading 1 Kings 12:1–19 alongside 2 Samuel 13 (and 1 Kgs 5), we recognize Amnon and Jonadab as belonging to the sector that would benefit most from an emerging monarchic tributary mode of production. Though only partially established under David, David does begin to establish a centralized, tributary (including labour, taxation, and tribute) mode of production, in which a small city-based elite (representing less than 1% of the population) extracts tribute from the mass (making up 95% of the population) of subsistence farmers.[41] What a trans-textual reading makes clear is that Amnon and Jonadab are 2 Samuel's equivalent of the "young men" of 1 Kings 12 (1 Kgs 12:8–11).

Confronted by the leader, Jeroboam, of the forced labour (1 Kgs 11:28) conscripted by Solomon from the subsistence families of the ten northern tribes ("Israel") in order to serve the economic and class interests of the Judahite monarchy in Jerusalem, Solomon's son, Rehoboam, consults with two quite different sectors, "the older men" (1 Kgs 12:6) and "the young men" (1 Kgs 12:8). The older men, "who had attended his father Solomon," remember a more egalitarian time, before the monarchic tributary mode of production, and so caution Rehoboam not to

---

41. Boer, "Sacred Economy"; West, "Tracking an Ancient Near Eastern."

exploit the people, urging him "to be a servant to this people" (1 Kgs 12:7). However, Rehoboam instead heeds the advice of his age-mates, the young men like him who have grown up among the economically elite ruling class. Their advice, which he embraces and employs, is to extract even more (1 Kgs 12:8–14).

By the time (both narrative and socio-historical time) of Solomon's son, Rehoboam, these elite "young men" (1 Kgs 12:10–11) will have considerable econo-patriarchal power, insisting on exploitative economic policies of extraction so that they can continue their lives of excessive consumption. Samuel (and God) warned the elders about the economic and class consequences of the monarchic tributary mode of production: "This will be the economic system of the king who will reign over you: he will take (*laqach*)..." (1 Sam 8:11). Econo-patriarchy "takes possession of" (*yaresh* or *yarash*, 1 Kgs 21:15, 16). And, as the story of Tamar tells, hetero-patriarchy "takes hold of" (*chazaq*, 2 Sam 13:11). Trans-textual readings expose exploitation.

Trans-textual Engagement: Peoples' Resilience and/as Prophetic Resistance (1 Kgs 21:20b and 2 Sam 13:12)

> And Elijah answered, "I have found you, because you have sold yourself to do evil in the sight of Yahweh."
> But Tamar answered him, "No, my brother, do not violate me, for such a thing is not done in Israel; do not do this disgraceful thing!"

The redactional processes by which the Bible has been produced interest me. I am persuaded by Itumeleng Mosala that "the texts of the Bible are sites of struggle."[42] Though Mosala acknowledges that the final literary form of the biblical text bear witness to these struggles, his primary focus is the socio-economic sites of struggle that produced and are evident within the various redactional editions of the biblical text.[43] While Mosala accepts the final form as a starting point for ideological redaction critical work, he recognizes that the final form "cannot provide inspiration to oppressed peoples because it is inherently a theology of domination and control."[44] So, for Mosala, ideological driven redactional work is

---

42. Mosala, *Biblical Hermeneutics and Black Theology*, 185.
43. Mosala, *Biblical Hermeneutics and Black Theology*, 40.
44. Mosala, *Biblical Hermeneutics and Black Theology*, 134.

a necessity if we are to appropriate the Bible for liberation. The enduring problem, according to Mosala, is that the final form of the Bible we have and use is a form shaped by the dominant classes of particular historical periods in the Bible's formation. Dominant classes have through the redactional processes of the Bible's composition co-opted the ideological perspectives of other socio-economic sectors. Collaborative work between socially engaged biblical scholars and ordinary readers from within the struggles of the poor and marginalized is therefore required in order to "discover kin struggles in biblical communities," for it is only then that there is the potential for "[t]hese biblical struggles . . . [to] serve as a source of inspiration for [their] contemporary struggles, and as a warning against their co-optation."[45]

Even biblical prophets "co-opt" the voices of the most marginalized.[46] So it was with some caution that I offered Question 6 in the 1 Kings 21 CBS. The question proved be enabling, offering additional textual resources for moving into forms of community-based action (Question 7). But, I wonder, is the prophetic voice required in order to hear the voices of Naboth, his wife, and children crying out against injustice? Perhaps, but Mosala reminds us that often a contemporary struggle "draws its poetry from a future that in this struggle's collision with . . . [much of the biblical text as we have it] is experienced as an 'absence.'"[47] In the language of the *Kairos Document*, "people's theology" may be as much a resource within the biblical text as it is in the construction of contemporary forms of "prophetic theology." The Revised Second Edition (1986) of the *Kairos Document* makes an important distinction between "people's theology" and "prophetic theology."

> It should also be noted that there is a subtle difference between prophetic theology and people's theology. The *Kairos Document* itself, signed by theologians, ministers and other church workers, and addressed to all who bear the name Christian is a prophetic statement. But the process that led to the production of the document, the process of theological reflection and action in groups, the involvement of many different people in doing theology was an exercise in people's theology. The document is therefore pointing out two things: that our present Kairos

---

45. Mosala, *Biblical Hermeneutics and Black Theology*, 188.

46. See my engagement with Mosala's analysis, pushing beyond the prophet to forms of "people's theology": West, "Redaction Criticism."

47. Mosala, *Biblical Hermeneutics and Black Theology*, 188.

challenges Church leaders and other Christians to speak out prophetically and that our present Kairos is challenging all of us to do theology together reflecting upon our experiences in working for justice and peace in South Africa and thereby developing a better theological understanding of our Kairos. The method that was used to produce the Kairos Document shows that theology is not the preserve of professional theologians, ministers and priests. Ordinary Christians can participate in theological reflection and should be encouraged to do so. When this people's theology is proclaimed to others to challenge and inspire them, it takes on the character of a prophetic theology.[48]

There can be no "Prophetic Theology" without there first being a "People's Theology," according to the *Kairos Document*. This is indeed the starting point of the Ujamaa Centre's work. We begin with the lived reality of local communities of the poor and marginalized as it is embodied within them. This is the "raw material" of Prophetic Theology. And CBS is a process that enables this People's Theology to become Prophetic Theology. What Mosala's ideological redactional work suggests is that we find something similar within the biblical text, "beneath" the redactional layers of dominant class voices.[49] We have come to recognize within the work of the Ujamaa Centre that forms of resilience, including interpretive resilience in the face of dominating interpretations of the Bible, are also forms of resistance.

Such is the case, I would suggest, in 2 Samuel 13. A trans-textual engagement with 1 Kings 21 recognizes the absence of a prophetic "word of Yahweh" (1 Kgs 21:17) or a "Thus says Yahweh" (v. 19) in 2 Samuel 13. There is a male voice that has the final word in direct speech in Tamar's story, but it is a disempowering and non-prophetic voice. It is a silencing voice: "Then Absalom her brother said to her, 'Has Amnon your brother been with you? But now keep silent, my sister, he is your brother; do not take this matter to heart.' So Tamar remained and was desolate/appalled in her brother Absalom's house" (2 Sam 13:20). However, if we resist the impulse to find a prophetic voice to re-present the people's voice, we will hear a people's theology voice. It is clear and articulate, and it belongs to Tamar, both in her direct speech (vv. 12–13, 16) and her embodied silent cry (v. 19), as well as in the resilient and resisting narrative shape

---

48. Kairos, *The Kairos Document*, 34–35, note 15.
49. West, "Redaction Criticism."

of 2 Samuel 13:1–22.[50] We are left to wonder whether Tamar might have spoken out in her brother's house against economic (as well as sexual) exploitation, for Absalom's house would have been an elite house, a house of the ruling class.

Conclusion: CBS as Trans-topia

Both 2 Samuel 13:1–22 and 1 Kings 21:1–16 have been redactionally incorporated and co-opted by hetero-patriarchal and econo-patriarchal agendas. The community-based work of the Ujamaa Centre, however, has discerned both the resilient presence and potential resistance of these texts.[51] A trans-textual reading of these texts constructs potentially trans-forming resonances, not least of which is the recognition, perhaps, of counter-hetero-patriarchal and counter-econo-patriarchal discourses seeking solidarity across biblical boundaries, transgressing even the boundary of time and space, forging not only a "hetero-topic" space but a "trans-topic" (or more theologically, "transcending") space across time with contemporary communities through Contextual Bible Study.[52]

Bibliography

Allen, Graham. *Intertextuality*. New Critical Idiom. New York: Routledge, 2000.
Boer, Roland. "The Sacred Economy of Ancient 'Israel.'" *Scandinavian Journal of the Old Testament* 21.1 (2007) 29–48.
Farisani, Elelwani Bethuel. "Land in the Old Testament : The Conflict between Ahab and Elijah (I Kings 21:1–29), and Its Significance for Our South African Context Today." M.Th. thesis, University of Natal, 1993.
Foucault, Michel. "Of Other Spaces (1967), Heterotopias." Translated by Jay Miskowiec. Michel Foucault, Info. https://foucault.info/documents/heterotopia/foucault.heteroTopia.en/.
Genette, Gérard. *The Architext: An Introduction*. Translated by Jane E. Lewin. Quantum Books. Berkeley: University of California Press, 1992.
Kotrosits, Maia. "How Things Feel: Biblical Studies, Affect Theory, and the (Im)Personal." *Brill Research Perspectives in Biblical Interpretation* 1.1 (2016) 1–53.

---

50. See for example Phyllis Trible's analysis of the text's chiastic structure: Trible, *Texts of Terror*, 37–57.

51. For our recent reflections on notions of "interpretive resilience and/as resistance" see: West, "Contextual Bible Study."

52. Foucault, "Of Other Spaces"; West, "Biblical Text as a Heterotopic Intercultural Site."

Maluleke, Tinyiko Sam, and Sarojini Nadar. "Alien Fraudsters in the White Academy: Agency in Gendered Colour." *Journal of Theology for Southern Africa; Scottsville*, no. 120 (November 2004) 5–17.

Masenya, Madipoane, and Hulisani Ramantswana. "Anything New under the Sun of South African Old Testament Scholarship? African Qoheleths' Review of OTE 1994–2010." *Old Testament Essays* 25 (2012) 598–637.

Mbembe, Achille. *On the Postcolony*. Johannesburg: University of Wits Press, 2015.

Mosala, Itumeleng J. *Biblical Hermeneutics and Black Theology in South Africa*. Grand Rapids: Eerdmans, 1989.

Nzimande, Makhosazana K. "Reconfiguring Jezebel: A Postcolonial Imbokodo Reading of the Story of Naboth's Vineyard (1 Kings 21:1–16)." In *African and European Readers of the Bible in Dialogue: In Quest of a Shared Meaning*, edited by Hans de Wit and Gerald O. West, 223–58. Studies on Religion in Africa 32. Leiden: Brill, 2008.

Nzimande, Makhosazana K. "Postcolonial Biblical Interpretation in Post-Apartheid South Africa: The Gvirah in the Hebrew Bible in the Light of Queen Jezebel and the Queen Mother of Lemuel." PhD diss., Texas Christian University, 2005.

Okure, Teresa. "Feminist Interpretation in Africa." In *Searching the Scriptures: A Feminist Introduction*, edited by Elisabeth Schüssler Fiorenza. New York: Crossroads, 1993.

"Pass Laws in South Africa 1800–1994 | South African History Online." https://www.sahistory.org.za/article/pass-laws-south-africa-1800–1994.

"SAHA—South African History Archive—You Strike the Women, You Strike the Rock!" http://www.saha.org.za/women/national_womens_day.htm.

Schüssler Fiorenza, Elisabeth. "Between Movement and Academy: Feminist Biblical Studies in the Twentieth Century." In *Feminist Biblical Studies in the Twentieth Century: Scholarship and Movement*, edited by Elisabeth Schüssler Fiorenza, 9–12. Bible and Women 9.1. Atlanta: Society of Biblical Literature, 2014.

Theologians (Group), Kairos. *The Kairos Document: Challenge to the Church: A Theological Comment on the Political Crisis in South Africa*. Grand Rapids: Eerdmans, 1986.

Trible, Phyllis. *Texts of Terror: Literary-Feminist Readings of Biblical Narratives*. Overtures to Biblical Theology. Philadelphia: Fortress, 1984.

Tshehla, Maarman S. "Africa, Where Art Thou? Pondering Post-Apartheid South African New Testament Scholarship." *Neotestamentica* 48.2 (July 2014) 259–81.

Vaage, Leif E., ed. *Subversive Scriptures: Revolutionary Readings of the Christian Bible in Latin America*. Valley Forge, PA: Trinity, 1997.

West, Gerald O. *The Stolen Bible: From Tool of Imperialism to African Icon*. Biblical Interpretation Series. Leiden: Brill, 2016.

———. "Tracking an Ancient Near Eastern Economic System: The Tributary Mode of Production and the Temple-State." *Old Testament Essays* 24.2 (2011) 511–32.

———. "Deploying the Literary Detail of a Biblical Text (2 Samuel 13:1–22) in Search of Redemptive Masculinities." In *Interested Readers: Essays on the Hebrew Bible in Honor of David J. A. Clines*, edited by James K. Aitken et al., 297–312. Atlanta: Society of Biblical Literature, 2013.

———. "Reading the Bible with the Marginalized: The Value/s of Contextual Bible Reading." *Stellenbosch Theological Journal* 1.2 (2015) 235–61.

———. "The Biblical Text as a Heterotopic Intercultural Site: In Search of Redemptive Masculinities." In *Bible and Transformation: The Promise of Intercultural Bible*

Reading, edited by Hans De Wit and Janet Dyk, 241–57. Semeia Studies 81. Atlanta: SBL Press, 2015.

———. "Redaction Criticism as a Resource for the Bible as 'a Site of Struggle.'" *Old Testament Essays* 30.2 (2017) 525–45.

———. "Contextual Bible Study and/as Interpretive Resilience." In *That All My Live: Essays in Honour of Nyambura J. Njoroge*, edited by Ezra Chitando and Esther Mombo, Forthcoming.

West, Gerald O., and Phumzile Zondi-Mabizela. "The Bible Story That Became a Campaign: The Tamar Campaign in South Africa (and Beyond)." *Ministerial Formation* 103 (2004) 4–12.

West, Gerald O., and Thulani Ndlazi. "'Leadership and Land': A Very Contextual Interpretation of Genesis 37–50 in KwaZulu-Natal, South Africa." In *Genesis*, edited by Athalya Brenner et al., 175–90. Texts@Contexts. Minneapolis: Fortress, 2010.

7

Ruth as Esperanza?
A Trans-textual Reading of Ruth with Foreign Domestic Workers in Singapore

CHIN MING STEPHEN LIM

Introduction

RUTH AS A BOOK has been received by communities seeking emancipation that ranges from feminist concerns of agency of women, solidarity under trial, and negotiating a place in a man's world, to more liberationist agendas of social justice and redemption from debt.[1] This paper is an effort to contribute another voice to this diverse discourse from the perspective of what Nicole Constable calls, "intimate labor."[2] Arguably, intimate labor constitutes one of the more relatively under-studied, yet increasingly widespread transnational flows of low cost labor that intersects class with gender and ethnicity, which I explore later. In this essay, while sharing the aspiration toward emancipation with other

---

1. See for instance, an exhaustive list given by Gale Yee. Yee, "She Stood in Tears," in *They were All in One Place?*, 119–20.

2. Constable, "Reproductive Labor." She points out that there is a tendency in many analyses of labor to avoid areas of sexual services, domestic work and marriage when mapping its entanglements with Empire.

liberation-minded people, the distinct contribution I wish to make is to read the text from the standpoint of privilege.

Therefore, I begin by situating Christian reading communities in Singapore as part of the middle class and explore the implications in light of the increasing presence of foreign domestic workers. Then, I look deeper into perceptions of foreign domestic workers and attempt to draw connections to the ideas of Moab that circulate in the Hebrew Bible. After which, I engage in a transtextual reading strategy that is what I argue elsewhere looking at contextual biblical hermeneutics as multicentric dialogue to interrogate my subject position.[3] In the interest of space, I focus on the need for Christian readers located in Singapore to engage in reading *from* context rather than what Gerald West and others have suggested as reading *with* local church communities.[4] In this regard, reading *from* as a reading strategy sees context as an epistemic terrain where standpoints are hierarchically organized based on its proximity to privileged social identities. In particular for this essay, the transtextual reading takes place between *Ruth* and a play produced in the tumultuous times of the 1980s in Singapore which focused on the plight of foreign domestic workers called *Esperanza*.[5] This is before concluding by outlining the discursive influences that reading *Ruth* would have on Christian communities in Singapore, which includes myself, who are ineluctably drawn into these "strange encounters" with the Other who is a poor, foreign woman in the intimate places we call "home."

Situating Christians in Singapore

No longer situated as the colonized Other in empires past and having largely attained middle class status, many Christians today in Singapore could well afford those whom could be seen as the modern day slave. As several studies have shown, most Christians, in addition to being part of the majority Chinese race, belong to the emerging or established middle class.[6] Achieving such a status would then put them in reach of employ-

---

3. Lim, *Contextual Hermeneutics*, 65–70.

4. Lim, *Contextual Hermeneutics*, 65–70.

5. Wong and Tay, "Esperanza." in *5 Plays from Third Stage*, 99–129. For the rest of this chapter, I will refer to the titles of both works in italicized form, i.e., "*Ruth*" and "*Esperanza*" and the protagonists in non-italicized form.

6. Chong and Hui, *Different Under God*, 40–66.

ing a domestic helper at home. So I wish to begin by situating middle class Christians in Singapore in relation to foreign domestic workers.

Middle class status in Singapore is associated with certain political connotations that are pertinent to the present reading. According to Beng Huat Chua and Joo Ean Tan, people who attain middle class status in Singapore may inadvertently consent to a form of social contract with the ruling elites, namely the current dominant political party. In Singapore where even the rich's participation in politics is largely restricted to philanthropy and charity work while being cautious of flaunting their own wealth, the middle class see their place in society as mainly precarious. In exchange for the current material comforts they enjoy such as property and car ownership and if I may add, the ability to hire a domestic helper, most middle class Singaporeans implicitly agree to becoming politically inert and refrain as much as possible from interfering in the public sphere of politics and policy making.[7] This general lack of enthusiasm in participating in politics such as labor movements could be because of what Lau-Fong Mak aptly sums up as "a combination of contentment, complacency, feeling of impotency and fear."[8] In western democracies, it would seem that attaining middle class status grants one the ability to participate more vigorously in politics.[9] In contrast, the middle class in Singapore likely harbor no such illusions about their own agency in the public sphere especially when it comes to issues of labor. While this is by no means representative of the *whole* of society, it is most probably the case with established Protestant denominations in Singapore. This is demonstrated, as I argue elsewhere, through the almost unproblematic embrace of social conservatism of North American Protestant fundamentalism that places more emphasis on the traditional family structure, personal morality, and evangelism.[10] In short, Christians in Singapore have largely accepted their middle class positions and the implicit political obligations that come with them.

That being said, when it comes to the foreign domestic worker, I find that this seeming state of equilibrium is destabilized as the home is transformed into a liminal space. Under the beat of modernity, the "home" appears increasingly segregated from the class struggle of wider

7. Chua and Tan, "Singapore."
8. Mak, "Between Materialism," 9–15.
9. Jones and Brown, "Singapore and the Myth," 79.
10. Lim, *Contextual Hermeneutics*, 33–39.

society especially after one is able to attain middle class status. Furthermore, as Terry Clark and Seymour Lipset point out, this "slimming of the family" has weakened social hierarchies within the family structure, thus giving way to "more egalitarian relations."[11] While this could be true of Singapore, the introduction of the domestic helper into these homes complicates matters. Now class differentiation acquires a different nuance as the helper is seldom seen as an equal in the home. In an uncanny fashion, we find a re-hashing of the old Marxist division of labor where one could possibly be emasculated as part of the middle class in wider society, but return home to as it were, become the ruling elite of one's little kingdom.[12]

It is in light of this paradoxical yet changing social dynamic that, in the next section, I position foreign domestic workers within the ethnoscape of Singapore society in order to distill their potential "danger" which largely accounts for the alleged abuses against them.

Foreign Domestic Workers in the Ethnoscape of Singapore

In the context of Singapore, a technical report on labor exploitation published in November 2017 shows that approximately 243,000 foreign domestic workers are employed on the city island-state with an average of one in every three households employing or being dependent on them for domestic chores and duties.[13] The report goes on to claim that 60% of 799 foreign domestic workers interviewed could be identified as exploited with 23% as victims of forced labor.[14]

Angelia Poon traces the ambivalence of foreign domestic workers in Singapore.[15] On the one hand they replace the role of the wife in the family to allow women to enter into the workforce and flourish there. On the other hand, their "strange" bodies pose all kinds of dangers from hygiene

---

11. Clark and Lipset, "Are Social Classes Dying?," 407.

12. Of course this presents its own set of distinct challenges. For instance, while working class in the factories given the communitarian working environment would have opportunities to organize and unionize (a task which is already in and of itself difficult in Singapore), foreign domestic helpers are not only hidden from the public eye, but also very often isolated from one another.

13. Wessels, Ong, and Daniel, "Bonded to the System," 18.

14. Wessels, Ong, and Daniel, "Bonded to the System," 74.

15. Poon, "Maid Visible."

and disease to sensuousness and greed. What is relevant to the current inquiry is how they are often perceived as a "contaminating presence" because their status as poor, foreign women often translate into sexualized objects and/or petty thieves. This justifies close management and supervision, sometimes even with close circuit television surveillance within the home itself.

It could be claimed that what mainly constitutes the "danger" of foreign domestic workers boils down to their "foreignness."[16] As Sara Ahmed argues, the stranger is often framed in terms of the differences that make him or her seem inferior and even dangerous.[17] This framing is not innate to a single individual but nurtured within wider society itself. Put differently, what undergirds our anxieties about the stranger/foreigner is not so much rooted in what we do *not* know but rather what we *presume* to know about the Other. Thus such "strange encounters" as she calls it are conditioned by how society structures our beliefs about who the Other is through governmentality, mainstream and social media, and other forms of cultural production. In the case of the foreign domestic worker, the foreignness is re-constructed as "the spectacle of contagion" which summons to our minds specters of hyper-sensuality, disgusting filth and backwardness.[18] As I highlight later, the play shows poignantly how such constructions could occur in everyday conversations.

What I wish to add to these studies on foreign domestic workers is exploring deeper the typical employer, particularly those who are part of the demographic of the church–majority Chinese who are relatively financially stable. As I argue elsewhere, Chinese privilege in Singapore has many elective affinities with white privilege in the U.S. such as mistaking one's raced and classed experiences of reality to be the universal frame of understanding that is often predicated on feminization of other subjects deemed inferior to oneself so as to valorize one's subject position. One decisive difference in Singapore is that by weaving in certain notions of Confucianism, those regarded as superior now have the right to discipline those seen as inferior.[19] In this essay, I further this through

---

16. A telling example is by comparing foreign domestic workers to the Cantonese *amah* who could be considered their antecedents. The latter was usually treated with more respect and dignity and even offered opportunities to be part of the family. Poon, "Maid Visible," 8–9.

17. Ahmed, *Strange Encounters*.

18. Poon, "Maid Visible," 14–24.

19. Lim, "Undoing Chinese Privilege," 2–4.

my reading of *Esperanza* together with *Ruth* by layering on how class difference moulds this desire to discipline inferior bodies.

Turning now to *Ruth*, while the dating of the book is still debated with no clear consensus emerging, part of the focus of the text is on the contaminating presence of Moab.[20] Therefore, I have preferentially taken the later date of post 650 BCE as my reference because regardless of when the book is written, *Ruth* would have been read (or heard) in light of the Israelites' evolving understanding of this Other called Moab. Robert Wafula offers one of the most comprehensive reconstructions of how Moabites are represented in the Bible along the lines of the politics of genealogy, land, and religion.[21] He traces the negative representations to how origins of the Moabites are constructed in the Hebrew Bible—descendants of an illicit union born between their primordial father Lot and his daughters as a result of a series of bad decisions beginning with his separation from Abraham to settle in the land of Sodom where "the people...were wicked, great sinners against the Lord" (Gen 13:13, NRSV; cf. Gen 13:8–13). Ultimately the city is destroyed and Lot loses his wife with no heirs to his name (Gen 19:1–38). Another particular instance he highlights is how the seduction of Israelite men by Moabite women could be traced back to the sin of the latter's primordial mother (Num 25:1; cf. 1 Kgs 11:1). Finally, in Wafula's evaluation of prophetic oracles, he mentions how certain parts, such as *ndd* (to flee) in Isaiah 16:2 and 3 and *'aro'er* in Jeremiah 48:6, are used to describe Moab as a land without food and water, marked by homelessness and destitution.[22] Therefore, in his assessment, the overall discourse within the Hebrew Bible positions the tainted genealogy and alleged Moabite aggression against Israel as the foundation of the prohibition that forbids their entry into Israelite community in perpetuity (Deut 23:2–5; cf. Ezra 9–10; Neh 13:23–27). It would seem from the monarchical period up until the postexilic era, the trajectory of Israel's understanding of Moab has hardly deviated. What his re-construction does for me is that it highlights the potential dangers of the Moabite Other—a kind of unbridled sensuousness that is at the same time, petty and calculative which resonates with typical ideological

---

20. See Sasson, *Ruth*, 241–52 for further discussion on dating.
21. Wafula, *Biblical Representations*, 101–78.
22. Wafula, *Biblical Representations*, 157–72. Much of his analysis primarily focuses on how Israel justifies its religious depiction of the judgment of Moab.

moves of the dominant to feminize the Other so as to subordinate and subjugate them.[23]

While it is possible to attribute some negative representations of Moab in the Hebrew Bible to conflicts in the past, there has not been an analogous, salient incident of bad blood between Singapore and the countries such as the Philippines and Burma that provide our domestic helpers. Rather in Singapore, the main factor that undergirds the less savory depictions of our neighboring countries is likely the possible hubris and arrogance because of its economic success. As Esperanza in the play highlights, being a maid in Singapore pays more than being a teacher there in the 1980s. Regardless of whether one chooses the postexilic dating or the time of the monarchy as the dating of the book, Judah in *Ruth* seems to be in a more prosperous position vis-à-vis its neighbors, of which the one in question here is Moab.

Despite the initial famine in Bethlehem, it ultimately fulfills its name's sake and is now full of food. It would also seem that wealthy landowners such as Boaz and Mr. So-and-So are doing well and even Naomi, surprisingly, still owns land there. Similarly, we find that the national narrative of Singapore is how it was transformed from a backward (and presumably, struggling) fishing village to a thriving cosmopolitan city filled with promise. Conversely speaking, the Philippines seems to be like Moab–a place of poverty and hopelessness. What interests me is how the commonality that strings the religious elite of Judah and Singapore would then be the pride of place conferred by their respective empires relative to other polities which do not enjoy similar levels of success. More pertinently, I show later how elitist constructions of the Other comes from a confidence founded on class difference. This would form the main intercontextual connection I develop in this paper while keeping in mind that other factors do shade into the ideological depictions of Moab in the imagination of the Hebrew Bible.

It is here where I venture a reflexive note on my own entanglements with domestic workers in Singapore. It should be apparent by now that my social identities as male, Christian, middle-class and part of the Chinese majority are socially constructed not only as their (almost complete) anti-thesis, but also superior to them. As mentioned earlier, this class difference becomes more acute in the sequestered space of the home. Recalling my personal involvement doing Bible study with a group of Filipina

---

23. See also Rendtorff, "The Gêr in Priestly Laws," 77; Begg, "Foreigner," 829.

domestic workers in a church for a year in 2011, there was hardly a single session facilitated by the foreign domestic worker herself. Most facilitators were Chinese middle class, including myself. It was not unusual that these sessions would involve a disciplinary element–for instance, the trope of gratitude was often repeated both by the Filipinas who had been in Singapore longer and the Chinese elite alike. Giving thanks became a cipher for being content with one's lot in life, and grateful that one had a job, no matter how demeaning and dehumanizing for the (economic) ends justify the means.

What really struck home for me was when my wife and I had to "take care" of a newly hired domestic worker from Myanmar for two weeks because her employers were on vacation. Ostensibly it was to ensure that she continued to do her allotted tasks around the house. Local employers often claim that the supervision is for their own good but in reality, it is to guard against the spread of the "contagion" that would bring unwanted filth (through neglect of their daily duties of housecleaning that arguably borders on obsessive-compulsiveness) and sexual impurity (mostly by failing to keep in check their unbridled passions to "uncover the feet" of the opposite sex). Therefore, I inevitably read *Ruth* through this nexus of relationships and experiences that I am enmeshed in.

Ruth and Esperanza: Similar Plights, Different Endings

It is here I turn to the play that is the transtextual, dialogical partner to *Ruth*. *Esperanza*, a play written in 1986, was the first of its kind to depict foreign workers onstage. According to Terence Chong, *Esperanza* was produced as a play at a time when there was increasing demand for authenticity among Singapore artists.[24] Authenticity in this regard meant that the work "engages sincerely with the pertinent issues of the day as it is with the construction of the artist as seeker of Truth."[25] While political cartoons were the mainstay during the time of British colonialism up until when the current dominant party, People Action Party (PAP) took over in 1959, it was banned in 1961 when the first Prime Minister Lee Kuan Yew blamed the media for some of PAP's losses in the General Elections. In this light, theater became the new "critical space," taking up the courageous mantle left behind by other forms of media. The Third Stage was a

24. Chong, *Theatre and the State*, 75–84.
25. Chong, *Theatre and the State*, 77.

prime example of a theater group that was willing to challenge the middle to upper class English educated Chinese masses. *Esperanza* was one of its productions that attempted to expose the plight of domestic workers in the private sphere of homes, which were far from public view. The group fell foul to the Marxist Conspiracy in 1987 with Souk Yee Wong and Suan Tze Chng being detained under the Internal Security Act. This play was subsequently banned.[26] As Joanne Leow traces, subsequent engagements with the issue of foreign domestic workers in Singapore became more ambiguous and less confrontational.[27]

The play focuses on a (stereo)typical Chinese family, Mr. Chee and his wife Cindy, employing a Filipina domestic worker whose name is Esperanza, which incidentally in Tagalog, means "hope." The play brings its (elite) audience into the hidden spaces of the home to show several of the potential abuses there. It could be said to be what many Chinese dread the most—washing dirty linen in public. Things come to a head when Esperanza, out of her own frustration, scratches Cindy's new watch. At that moment, Mr. Chee walks in, looking for that watch and finds her hiding it in her pocket. The obvious conclusion is that she is trying to steal the watch and she is sent back to the Philippines.

One key connecting point is that both Ruth and Esperanza could be seen as banal forms of indentured labor. As Jack Sasson points out in his commentary on Ruth 1:15–19, the formula in this text suggests a binding contract.[28] Implicit to Esperanza is the contract that is signed between employer and foreign domestic worker. It may seem at first blush that Ruth is motivated by love where a tragic preamble leads up to her pledge to Naomi, but as for Esperanza, her "only reason for . . . being in this strange land" is to earn enough money to send back home by laboring for a foreign master.[29] Athalya Brenner points out that "love" here is closer to that of the slave for the master (cf. Exod 21:2–6), which then implies that this is "a legal rather than emotional concept."[30] In this contractual relationship, she points out that Ruth (re)solves the issue of Naomi taking care of herself, just as foreign domestic workers like Esperanza are supposed to enable women in our society to be free to do what they like

26. See also Peterson, *Theater and the Politics*, 107–8.
27. Leow, "Strangers, Surrogates, Lovers," 203.
28. Sasson, *Ruth*, 28–31.
29. Wong and Tay, *Esperanza*, 118.
30. Brenner, "Ruth as a Foreign Worker," 159.

to achieve. Thus it would seem that Ruth's motivations of moving out of Moab may not be so diametrically different when viewed through the relationship of a foreign younger woman helping an older woman from the host culture to live her life.

In this light, the external motivations that string *Esperanza* and *Ruth* together could be summed up by what Katherine Doob Sakenfeld describes as "the theme of migration in search of economic survival."[31] Thus, both stories portray a common struggle of such foreign women being brought into foreign homes in foreign countries. Both women inevitably struggle with adjusting to a completely new environment and try their best to eke out a living for themselves and their families. What is also crucial here are the differences. Ruth seems to have successfully integrated into Israelite culture, giving birth to the son who will be part of the lineage of King David. Esperanza leaves Singapore in shame and fear of what the future holds for her. So we have two stories of foreign women in foreign homes with very different endings. In the interest of space, I look mainly at how the label of being a poor, foreign woman is handled in both texts.

Being the Other Woman

As mentioned earlier, Moab is constantly associated with deprivation, economic and otherwise. Musa Dube points out that the contrasting images of Israel to Moab shows how the latter is synonymous with barrenness, famine, and even death.[32] It also seems that marrying the people of the land whom in *Ruth* are foreign women, results in the death of all men in the family. This is not to mention that they are left with no sons.[33] Furthermore, it is possible to think of Boaz's subtle coercion of Mr. So-and-So to give up his right to Naomi's estate toward the end of the story as demonstrating similar tropes about Moab. While it is debated how this would impoverish his estate, it is difficult to miss that the invoking of Ruth's Moabite status is yet another association of Moab with potential loss and barrenness (Ruth 4:5–6). In light of this, it is hard to ignore that

31. Sakenfeld, *Just Wives?*, 32.
32. Dube, "Divining Ruth,"186.
33. Nonetheless, the reason why we find Elimelech and Naomi in Moab is because of famine in Israel itself which compels the family to relocate to Moab which is relatively wealthier. In my view, the opening prologue in *Ruth* gives the impression that abundance elsewhere is more often transient and almost illusory.

Ruth's Moabite status is consistently emphasized throughout the narrative (Ruth 1:4, 22; 2:2, 6, 21; 4:5, 10).

In a similar fashion, Esperanza's status as a Filipina is evoked in the play mainly to reinforce her inferiority. She is ignorant and incompetent, a poor cook[34] and is apparently incapable of performing "simple" housework properly.[35] Furthermore, her hygiene is often called into question culminating in her mistress spraying insecticide on her hair in a bid to rid her of "head lice."[36] Furthermore, such unsavory ideas about the other become salient during banal, everyday activities. When Cindy plays overnight mahjong with her friends, we find them picking on their hypersensuality and incompetence which is often interpreted as laziness. This is to say that one cannot underestimate how such activities contribute to what we *presume* to know about the Other.

Reading *Ruth* through Esperanza's struggle to please her employers makes me wonder how she would view Ruth. Phyllis Trible applauds Ruth's determination when she remarks "how difficult and courageous for a foreign woman to glean in the field" while at the same time "how healing and fulfilling for the empty Naomi to embrace Ruth the Moabite in the language of kinship [Ruth 2:20]."[37] So we have a Moabite woman who is willing to work jobs that mark the workers as poor and disenfranchised. Furthermore, she not only does what she is told, but also takes initiative to ensure her mother-in-law or as Esperanza would call Cindy, "ma'am" is well taken care of. However, it would seem to me that in the eyes of Esperanza, Ruth is closer to Bonnie Honig's model emigrée or Gale Yee's model minority and perpetual foreigner.[38] What makes Ruth exceptional is that the needs of Naomi (as a woman of the host culture) will always supersede her own (as a foreign woman).

This brings me to my next point. In *Esperanza*, Cindy and her friends who are middle class members of the host culture often see themselves as benevolent to the lower class such as foreign domestic workers. For instance, Cindy compares herself to employers of old who would not allow their maids to sleep before they do or give them Sundays off so as to justify the way she treats Esperanza. Recalling the earlier point about

---

34. Wong and Tay, *Esperanza*, 103–4.
35. Wong and Tay, *Esperanza*, 105–6.
36. Wong and Tay, *Esperanza*, 123–24.
37. Trible, *God and Rhetoric of Sexuality*, 180.
38. Honig, "Ruth"; Yee, "She Stood."

how Ruth as a Moabite could potentially impoverish Mr. So and So, it would contrast Boaz as all the more courageous in taking up what could be potentially disastrous to him (Ruth 4:10). While we do not have direct access to the thoughts of Naomi and Boaz, it is hard not to think of such portrayals as anything more than thinly veiled references about the inferiority of Moab so as to shore up Israel's benevolence to them. Ruth is given financial security. What more could she ask for?

I would go further to claim that it is this presumed benevolence on the part of the middle class that makes us blind to our privilege. The playwrights seem cognizant of this as they attempt to not only keep Esperanza's association with being Filipina alive, but also reverse negative stereotypes. For instance, we are told that Esperanza is well educated having graduated with a degree in English and Political Science and has worked previously in the Philippines Embassy as the first secretary to the Ambassador of the Philippines. Furthermore through Esperanza writing a letter back home, we come to know about her family and life in the Philippines. In contrast, little is known about Ruth's previous Moabite past other than her dogged persistence in following Naomi back to Bethlehem.[39] As Jione Havea points out, the locals of Moab as compared to that of Bethlehem are given relatively little attention in the narrative.[40] In the next section, I argue that this lack of information is problematic for middle class readers such as myself and how this could be subverted through reading *Ruth* with *Esperanza* to as to conscientize us not only to the realities of foreign domestic workers like Esperanza, but also to our own class desires.

Re-reading Ruth for Singapore

I would like to begin this act of reconfiguring the text for "common Singapore use" with a rather mundane observation that both the play and the book are named after their respective protagonists. Both in their unique ways bring up the trope of sensuality of foreign women—Ruth on the threshing floor and Cindy gossiping with her mahjong friends about flirtatious maids. Yet in neither story is the sexual potential played out to its (climactic) end though I would concede that *Ruth* is more tantalizingly

---

39. In this regard, Musa Dube attempts to fill in the missing Moabite background of Ruth and Orpah. See Dube, "Unpublished Letters," 145–50.

40. Havea, "Stirring Naomi," 120–21.

vague.[41] At least for Wong and Tay, it would have made for a truly shocking and sensational story had Mr. Chee raped Esperanza that might have conceivably worked in favor of advocacy. Yet these expectations of dominant culture with an appetite for sex and violence seem relatively muted in both accounts which then deprives their respective, likely elite audiences of their orgasmic release. Perhaps as one brought up in more fundamentalist Christianity, the expectation would be less of the sacred text. Yet in inflecting the desire for a sordid, sensuous twist in *Esperanza* through *Ruth* would highlight that attention on the protagonists is meant to be less so as to allow the spotlight to shift back onto the reader. In other words, the text resists our entry into its world predicated on certain class desires so as to reflect more light onto the world of the readers.

Put more personally, both texts are synergistically calling into question my position in relation to the Ruths and Esperanzas of my society. The shock and horror of maids abused physically, emotionally, and sexually continue to grace the headlines of mainstream media on a far more regular basis than one would expect of such a clean and prosperous city. Somehow the unsavory portrayals not only has shocked the system especially middle class readers into numbness, which causes the failure to recognize this as a form of *systemic* injustice, but also makes it difficult to see oneself as complicit, folded together with these realities because the mundane, everyday nature of these strange encounters have been undermined. Reading *Ruth* and *Esperanza* transtextually along the lines of the mundane draws in the reader through the familiarity of home before rendering the otherwise banal interactions between the local and foreigner uncanny. Put differently, paraphrasing Ivan Petrella, juxtaposing the "horrendous" with the banal breaks the "normalcy of everyday life" and shows the "shame in forgetting the horror is not exception but rule."[42] Thus, there is something potentially misleading in the names of both stories because attention directed toward named protagonists seems to be (mis?)directed to other actors such as Naomi or Mr. So-and-So/Mr. Chee or Cindy so as to boomerang back onto the readers themselves. In other words, is the story truly about Ruth/Esperanza?

If the above assertion that the readers needed to be foregrounded more in reading *Ruth* were true, then I wish to explore further how class

---

41. Several commentators have argued that sexual intercourse did take place on the threshing floor. See for instance, Yee, "She Stood," 132–33. Nonetheless, the presence of the debate signifies that the text is at best ambiguous.

42. Petrella, *Beyond Liberation Theology*, 124.

privilege could possibly domesticate the text in the context of Singapore. Arguably both cultures have conditioned their respective readers to think of marriage and children as "happy endings." Therefore, it is not unusual to think of *Ruth* as a fairy tale that ends happily ever after and *Esperanza* as a tragic microcosm reflecting a clash of civilizations. Reading *Ruth* by itself, most Singaporean Christian readers would choose to do so according to their own class sensitivities. Assuming that Moab is a land of famine and destitution, Ruth is easily read as being granted social mobility through her persevering pursuit of Naomi which lands her a marriage with a wealthy landowner, Boaz. Furthermore, as mentioned earlier, Christians, especially Protestants in Singapore have to a large extent embraced dominant ideas of North American Protestant fundamentalism, particularly tropes revolving around the traditional family. To compound this further, Chinese privilege values sons more than daughters because of its affiliation to Confucianism, albeit such desires are eroding under the pressure of modernizing Singapore. Therefore, the seemingly happy ending of boy meets girl culminating in the birth of a son with the subtle trope of women being saved through childbirth would most likely resonate with the desires of many middle class Christian readers. This would have a synergistic effect with class desire refracted through Chinese privilege. In the case of *Ruth*, the disciplining of inferior bodies produces results. Put more bluntly, Ruth's willing submission results in her finding financial security. Thus, it is not too far-fetched to argue that this could possibly lead Singaporean readers to think of Singapore as a land of promise and prosperity for domestic helpers who then ought to be grateful for this opportunity and emulate Ruth in her willingness to "assimilate" into her host culture. The end-result, of course, is that it leaves the issue of privilege associated with class and ethnicity relatively unquestioned and the problems of labor exploitation mostly hidden.

Unlike other forms of foreign labor such as white people from Europe and North America or wealthy Asians typically from China and India taking up specialized jobs, there is no expectation that workers like that of the foreign domestic helpers to integrate into Singaporean society.[43] On this note, it deserves mention that one important redeeming point of the narrative is the impossible status that Ruth as a Moabite has attained in the Israelite community as the ancestress of the great King David himself. Or as Stephanie Day Powell, Amy Beth Jones, and Dong

43. Poon, "Pick and Mix," 81–84.

Sung Kim put it, "an unlikely candidate—a Moabite woman—ushers in a new future."[44] Perhaps this is something even the writers of this tale find (mildly?) intolerable as they conveniently report that "a son has been born to Naomi" instead of Ruth (Ruth 4:17, NRSV).[45] Yet, I still wish to claim that even this seeming advantage of the narrative could be easily elided over so as to demonstrate the benevolence of the superior class to the inferior.

As a corrective, what if I were to choose to read both stories in a similar vein? What if I heed the insights of *Esperanza* on the potential points of misrepresentation of the foreigner? Incidentally, this resonates with a growing number of readings from Third World spaces within the Global North and Global South that could be summed up in Brenner's suspicions that Ruth is "be[ing] *absorbed* rather than *integrated*."[46] Perhaps the point of rehabilitation for *Ruth* is to read it as a *cautionary tale*.[47] Or for the domestic helper, reading *Ruth* in this way gives voice and dignity to her struggle without being eclipsed by happy endings. Therefore, in order to read *Ruth* in the manner of how *Esperanza* resists any resolution to the matter of foreign domestic workers other than foregrounding the tragedies of these "strange encounters," modern Singaporean Christian readers such as myself who have grown accustomed to such desires need to reorient our postures to accommodate a significant degree of counter-intuition in approaching this tale. In other words, the trace of "the Moabite" in the text should be seen as an invitation to employ a hermeneutic of suspicion rather than contributing to its further erasure. In doing so, it interrogates our presumed benevolence and hopefully, exposes our potential hubris.

Conclusion?

In conclusion, what I am led to see through this transtextual reading with *Esperanza* is that what *Ruth* offers as resolution of "strange encounters" with foreign domestic workers could at best be cleansing of the

---

44. Powell, Jones, and Kim, "Reading Ruth, Reading Desire," 253.
45. Fewell and Gunn, "Son is Born to Naomi!," 233–39.
46. Brenner, "Ruth as a Foreign Worker," 162, emphasis hers.
47. Honig makes a similar point that the story is a "tale of incomplete mourning, a fable of failed transition" which highlights the need to provide safe spaces for immigrants to mourn their loss and attain closure. Honig, "Model Emigrée," 128.

foreign contagion through assimilation.[48] The structures that construct the other as "other" remain relatively intact as the signifier "Moabite" is not properly interrogated in the text on its own terms but rather relative to what makes it "right" in the eyes of the Israelites. This process of re-appropriation of the text to the present context with the help of the Other's, namely Esperanza's, standpoint foregrounds the dangerousness of this text. Perhaps I should be compelled like Musa Dube and Laura Donaldson who look elsewhere by attempting a revisionist reading of the figure of Orpah that favors her choice of leaving to engage with this problematic text.[49] Instead, I have chosen in this essay to disrupt such class desires that transform Ruth into a model worker while ignoring the systemic issues with her being a poor, foreign woman.

Reading *Ruth* transtextually through *Esperanza* then forces my community, including myself, to confront how our own class desires have domesticated this text. By alienating this (over)familiar book, the biblical text then becomes what Justin Ukpong calls a "site of struggle"[50] that facilitates the process of exposing and interrogating our stereotypes of the Other, both in biblical Israel and contemporary Singapore. Put more concretely, it serves as a constant reminder that while the middle class might be limited in bringing about social transformation in wider society, we should at the very least begin to dismantle such "strange encounters" in our little kingdoms called "home." Perhaps like all good medicine, it is better to take *Ruth* in small doses to keep us alert to our xenophobic tendencies, but taking (in) too much of it would turn a relatively useful treatment of symptoms of classism and ethnocentrism into a fatal dose that might confer (unintended?) death to the foreigner.

Bibliography

Ahmed, Sara. *Strange Encounters: Embodied Others in Post-Coloniality*. New York: Routledge, 2000.

Begg, Christopher T. "Foreigner." In *Anchor Bible Dictionary*, edited by David Noel Freedman, 2:829–30. 6 vols. New York: Doubleday, 1992.

---

48. The idea of "assimilation" is also reinforced through Laura Donaldson's reading through the experiences of Cherokee women during the time of Anglo-European expansion into the Americas. Donaldson, "The Sign of Orpah," 164.

49. Dube, "Unpublished Letters"; Donaldson, "Sign of Orpah."

50. Ukpong, "Inculturation Hermeneutics."

Brenner, Athalya. "Ruth as a Foreign Worker and the Politics of Exogamy." In *A Feminist Companion to Ruth and Esther*, edited by Athalya Brenner, 158–62. Sheffield: Sheffield Academic, 1999.

Chong, Terence. *The Theatre and the State in Singapore: Orthodoxy and Resistance*. New York: Routledge, 2011.

Chong, Terence and Yew Foong Hui. *Different under God: A Survey of Church-Going Protestants in Singapore*. Singapore: Institute of Southeast Asian Studies, 2013.

Chua, Beng Huat and Joo Ean Tan. "Singapore: Where the Middle-Class Sets the Standard." In *Culture and Privilege in Capitalist Asia*, edited by Michael Pinches, 138–59. New Rich in Asia Series. London: Routledge, 1999.

Clark, Terry Nichols, and Seymour Martin Lipset. "Are Social Clasess Dying?" *International Sociology* 6.4 (1991) 397–410.

Constable, Nicole. "Reproductive Labor at the Intersection of Three Intimate Industries: Domestic Work, Sex Tourism, and Adoption." *Positions: East Asia Cultures Critique* 24.1 (2016) 45–69.

Donaldson, Laura. "The Sign of Orpah: Reading Ruth through Native Eyes." In *Postcolonial Biblical Reader*, edited by R. S. Sugirtharajah, 159–70. Oxford: Blackwell, 2006.

Dube, Musa W. "Divining Ruth for International Relations." In *Other Ways of Reading: African Women and the Bible*, edited by Musa W. Dube, 179–98. Global Perspectives on Biblical Interpretation 2. Atlanta: Society of Biblical Literature, 2001.

———. "Unpublished Letters of Orpah to Ruth." In *Ruth and Esther*, edited by Athalya Brenner, 145–50. Feminist Companion to the Bible. Sheffield: Sheffield Academic, 1999.

Fewell, Danna Nolan, and David M. Gunn. "'A Son Is Born to Naomi!': Literary Allusions and Interpretation in the Book of Ruth." In *Women in the Hebrew Bible: A Reader*, edited by Alice Bach, 233–39. London: Routledge, 1999.

Havea, Jione. "Stirring Naomi: Another Gleaning at the Edges of Ruth 1." In *Reading Ruth in Asia*, edited by Jione Havea and Peter Lau, 111–24. International Voices in Biblical Studies 7. Atlanta: Society of Biblical Literature, 2015.

Honig, Bonnie. "Ruth, the Model Emigrée: Mourning and the Symbolic Politics of Immigration." *Political Theory* 25.1 (1997) 112–36.

Jones, David Martin, and David Brown. "Singapore and the Myth of the Liberalizing Middle Class." *The Pacific Review* 7.1 (1994) 79–87.

Leow, Joanne. "Strangers, Surrogates, Lovers: Foreign Domestic Workers in Contemporary Singapore Texts." In *Singapore Literature and Culture: Current Directions in Local and Global Contexts*, edited by Angelia Poon and Angus Whitehead, 198–216. Routledge Studies in Twentieth-Century Literature. New York: Routledge, 2017.

Lim, Chin Ming Stephen. *Contextual Biblical Hermeneutics as Multicentric Dialogue: Towards a Singaporean Reading of Daniel*. Biblical Interpretation Series 175. Leiden: Brill, 2019.

———. "Undoing Chinese Privilege through Reading with the Other." *Journal of Law and Social Sciences* 7 (2018) 1-8.

Mak, Lau-Fong. "Between Materialism and Post-Materialism: The Addicted Middle Class of Singapore." Program for Southeast Asian Studies Occasional Paper no. 8: Academica Sinica, 1997.

Peterson, William. *Theater and the Politics of Culture in Contemporary Singapore.* Middletown, CT: Wesleyan University Press, 2001.

Petrella, Ivan. *Beyond Liberation Theology: A Polemic.* London: SCM, 2008.

Poon, Angelia. "Maid Visible: Foreign Domestic Workers and the Dilemma of Development in Singapore." *Crossroads: An Interdisciplinary Journal of Southeast Asian Studies* 17 (2003) 1–28.

———. "Pick and Mix for a Global City: Race and Cosmopolitanism in Singapore." In *Race and Multiculturalism in Malaysia and Singapore*, edited by Daniel P. S. Goh et al., 70–85. Routledge Malaysian Studies Series 8. London: Routledge, 2009.

Powell, Stephanie Day, Amy Beth Jones, and Dong Sung Kim. "Reading Ruth, Reading Desire." In *The Oxford Handbook of Biblical Narrative*, edited by Danna Nolan Fewell 245-254. Oxford Handbooks. Oxford: Oxford University Press, 2016.

Rendtorff, Rolf. "The Gêr in Priestly Laws of the Pentateuch." In *Ethnicity and the Bible*, edited by Mark G. Brett, 77–88. Biblical Interpretation Series 19. Leiden: Brill, 1996.

Sakenfeld, Katharine D. *Just Wives?: Stories of Power and Survival in the Old Testament and Today.* Louisville: Westminster John Knox, 2003.

Sasson, Jack M. *Ruth: A New Translation with a Philological Commentary and a Formalist-Folklorist Interpretation*, 2nd ed. Biblical Seminar 10. Sheffield: JSOT Press, 1989.

Trible, Phyllis. *God and the Rhetoric of Sexuality.* Overtures to Biblical Theology. Philadelphia: Fortress, 1978.

Ukpong, Justin. "Inculturation Hermeneutics: An African Approach to Biblical Interpretation." In *The Bible in World Context: An Experiment in Contextual Hermeneutics*, edited by Walter Dietrich and Ulrich Luz, 17–32. Grand Rapids: Eerdmans, 2002.

Wafula, Robert Sammy. "Biblical Representations of Moab: A Kenyan Postcolonial Reading." PhD diss., Drew University, 2013.

Wessels, Anja, Madeline Ong, and Davinia Daniel. "Bonded to the System: Labour Exploitation in the Foreign Domestic Work Sector in Singapore." https://www.researchgate.net/publication/321298753_Bonded_to_the_system_Labour_exploitation_in_the_foreign_domestic_work_sector_in_Singapore.

Wong, Souk Yee and Hong Seng Tay. "Esperanza." In *5 Plays from Third Stage: A Collection of Five Singaporean Plays*, edited by Anne Lim and Suan Tze Chng, 99–129. Singapore: Third Stage, 2005.

Yee, Gale A. "She Stood in Tears amid the Alien Corn: Ruth, the Perpetual Foreigner and Model Minority." In *They Were All Together in One Place? Toward Minority Biblical Criticism*, edited by Randall C. Bailey, Tat-siong Benny Liew and Fernando Segovia, 119–40. Semeia Studies 57. Atlanta: Society of Biblical Literature, 2009.

Section III

Gender, Race, and Class

8

Proletarianized Sexuality of Soldiering and Prostitution

Making a Christian Ethic of Peace Countering Necropolitics of War

Keun-Joo Christine Pae

A Necropolitics of War

As Susan Hayward and Katherine Marshall state, our understandings of war and war itself become far more complex in the modern era.[1] If our understandings of war were influenced by our social locations such as class, race, gender, experiences of war, and perceptions of peace, how would we, progressive Christians, who are committed to God's peace and justice on earth, talk about war without ignoring its brutal and complex realities? The ethical discourse on peace and war that this chapter constructs aims at disrupting the commonly shared belief that the military is inevitable for global peace and security. For this purpose, I employ the lens of "necropolitical labor" to analyze the realities of war and militarism through the raw stories of soldiers and military prostitutes whose sexualized and racialized labors are proletarianized, commodified, and finally

1. Hayward and Marshall, *Women, Religion, and Peacebuilding*, 2.

extracted to serve "the labor demands of the state or empire."[2] Korean American cultural theorist Jin-kyung Lee conceptualizes necropolitical labor in interrogating the deadly aspects of gendered, sexualized, racialized, and classed labors in service of the state (e.g., service economies or surrogate economies).

Reconceptualizing "the notion of biopower and labor through their connection to death or possibilities of death," Lee articulates that:

> The notion of necropolitical labor highlights an intermediate stage where the extraction of labor is related to and premised on the possibility of death, rather than the ultimate event of death itself . . . *necropolitical labor as the most disposable labor* . . . [is] the ultimate labor commodity or worker, something or someone to be thrown out, replaced, and/or (both literally and figuratively) killed after or as the labor is performed.[3]

As the concrete sites of knowledge about war and militarism, military prostitution and soldiering make up the two distinctive forms of "necropolitical labor." If, as postcolonial theorist Achille Mbembe argues, war is understood "as much a means of achieving sovereignty as exercising the right to kill," soldiers embody sovereignty by exercising its right or mission to kill (enemies).[4] Soldiering or military labor represents "the state's necropower" to kill and conquer anyone perceived as the enemy to the state. At the same time, soldiers are "the state's very potential victims" who carry "the risk of being exterminated by the enemy."[5] For this reason, Lee calls military labor "surrogate labor" to the state.[6] Due to the contradictory nature of soldiering, in order to understand the realities of any war, we must scrutinize who are recruited to military labor. This question is particularly important in the United States where the military has become a competitive employer of African American youth, poor whites, and immigrants of color in the market sector, while soldiers' lives are mystified, and the military is generally isolated from the civil society.

At the other side of the spectrum of militarized necropolitical labor is military prostitution. The prostitution industry relies on the commodified body and acts of prostitutes. As Lee argues, similar to other

2. Lee, *Service Economies*, 6.
3. Lee, *Service Economies*, 6; emphasis added by the author.
4. Mbembe, *Necropolitics*, 66.
5. Lee, *Service Economies*, 6.
6. Lee, *Service Economies*, 6–7; 37–38.

necropolitical labors, "the possibility of death, the ultimate disposability, is an integral element of prostitution as occupation."[7] As Australian feminist Sheila Jeffreys rightly points out, in the second half of the 20th century, the transnationalization of the U.S. military industrialized prostitution on a global level.[8] Especially during the Cold War, the construction of Rest and Recreation businesses in East and Southeast Asia, including the Philippines, Thailand, Okinawa, Vietnam, and South Korea, was an integral part of U.S. overseas military bases. In contrast to soldiers' glorified bodies, those of military prostitutes are morally condemned, although the state demands their necropolitical labor to ease soldiers' anxiety and fear, and to control venereal disease to protect soldiers' readiness to fight. Military prostitution shows not only the proletarianization of sexuality but also the extraction of sexuality from the proletariat. During the time of war, poor women are routinely mobilized as the collective labor forced to respond to the sexual needs of men—male soldiers, in particular. Despite the long historical presence of prostitution in the global war theater, poor women's sexualized labor has been generally ignored in Christian discourse on war and peace.

In the meantime, a necropolitical approach to war shows that war is a lucrative business fueled by deadly labors of gendered, classed, racialized, and sexualized low-ranked soldiers and military prostitutes. With attention to the U.S.-Korea relations, I transnationally contextualize this lucrative war business. More specifically, I examine the complex and antagonized relationship between American soldiers and Korean prostitutes who share the proletariat class background, arguing that the state recruits the racialized and sexualized proletariats into its war business. Based on the analysis of war through the lens of necropolitical labor, this chapter elaborates on (1) why Christian ethics of war and peace should be re-read through the lens of class transected with race and gender/sexuality; (2) how this ethical discourse would make the proletarianized human sexuality in the state's military projects more visible; and (3) how "God's preferential option for the poor" can help us creatively imagine a world of peace liberated from militarism or militarized fear.

7. Lee, *Service Economies*, 7.
8. Jeffreys, *The Industrial Vagina*, 107.

Rethinking Christian Ethical Discourse on War and Peace

The Christian church's views on war, militarism, and violence are often contradicted with one another. While the church argues that to use violence, the intention and the acts of violence should be justified in the court of nonviolence, the church has rarely endorsed nonviolence during armed conflict. However, pacifism, epitomized as nonviolence, is arguably Christianity's oldest response to war. Pacifism is often misunderstood as "passive submission" to violence by its exponents, but the idea means "active" resistance of violence through nonviolence. Ghandi's nonviolent resistance against the British Empire's ruling of India, Dr. Martin Luther King Jr.'s nonviolent civil rights movement, and Zen Master Thich Nhat Hanh's anti-Vietnam War peace movement are the good examples of pacifism. As many people doubt the practicability of nonviolence in the real war situation, influenced by modern pacifist theologian Howard Yoder, Christian ethicist Stanley Hauerwas presents nonviolence as a way of life manifested by the followers of Jesus rather than a strategy to end war.[9]

In spite of many noble values from pacifism, and religiously motivated pacifists' courageous practices of nonviolence even when their own lives are jeopardized, pacifist discourse is generally challenged when "crimes against humanity" such as massacre, genocide, ethnic cleansing, and systemic rape against women and girls happen. These cases call the international community to take Responsibility to Protect (R2P) and urge immediate military intervention (e.g., U.N. Peacekeeping Corps) to stop atrocities against the vulnerable.[10]

R2P is not simply a secular humanitarian discourse but also a crucial part of Christian Just War Tradition (JWT). As the term suggests, JWT focuses on "justice," namely, which war is morally justifiable enough to fight. Traditional just war criteria applied to R2P include "right intention, last resort, proportional means, and reasonable prospects."[11] To protect the vulnerable from crimes against humanity is usually considered a right intention to enter a war.

---

9. Pae, "Peace and War," 87.

10. Welch, *Real Peace, Real Security*, 31–32. I should emphasize that R2P raises questions regarding the effectiveness of military intervention, morality or intention behind intervention in a sovereign state. It is also morally complex to determine which case falls into the category of R2P.

11. Welch, *Real Peace, Real Security*, 37.

Contemporary just war theory is divided into three parts: (1) the conditions that must be obtained before a war is considered "just" (*jus ad bellum*); (2) right conducts during the warfare (*jus in bello*), for example, not killing civilians, and humanely treating the prisoners of war; and (3) the just way to exit or cease a war (*jus post bellum*).[12] JWT is intended to offer moral checkpoints to enter and exit a war. These moral checkpoints are important to scrutinize and limit the use of violence. For, as feminist ethicist Sharon Welch reminds us, cruelty can be intoxicating, and therefore, the use of violence even for noble ends can sparkle the excessive use of violence during the time of conflict.[13]

JWT does not have a biblical foundation for its principles. However, the tradition has dominated both theological and philosophical discourses on war and peace in the West. The major critique of JWT is that the theory often fails to map out how to create just social structures before and after a war so that the cultural, social, and political breeding of war can be aborted. Thus, contemporary just war theory with attention to *jus post bellum* accentuates the necessity of reconciliation between warring parties, restorative justice, forgiveness, and healing of post-war trauma. In response to the theoretical and practical shortcomings of pacifism and JWT, a group of religious and philosophical ethicists and peace activists propose the "just peacemaking paradigm" or the fourth paradigm beyond the historic address of peace and war. The core concern of the just peacemaking paradigm is about how to create just socio-political, economic structures in weak society because social injustice is the root cause of armed conflict and undermines the stability of society.

Christian discourses on war and peace represented by pacifism, just war tradition, and just peacemaking all underline moral danger behind the use of violence, the destructive power of war, human suffering and injustice caused by war, and particular concerns about the vulnerable. However, gender, race, class, and sexuality of the real people are invisible in these Christian theories. Ungendered, unclassed, unsexualized, and unracialized theories may unintentionally benefit only a certain group of people whose social locations are not challenged by mainstream society—the heterosexual white male bourgeoisie. As transnational feminist theorist M. Jacqui Alexander insightfully points out, modern warfare is built upon the heteropatriarchal capitalist nation-building with the territorial

12. Pae, "Peace and War," 89.
13. Welch, *Real Peace, Real Security*, 38.

marking of land and property, coincident with the territorial marking of whiteness and with inscribing particular gendered and sexualized bodies and communities (same-sex and sex workers).[14] The practices of patriarchal nation-building further include securing the borders of the nation from sexually devious terrorists of color, folding Judeo-Christian conjugal tradition into the regimes of rule, and "aligning corporate and state interests in ways that benefit imperialism and render the neocolonial class as complicit in global capital's project of recolonization."[15] Thus, any Christian discourse that truly aims at preventing war and violence while promoting peace should more actively search for how to dismantle heteropatriarchal capitalist nation-building at the cost of sexually gendered and racially minoritized people. Unfortunately, Christianity's representative theories of war and peace often fail to challenge the existing power structure built upon gender, race, class, and sexuality.

Furthermore, the said Christian traditions of war and peace assume three different parties involved in a war: decision-makers of war, the vulnerable to be protected, and active participants of flesh and blood either in just peacemaking or in fighting a war. The theories potentially create a division among these parties rather than seeing interconnection among them. Especially, the moral agency of the vulnerable, who are likely to be gendered and racialized others in their respective societies, is hardly respected but silenced in the Christian theories of war and peace. The adherent to the theories may treat the vulnerable as the objects to be protected because they are presumed not to protect themselves. Although social injustice and discrimination against racial, gender, and religious minorities are sources for armed conflict, just peacemaking and just war tradition may see the oppressed as potential insurgents. The oppressed population may be presumed to revolt violently against the unjust regime or take a revenge on their oppressors in the post-war context.

Due to its blind spots, any theory detached from the real bodies of people, who are forced to fight a war or sexually enslaved by the military, survive armed conflict, witness crimes against humanity, and painfully watch their children die one by one at refugee camps, becomes impotent before armed conflict. Such a theory fails to prevent violence against the vulnerable, too. For this reason, Christian theologian Susan Thistlethwaite criticizes major Christian traditions of war and peace for lack of

---

14. Alexander, *Pedagogies of Crossing*, 195.
15. Alexander, *Pedagogies of Crossing*, 196.

gender analysis and sexism embedded in those traditions while women's bodies experience deadly violence every day.[16] How can we make the real human bodies visible in the Christian discourse of war and peace? Now we turn to this question.

Making the Invisible Visible: Proletarianization of Sexuality and Race in the United States, Korea, and Somewhere in Transnational Context

With a focus on the U.S.–Korean context, I show the necropolitical realities of soldiering and military prostitution. These realities of war eventually lead to an alternative Christian discourse on peace that aims to overcome necropolitics.

War Profits at the Cost of Soldiers

In his antiwar classic, *War Is a Racket*, America's most decorated soldier, Major General Smedley Butler, called war a racket because "it is conducted for the benefit of the very few at the expense of the very many."[17] During World War I, the major war that allowed the U.S. to emerge as a global power, a small number of capitalists reaped profits as much 1400% as before the wartime by selling copper for weapons, boots for soldiers, and mosquito nets for the use of the soldiers overseas.[18] They manufactured excessive products often with poor qualities, and some of them would not be used by soldiers at all. While war profits created 21,000 new billionaires, $13 billion deficits fell on American citizens' shoulders, which would result in increasing taxation.[19]

Butler's analysis of the cost and profits of World War I is arguably relevant to any war in America's modern history. For instance, during the early Cold War period, America's two hot wars in Korea and Vietnam respectively congealed American hegemony in the free market world. The Vietnam War was also the crucial moment for South Korea (ROK— Republic of Korea) to construct its platform for economic prosperity. ROK participated in America's war in Vietnam by dispatching the second

16. Thislethwaite, *Women's Bodies as Battlegrounds*, 147–49.
17. Butler, *War Is a Racket*, 5.
18. Butler, *War Is a Racket*, 20, 23.
19. Butler, *War Is a Racket*, 28, 31.

largest troops and civilian workers to Vietnam—more than three hundred thousand troops and over one hundred thousand civilian workers were sent to Vietnam between 1965 and 1973.[20] During the War, Korean soldiers remitted a substantial sum of their earnings to their families in Korea, and their remittance made up the second highest source of foreign currency.[21] Not only soldiers but also Korean corporations took the Vietnam War as an opportunity to expand their overseas businesses and export industries. Among these corporations are Korea's multinational corporations today such as Samsung, Hyungdai, and Hanjin.[22] About seventy-one percent of approximately 56,000 Korean civilian laborers in Vietnam between 1965–1972 were hired by 35 American companies and the rest by 52 Korean companies.[23] Butler's story of World War I was repeated in Vietnam, and now in Iraq, Afghanistan, Yemen, and elsewhere. In America's contemporary wars, necropolitical labor is conducted both by soldiers and private contractors, who do the jobs traditionally done by soldiers. In 2008 when the country fought two major wars abroad, about $33 billion dollars were paid to these private contractors. At that time, in Iraq alone, "163,900 private contractors supported 160,000 troops."[24]

The true cost of war is paid by low-ranked soldiers whose bodies and souls are often destroyed and maimed. Their deaths, disfigurement, dismemberment, and psychological and moral injury are the true cost of war. Butler underlines that (1) military training (e.g., a boot camp) remolds civilians to necropolitical laborers; and (2) the state does not provide a sufficient support system for the soldiers when their duties are over.[25] Thus, soldiers should often endure the detrimental consequences of necropolitical soldiering on their own.

Military training, an important tool for necropolitical labor, relies on the ideology that requires a soldier's body to be suppressed and disciplined to intentionally kill the enemy and to overcome fear. The

20. Lee, *Service Economies*, 37.
21. Jo, "Fighting for Peanuts," 72.
22. Jo, "Fighting for Peanuts," 73.
23. Jo, "Fighting for Peanuts," 73.
24. Taylor, *Military Service and American Democracy*, 170, 172, quoted in Curtin, "A Necropolitical Analysis."
25. Butler, *War Is a Racket*, 31–33. The reader should be noted that Butler did not use the term, "necropolitics" or "necropolitical labor." However, his description of a soldier's status resonates with Jin-kyung Lee's example of soldering as a form of necropolitical labor.

construction of the warrior's body is intertwined with masculinized ideologies such as dominance over femininity and direct denial of human vulnerability. Sex, then, is used as a vehicle to suppress soldiers' fear and vulnerability or to show their superiority to women and the (feminized) enemy. Susan Thistlethwaite argues that militarism is both a product of and a support for "the gnosticizing tendency in Christianity to denigrate the body and sexuality and to exclude them from the realm of the spirit."[26] In this case, necropolitical labor should be understood as the extraction of labor from both the body and the spirit of those who are condemned to death. Namely, alienation of one's body from the spirit is inevitable in necropolitical labor.

The separation between the body and the spirit can further damage soldiers' personhood, their sense of who they are. Various psychologists and theologians have proved how the necropolitical labor of soldiering is truly necropolitical by harming soldiers' bodies, minds, spirits, and moralities, especially after they had been involved in killing enemies or witnessing the tragic deaths of their comrades. According to military psychologist David Grossman, human beings, even soldiers, inherently have tremendous resistance to killing other human beings.[27] If soldiers are forced to kill enemies in a close range, they experience unspeakable stress. For this reason, only 50–55% of soldiers fired their arms during the Korean War (1950–1953) but with new training, 90–95% of soldiers did in the Vietnam War (1955–1975).[28] The increased firing rates do not mean the success of the army's training programs. Rather, soldiers are conditioned to fire their arms (e.g., reflexive shooting) which results in even deeper wounds of pain and guilt on their minds, known as PTSD and moral injury.

Since the burden of killing is so great, most soldiers try not to admit that they have killed, so they deny it to others and try to deny it to themselves.[29] Denial or intentional forgetfulness is a survival strategy for combat soldiers, who live with PTSD and moral injury for an indefinite period, but this also causes a further split between the body and the spirit. According to Rita Nakashima Brock and Gabriella Lettini, moral injury results:

26. Thistlethwaite, "Militarism in North American," 120–21.
27. Grossman, *On Killing*, xxxi.
28. Grossman, *On Killing*, 36.
29. Grossman, *On Killing*, 90–92.

> . . . [W]hen soldiers violate their core moral beliefs, and in evaluating their behavior negatively, they feel they no longer live in a reliable, meaningful world and can no longer be regarded as decent human beings...Killing, torturing prisoners, abusing dead bodies, or failing to prevent such acts can elicit moral injury. Seeing someone else violate core moral values or feeling betrayed by persons in authority can also lead to [moral injury]. It can also even emerge from witnessing a friend get killed and feeling survivor guilt. In experiencing a moral conflict, soldiers may judge themselves as worthless; they may decide no one can be trusted and isolate themselves from others; and they may abandon the values and beliefs [even God] that gave their lives meaning and guided their moral choices.[30]

Grossman, Brock, and Lettini point out one truth about war: soldiers' war never ends. Once they step into a war, they can hardly re-enter the civilian world. There is no boot camp for them to get readjusted to the civil world. Their broken bodies and minds can be compared to those of zombies. The result of militarized necropolitical labor is a "living death."

Proletarianization of Sexuality and Race: Recruitment of Soldiers

Jin-kyung Lee defines "sexual proletarianization" as a process of "mobilizing respectively gendered sexualities into various working-class service labors," including military labor, and military and industrial sex work.[31] Soldiering is "a particular kind of sexual proletarian labor, where certain aspects of masculine sexuality are [re]constructed, [re]appropriated, and deployed as a range of tasks."[32] The U.S. military is not an all-male institution but is masculinized space where all soldiers are expected to perform hypermasculinity marked with physical and mental strength, domination, aggression, hierarchy, and the patriarchal rank system. As mentioned earlier, female sex is often used to create or sustain this patriarchal military morale.

If a universal draft system may present the entire (male) population as potential victims and agents of the state's necropolitics, the draft

---

30. Brock and Lettini, *Soul Repair*, xv.
31. Lee, *Service Economies*, 38.
32. Lee, *Service Economies*, 38.

system's abstract equality renders "the substitutability of labor possible."³³ Within the system of a volunteer force (e.g., America's All-Volunteer Force [AVF] enacted in 1973 and ROK's use of voluntarily enlisted men during its involvement in the Vietnam War), the only coercive force for people to join armed forces is an economic one. This market model of the military illustrates the unequal conditions of class, race, gender, and nationality as a proletarianization of sexuality and race.

The Vietnam War led the U.S. military to an All-Volunteer Force (AVF) in 1973. Through the Vietnam War, American society critically re-examined its military system beyond the notions of patriotism and the obligations of citizenship. America's draft system was, in fact, a selective service system that created a working class war by protecting the economically successful and the socially-well positioned.³⁴ In the meantime, right conservatives saw conscription as "one more loss of individual liberty to government power."³⁵ In the meantime, the Pentagon's concern was about how to attract large numbers of volunteers to make the military more effective, as reluctant draftees ruined the military institution. A group of free-market economists and libertarian thinkers who gained influence in the Nixon administration shaped the initial and determining structure for an all-volunteer force. Their moral assumption was simple:

> The draft . . . could be replaced by the free market; whatever inequities and inequalities that stemmed from either random chance or government-sponsored engineering…could be avoided by creating a free-market arena in which individuals made decisions based on rational understandings of their own economic best interest.³⁶

Unfortunately, the logic of the market that replaced the logic of citizenship attached to the institutionalized military has generally failed to overcome social inequalities, because libertarian economists could not comprehend the complexities and irregularities of human decisions affected by moral agents' social locations.

In terms of race, until World War II African Americans demanded their right to fight for the state to be recognized as legitimate citizens.

---

33. Lee, *Service Economies*, 39.
34. Bailey, *America's Army*, 3–6.
35. Bailey, *America's Army*, 3.
36. Bailey, *America's Army*, 4.

The military was racially segregated until the Korean War.[37] The AVF has been often considered a new opportunity for African American men and women, who have traditionally experienced racial, gender, and sexual discrimination in employment. Perceiving less discrimination in the military than in the civil market sector, African American men disproportionately volunteer for the military service and are overrepresented in the military. For many of them, the military is a competitive career option, compared to many entry level jobs in the civil sector. However, African American military personnel are paid less than their white counterparts mainly because the majority of African Americans are enlisted at a low rank. Entry to the enlisted ranks across armed forces generally requires a high school diploma (not GED), and here African Americans' overrepresentation is pronounced. The military is the largest employer of African American high school graduates. In 2000, 22% of enlisted personnel across services were African Americans and in the army 30% of all enlisted soldiers.[38]

African American enlistment rates have fluctuated since 2000 due to African American youth's fear of death as the United States has entered various "hot" wars across the globe. Since they look for money for college, leadership skills, and proper job training through the military service, the re-enlistment rates of African Americans have fluctuated, too.[39] The U.S. military does not enlist those who fail to finish high school and demonstrate healthy body and mind (e.g., people with obesity, underweight, or psychological instabilities), or anyone who is convicted of sexually violent crimes, drug trafficking, and more than one felony.[40] The bottom of the economic ladder has been excluded from the military service because many poor youth, especially blacks and Latinos in inner-city school districts, cannot even finish high school.

While the majority of soldiers identify themselves with (lower) middle class, whites from economically struggling geographic locations

---

37. In 1948, President Harry S. Truman issued Executive Order 9981: Desegregation of the Armed Forces but faced public resistance due to Americans' deep belief in the military service as a sacred duty of citizens. By the end of the Korean War (1950–1953), almost all the military was racially desegregated. (Executive Order 9981: Desegregation of the Armed Forces, https://www.ourdocuments.gov/doc.php?flash=false&doc=84).

38. Booth and Segal, "Bringing the Soldiers Back" 35.

39. Bailey, *America's Army*, 258.

40. Bailey, *America's Army*, 253.

are overrepresented in the military. For example, in 2007 when 62 percent of the male population between 18 and 24 were classified as white, the recruitment-to-population ratio was 1.05 for whites and 1.08 for blacks. Hispanics were significantly underrepresented with a troop-to-population ratio of 0.65. However, Southerners made up 40 percent of new military recruits in the same year.[41] During the war in Iraq (2003–2011), soldiers from Appalachian regions disproportionately died, compared to soldiers from other regions. Appalachian soldiers' hometowns are characterized by less educational attainment, lower household per capita incomes, and higher poverty rates, compared to the rest of the United States.[42] Spatial inequalities matter with soldiers' deaths and the military recruitment. To meet the enlistment goals, the military targets public schools in poverty-stricken areas such as Appalachian regions. Thus, spatial inequalities help sovereignty determine more carefully who can make effective soldiers among those whose lives can be disposable rather than those who are "already" condemned to death.

Race, gender, class, poverty, or spatial inequalities alone cannot sufficiently explain who are recruited into the business of death or who pay the true cost of war. These categories of analysis should be considered transectionally in order to unpack the complexities of necropolitical labor of soldiering. Since war affects every part of society, we should also critically question how the urban and rural poor who are not used by the military silently pay for America's wars, for example, by enduring the severe budget cuts for various social welfare programs, public education, and healthcare.

Surrogacy of Soldiering and Military Prostitution in South Korean Context

ROK still practices a universal draft due to its confrontation with North Korea. During the Vietnam War, however, the country used volunteer forces: over 60 percent of Korean soldiers were voluntarily enlisted.[43] South Korean military labor in the Vietnam War functioned as intranational class surrogate labor for South Korea, and as transnational

---

41. Bailey, *America's Army*, 259.

42. Scalan, "Mined for Its Citizens?," 44. All statistical numbers come from Scalan's article.

43. Jo, "Fighting for Peanuts," 63.

racialized surrogate labor for the U.S.[44] ROK's Park Jung Hee regime during the Vietnam War simultaneously reconstituted such military proletarian labor as "a supra-class, ethnonationalist, and masculinist service."[45] Since soldiers are the agents of the state's right to kill, as I analyzed earlier, their labor embodies surrogacy of the state in fostering the lives of others. Surrogate labor is both substitutable and unsubstitutable, because only those who have desirable skills and physical and mental conditions can perform the labor (unsubstitutable), but they can be always replaced by skilled laborers with lower wages. During the Vietnam War, the extraction of labor from poor Korean men was justified for the sake of peace and security against communism, but in reality, their labor was bought by the U.S. and used for the economic development of ROK. The economic reason was a driving force for many Korean men to be enlisted for the Vietnam War. In the poverty-stricken country where unemployment rates were high, Korean military laborers in Vietnam also wanted to prove their manhood by providing financial resources for their families.

U.S. camptown prostitution in ROK is another example of surrogate labor supplied by the Korean government for American soldiers. In the context of camptown prostitution, American soldiers are both surrogate laborers of the U.S. and consumers of Korean prostitutes' surrogate labor. Korean prostitutes are the surrogates for "good" and "respectable" Korean women to be protected from wild American soldiers. The prostitutes have also performed surrogate labor for Korea that should provide entertainment for American soldiers for the sake of national security. In reality, these prostitutes were the largest group of dollar earners in Korea in 1960s through 1970s, and the second largest were military laborers in Vietnam. As Lee analytically points out, an essential dimension of South Korean modernization consists of "commodifying the transformation of sexuality and race into labor power."[46] In modern Korea, the mobilization of female sex has two related stages: the militarization of prostitution and the industrialization of prostitution.[47] Military prostitution is built upon the heterosexual masculinist assumption that soldiers' sex drives are uncontrollable. Hence, to ensure their willingness to kill and to be

---

44. Lee, *Service Economies*, 38.
45. Lee, *Service Economies*, 39.
46. Lee, *Service Economies*, 39.
47. Lee, *Service Economies*, 40.

killed in war, a means of easy, cheap, and safe sex must be provided.[48] It is worth tracing the history of U.S. military prostitution in ROK to understand how the state has systematized military prostitution as a form of necropolitical labor, and how entertaining camptowns in the country are the sites where different necropolitical laborers (e.g., American soldiers and Korean prostitutes) encounter one another.

U.S. military prostitution in South Korea began in 1945, only a few months after the arrival of the U.S. Twenty-Fourth Army Corps, consisting of some 72,000 soldiers who were expected to transfer power from Imperial Japan to Korea.[49] Since then, camptown prostitution has evolved in different stages: the early stage (1945–49), the foundation of the Relaxation and Recreation business (1950s), the golden days (1960s), the systematic corporation (1970s to mid-1980s), and the declining period (mid-1980s to present). These stages correspond to the number of American G.I.'s stationed in ROK, changes in American military policy, and the economic development of ROK.

During the Korean War, the South Korean government adopted the Japanese institution of "comfort stations" to serve U.N. Allied Forces and Korean soldiers. The Korean version of the "comfort women" system was justified in the name of "protecting respectable women and rewarding soldiers for their sacrifice."[50] Since its arrival on Korean soil, the U.S. military had fought two wars: one against communism and the other against venereal disease, which directly threatened the soldiers' readiness to fight in the war. Unfortunately, the U.S. military could not control the soldiers' sexual behaviors. Wherever the soldiers were stationed, they could take sexual advantage of poverty-stricken Korean women, mostly war widows and orphans who had multiple dependents. The soldiers' attitudes toward the Korean women resembled those of white European colonialists toward the colonized women of color, who were seen as sexually exploitable.

As the Korean War ended in a truce in 1953, the U.S. military has remained stationed in ROK for an indefinite period. The majority of strategic areas in ROK, close to the border with North Korea, developed into Rest and Relaxation (R&R) boomtowns beginning in the mid-1950s.[51]

48. Enloe, *Maneuvers*, 51–52.
49. Moon, "Regulating Desire," 40.
50. Moon, "Regulating Desire," 45.
51. Moon, *Sex among Allies*, 28.

Entertaining camptowns sprang up all around U.S. bases, becoming the borderlands between the U.S. and South Korea and the quasi-colonies of the U.S.

In the early 1970s, in response to the Nixon Doctrine that announced the reduction of the number of G.I.'s in Korea, the ROK government launched the Camptown Clean-up Campaign, which was intended to improve channels of communication and cooperation in racial and sexual politics of camptown.[52] This Campaign is the prime example of how the state systematically controlled necropolitical labor. Through the Campaign, ROK modernized camptowns with new lights, roads, buildings, and tried to alleviate the racial tension among American soldiers. At that time, Korean prostitutes were divided into "white-only" and "black-only" because white soldiers, the majority of the United States Forces in Korea (USFK), did not want to buy sex from the women who catered to soldiers of color. In the meantime, associating with blacks further stigmatized the prostitutes, not only to white soldiers but also to local Koreans. For most prostitutes, racial discrimination against black men was a means to exercise their limited agency to choose customers and retain their compromised sense of self-dignity.[53] The Clean-up Campaign subcommittee educated Korean prostitutes not to discriminate soldiers of color and made bars and clubs to play blues and jazz more frequently. However, the prostitutes' anti-black racism only mirrored the practice inside the USFK and larger Korean society. Racial division in camptown prostitution industries still exists today.

The Korean government relied on prostitutes' sexualized labor for its economic development, national security, and relationship with the USFK, in particular. For this reason, the Clean-up Campaign subcommittee regularly gathered the camptown prostitutes to indoctrinate them to the belief that they contributed to the modernization and security of their country through prostitution.[54] In order to survive in camptowns, the prostitutes internalized the patriotic dimension of their work like soldiers but had no illusions about prostitution being viewed as dirty work condemned by society. One paradoxical aspect of military prostitution as necropolitical labor is that sovereignty knows its reliance on the condemned population for its livelihood.

---

52. Moon, *Sex among Allies*, 128.

53. Moon, *Sex among Allies*, 129.

54. Moon, *Sex among Allies*, 135.

The ROK government designed U.S. camptowns to be segregated from the rest of Korean society, disciplining and regulating the prostitutes' bodies through mandatory venereal disease check-ups and sex education. Camptowns were also neo-colonies of the United States until recently, so most South Koreans and Americans do not know what has happened inside the said neo-colonies. At the turn of the 21st century, as ROK emerged as a sub-imperialist state, camptown prostitution industries smuggled women from the Philippines, Central Asia, and Russia while exporting Korean women to prostitution in the U.S., Australia, and Japan. Since the early 1990s, camptown prostitutes have moved to domestic prostitution industries or to foreign countries to make more money.[55] Necropolitical labor of military prostitution does not know national borders.

Ironically, military prostitutes see the necropolitical nature of soldiering that many soldiers do not comprehend. Camptown prostitutes know that American soldiers came to Korea to make money rather than to protect the country, and that these soldiers were recruited among the poor in the United States. These women have no illusions about America but criticize U.S. mismanagement of its economy, high unemployment rates, low educational standards in public schools, racial discrimination, and imperialistic actions toward developing countries.[56] Thus, Korean prostitutes know that they share similar class backgrounds with their G.I. customers, although G.I.'s act as if they were the protectors, liberators, and conquerors of Koreans. Here, political theorist Katherine Moon offers a crucial analysis. Since the relationship between Korean prostitutes and G.I.'s is closely tied with the U.S.-Korean relationship, it is almost impossible to imagine the genuine and autonomous relationship between them.[57] In the women's eyes, the fate of their lives depend on the economic and political strength or weakness of their own nation-state that has never been treated as a sovereign nation by the U.S. or other big powers.[58] On the contrary, G.I.'s consider themselves as the representatives of

55. Durebang, *Durebang Report*.
56. Moon, *Sex among Allies*, 30.
57. Moon, *Sex among Allies*, 158.
58. Moon, *Sex among Allies*, 158. In 2013–2014, during my field research at the Sunlit Center for elderly women in the Anjung-ri camptown, adjacent to Camp K-6, I learned that the center women, who had been involved in military prostitution for a long time, filed a law suit against the Korean government based on the state's violation of human rights. It might not be a coincident that as ROK became a sub-imperialist state,

the world's most powerful country. The power gap between ROK and the U.S. has rarely made the prostitutes and G.I.'s empathetically understand one another as necropolitical laborers. Additionally, camptown prostitution confirms that necropolitical labor is not a result of an individual choice but is always bound with the international political and economic power structures.

Historically speaking, poor women across the globe have been forced to respond to the public needs of sex by their governments, and (neo)colonial powers. War and militarism only intensify this demand through forced prostitution, organized rape, and military sexual enslavement. Without critically analyzing the proletarianization of sexuality, we cannot understand the socio-political-economic complexities of war and militarism.

Searching for an Alternative Christian Discourse on Peace

So far I have analyzed the complex inter/transectionality of race, gendered sexuality, class, and spatial inequalities in militarized necropolitical labor. If we are conscientized with how a sovereign state operates its war business in a neoliberal world at the cost of necropolitical labors such as soldiers and military prostitutes, we, Christians, would not support any war. As I argued earlier, however, nonviolent resistance to war would not be enough, if we also considered our globally shared responsibilities to protect the vulnerable from war and violence. Closing this chapter, I tentatively suggest "God's preferential option for the poor" as a metaphor for Christian peacemaking. The phrase is a metaphor because classical liberation theology's understanding of the poor is often monolithic, ignoring gender, race, sexuality, citizenship, and religion of the poor. The poor for Christian peacemaking in this chapter refer to the vulnerable population to necropolitical labor whose race, gender, sexuality, and experiences of spatial inequalities can be commodified and extracted for the sake of fostering the lives of others on demand of the state and empire. Hence, the poor should be always historically concretized to avoid the rhetorical abstraction in theological discourse. In light of God's preferential option for the poor, I make five suggestions in the making of a Christian ethic of peace.

---

the prostitutes finally broke their silence and demanded justice from the government.

First, God's preferential option for the poor accentuates that God is on the side of justice for the poor because the poor have epistemic privilege to understand God's love and justice owing to their experiences of necropolitical labor. Since their lives are constantly exposed to the state-sanctioned violence and military recruitment to an entry level, we should listen to the poor—their visions for peace and a just world order. Merely listening is not enough. We must develop spiritual skills of deeply listening to the poor because necropolitical laborers often lose words to describe their experiences due to the damages done to their bodies and spirits.

Second, through the stories of the poor's experiences of war, militarism, military labor, and military prostitution, we should rewrite war stories. By re-examining historical wars through the lens of necropolitical labor, we can unpack the horrible realities of war intertwined with sovereignty's right to kill, and more specifically, heteropatriarchal capitalist nation-building at the cost of those who are condemned to death. We need the alternative epistemology of war in order to re-memorialize history's victims more intentionally, including low ranked soldiers in active combats, and military prostitutes.

Third, we continue to intentionally make the invisible faces of the poor more visible in any Christian discourse on war and peace. In 1999, less than 6 percent of adults under 65 years of age in America have an experience of the military service. As a result, the majority of Americans cannot imagine what it is like to fight a war far away from home, or how female sex is used to appease a soldier's vulnerability, fear, and anxiety.[59] If we do not have proper knowledge of war and militarism, we should at least refrain ourselves from mystifying the lives of soldiers and from blindly praising soldiers' sacrifices. In addition, society should render soldiers more opportunities to decide which war they want to fight, because they have experiential knowledge of war, and we, as a society, should not expect anyone to risk their life for the sake of ours.

Fourth, it is time for us to critically reexamine our assumptions about the military—whether and why we need the institutionalized military for peace and security. How can the Christian church educate its people to re-examine the necessities of the military, and search for the possibilities of disarming the world? Similarly, we should examine why military prostitution has been normalized, and search for the concrete

---

59. Bailey, *America's Army*, 261–62.

ways in which we can prevent female sex from being exploited by the state.

Fifth, an ethic of everydayness is a Christian alternative to militarized peace and security. For example, how can we change the militarized languages, such as "the soldiers of the Christ" used in the Christian church where the images of soldiers are used for the faithful, while those of the whore for the condemned and the unfaithful? How can we critically examine our everyday use of the militarized language? Peacemaking requires radical changes in every part of human life. From where we stand, we should critically analyze our gendered, racialized, and classed relationships with one another, our participation in the state's war project built upon neoliberal profit-making, and the militarization of our communities. Our concrete knowledge firmly rooted in our communities can help us see our locations in transnationalized militarism, and lead us to see ourselves among the poor, as in the current neoliberal world of heterosexual patriarchal militarism, anyone can be recruited to necropolitical labors.

On an ultimate level, Christianity is and should be antithetical to necropolitics or the state's right to kill. If the state claims its sovereign power by exercising the right to kill, the Kin-dom of God manifests its power by exercising the right to foster the life of every living being. Christianity is a life-affirming system. If we see war through the lens of necropolitics, peace is no longer about how to resist and prevent war but about how to liberate ourselves from the fear of necropolitics by affirming the sacredness of every life.

Bibliography

Alexander, M. Jacqui. *Pedagogies of Crossing: Meditations on Feminism, Sexual Politics, Memory, and the Sacred*. Perverse Modernities. Durham: Duke University Press, 2005.

Bailey, Beth L. *America's Army: Making the All-Volunteer Force*. Cambridge, MA: Belknap, 2009.

Booth, Bradford, and David R. Segal. "Bringing the Soldiers Back In: Implications of Inclusion of Military Personnel for Labor Market Research on Race, Class, and Gender." *Race, Gender & Class* 12.1 (2005) 34–57.

Brock, Rita Nakashima, and Gabriella Lettini. *Soul Repair: Recovering from Moral Injury after War*. Boston: Beacon, 2012.

Butler, Smedley D. *War Is a Racket*. New York: Round Table, 1935.

Curtin, Sara. "A Necropolitical Analysis of American Military Recruitment." *Denison Journal of Religion* 18 (2019) article 2. https://digitalcommons.denison.edu/religion/vol18/iss1/2.

Durebang (My Sister's Place). "Durebang Report: Concerning Migrant Women Involved with U.S. Bases from 2002–2009." Uijeongbu, Gyeonggi-Do, South Korea: Durebang, 2009.

Enloe, Cynthia H. *Maneuvers: The International Politics of Militarizing Women's Lives.* Berkeley: University of California Press, 2000.

Grossman, David. *On Killing: The Psychological Cost of Learning to Kill in War and Society.* Boston: Little, Brown, 2009.

Jeffreys, Sheila. *The Industrial Vagina: The Political Economy of the Global Sex Trade.* RIPE Series in Global Political Economy. New York: Routledge, 2009.

Jo, Eun Seo. "Fighting for Peanuts: Reimagining South Korean Soldiers' Participation in the Wŏllam Boom." *Journal of American–East Asian Relations* 21.1 (2014) 58–87.

Kao, Grace, ed. *Asian American Christian Ethics: Voices, Methods, Issues.* Waco, TX: Baylor University Press, 2015.

Lee, Jin-kyung. *Service Economies: Militarism, Sex Work, and Migrant Labor in South Korea.* Minneapolis: University of Minnesota Press, 2010.

Mananzan, Mary John, ed. *Women Resisting Violence: Spirituality for Life.* 1996. Reprint, Eugene, OR: Wipf & Stock, 2004.

Marshall, Katherine, and Susan Hayward, eds. *Women, Religion, and Peacebuilding: Illuminating the Unseen.* Washington, DC: United States Institute of Peace, 2015.

Mbembe, Achille. *Necropolitics.* Translated by Steven Corcoran. Durham: Duke University Press, 2019.

Moon, Katharine H. S. *Sex among Allies: Military Prostitution in U.S.-Korea Relations.* New York: Columbia University Press, 1997.

Moon, Seung Sook. "Regulating Desire, Managing the Empire: U.S. Military Prostitution in South Korea, 1945–1970." In *Over There: Living with the U.S. Military Empire from World War Two to the Present*, edited by Maria Höhn and Seungsook Moon, 39–77. Durham: Duke University Press, 2010.

Pae, Keun-Joo Christine. "Peace and War." In *Asian American Christian Ethics: Voices, Methods, and Issues*, edited by Grace Y. Kao and Ilsup Ahn, 85–107. Waco, TX: Baylor University Press, 2015.

Scanlan, Stephen J. "'Mined' for Its Citizens? Poverty, Opportunity Structure, and Appalachian Soldier Deaths in the Iraq War." *Journal of Appalachian Studies* 20 (2014) 43–67.

Taylor. William A. *Military Service and American Democracy.* Lawrence: University Press of Kansas, 2016.

Thistlethwaite, Susan Brooks. *Women's Bodies as Battlefield: Christian Theology and the Global War on Women.* New York: Palgrave Macmillan, 2015.

———. "Militarism in North American Perspective." In *Women Resisting Violence: Spritiuality for Life*, edited by Mary John Mananzan and Mercy Amaba Oduyoye, 119–25. 1996. Reprint, Eugene, OR: Wipf & Stock, 2004.

Truman, Harry S. "Executive Order 9981: Desegregation of the Armed Forces." July 26, 1948. https://www.ourdocuments.gov/doc.php?flash=false&doc=84).

Welch, Sharon D. *Real Peace, Real Security: The Challenges of Global Citizenship.* Facets. Minneapolis: Fortress, 2008.

9

Class and Privilege—Salient Racism
The Case or Curse of Being Black!

Sifiso Mpofu

Introduction

THROUGHOUT HUMAN HISTORY, IN many cultures and societies, black and white have stood as strong opposites. The white color has been perceived to be associated with positive things such as intelligence, brightness, and purity. On the other hand, its black counterpart is widely associated with negativity: for example, "black magic," an undesirable element of witchcraft or medicine; "black spot," a term that describes a popular place where accidents usually occur; and "black market," a term that suggests an illegal and unauthorized way of doing business. In modern history, black has been associated with failure and or death; and "Black Friday" is an example. Historically, Black Friday was a stock market catastrophe that took place on September 24, 1869. On that day, the price of gold plummeted and the markets crashed. Against this background, "black" has become a social label. In line with the negativity carried by the phrase "being black," I will demonstrate how the issues of salient racism and the social structures have historically subjugated black people to perpetual "second class citizens" and poverty. The roots of the political, social, and economic discrimination of black people lies in the history of slavery—a humanly degrading period that gave birth to historical perceptions and misconceptions about black people and how blackness is traditionally translated into being cursed and associated with poverty. I will further demonstrate how this misconception is merely a social construct and not a reality or a fact of creation.

Today, any discussion of class and privilege (fundamental cases of societal and racial inequality) is ideologically polarized. However, those who claim to be true and just in their mandate—and as a fact of their religious concern—will always dare to consider tackling the institutional and cultural factors that have persistently been couriers of class and racial inequality in the postmodern era. While structural and cultural forces are inextricably linked to salient racism, public policy is also antagonistic to changing the racial status quo and perceptions of black people by reforming the institutions that tend to reinforce the gap between those who are privileged in terms of class and those who are undermined and marginalized because of their skin color. It is sad that—despite the claims of our postmodern world—the reality of class polarization has remained with us!

In my discourse on the effects of class and privilege in the context of being black and poor, I am inspired by David Livingstone's consciousness of a fully empowered human being; be it white or black! Even though Livingstone has been viewed negatively—perceived to be a pioneer of Western colonialism—he believed that the source of endemic poverty amongst black people was not the depravity of being black, but the white man had deprived their land and thus their pride. Therefore, "Christianity could not be preached without developing the autonomy of all individuals—or without political, social, and economic freedom and civil rights for all."[1] But this does not mean that Christianity was without its own problems. The Gospel narratives assume a superior narrative above everything: "I am the way, the truth, and the life" (John 14:6). Hence in 1890 King Lobengula of the Matebele people retorted: "I believe that God has made the (African) just as he wished them to be; it is wrong for anyone to seek to alter them."[2]

Respect and dignity for black people can only be restored not by way of giving mere grants to them but through deliberate change of people's mindset towards Africa—from a neo-colonial mentality which

1. Nkomazana, "Livingstone's Ideas of Christianity, Commerce and Civilization," 47.
2. Clinton, *These Vessels*, 54.

views black negatively. This change must be visible through economic policy formulations, equal opportunities, and political treatment at international institutions that must result in non-discriminatory and class perceptions. The solution towards building non-discriminatory communities is possible through an honest and open dialogue culminating in the combination of inclusive and non-discriminatory religious values with legitimate public and institutional policies built on the premise of both constitutionalism and legislation. This must deliberately include discussions "on why poverty and unequal opportunity."[3] In the search for classless and non-racial societies, this must be the agenda for the politician (podium) and the pastor (pulpit) alike!

Class System and Racism: Eternal Partners in the Making

In simple terms, class defines a system of ordering society whereby people are divided into sets based on perceived social or economic status. While social class refers to divisions in society based on economic and social status, classism is not just ideology but a system of inequality. In a class system, people in a "particular" social class typically enjoy a common level of wealth, income, educational achievement, and type of job. Sociologically, a social class shapes an individual's material resources as well as perceptions of rank vis-a-vis others in society. Keltner posit that, "an individual's social class is a context rooted in both the material substance of social life (wealth, education, work) and the individual's construal of his or her class rank, and is a core aspect of how he or she thinks of the self and relates to the social world."[4]

In my argument on class and privilege, I do not seek to pretend that class issues rank higher than any other social ill. The class system influences our daily lives, hence it cannot be wished away by mere pretense when people exchange mere greetings in the public arena. The location of my discourse is inspired by the observation that the system of class has often been ignored when people talk about racism, sexism, and homophobia when the reality is that such social ills tend to be directed towards people of lower or under-privileged classes. The employment trends in many private and public institutions indicate that issues of gender, race, and class dynamics are observable in terms of the hiring

---

3. Wilson, *More than Just Race*, 3.
4. Kraus et al., "Social Class, Solipsism, and Contextualism," 546.

practices and decisions on promotions.⁵ The issues related to class follow very much the streams characteristic of racism. Just like classism, which functions around social setting and privileges, the whole subject of race being a social construct evolves around different physical traits of peoples (curly hair, lighter skin, etc.). Race is dependent on skin color, geography, language, and some vague social constructed impressions as its basis. In this logic it becomes clear that race is an idea, not a fact. And, racism is undeniably a social construct and a political concept.⁶

An emphasis on the social construction of race does not seek to deny the biological traits of race since through the fate of Mother Nature, all human beings are born into a system they did not create, initially unaware of their family's status, and they are gradually socialized into the upside or the downside of class, race, gender, and other hierarchies. But as they become aware of the social meaning of their identities, they can then choose whether to accept or resist systems of domination. What is an undeniable fact is that the social construction of race has a huge bearing on human conduct and behavior! Just as race has a biological route and a sociological route, it can be misleading and counterproductive to treat the two issues of class structures and racism as unrelated ideologies. But what is clear is that the intersection of class and race is complex hence it is argued that:

> The same systems that brought slavery to the New World also planted the early seeds of the unequal classes we see today. Wealthy landowners and slave-owners deliberately set up different rules for poor whites than for African slaves and Indigenous peoples in order to prevent joint rebellions. That same choice of whether to take the "racial bribe" of white advantages or to band together with people of color for the common good still faces [many white people today].⁷

---

5. "Class Action's Vision."

6. For example, Robin O. Andreasen argues, "What is race if it is not a biologically objective category? Some constructivists argue that 'race' is a social fiction; it is entirely a product of the ways that people think about human differences. Others argue that race plays a prominent role in human social practices; hence, the social reality of race cannot be denied." This understanding of race is based on the social construction theory which is "interested in the sociology of race and race relations." Andreasen, *Race: Biological Reality or Social Construct?*, 655, 662.

7. "What about Race?"

When racism becomes the single focus in issues of social disintegration we may run the risk of overlooking the millions of working-class and poor white people who face the challenge of the class system in their daily lives. On the other hand, when our focus for a healthy society is only in class issues then we create obstacles in the paths of people of color in their struggles for self-affirmation in a society that sees them as an inferior race.

Sociologically, class is a system of ordering society whereby people are divided into sets based on perceived social or economic status. It is a social division based on social or economic status and privileges. Today, the experience of the being black and being poor cannot be divorced from the challenges of class hierarchy and racism. By way of the class system, black people were socially located in a variant class, which defined their social and economic conditions. As we delve into the complex nature of class and racism, we need to understand what is meant by the phrase "being black and being poor." Being "black" is a term used often in socially-based systems of racial classification or of ethnicity to describe persons who are perceived to be dark skinned.[8] Being "poor" is a social term used to refer to a state of having insufficient wealth to meet the necessities or comforts of life or to live in a manner considered acceptable in a society.

Semantically, poverty is a multifaceted concept that includes economic, social, and political elements, but also defines one's social class. While poverty is characterized by the scarcity or lack of resources necessary for basic survival or necessary to meet a certain minimum level of living standards expected in the context of one's existential needs, class defines poverty in relation to wealth. The experience of many black people is no longer talk of the cases of being black but the curse of being black! Why? Being black is, in most cases, associated with negativity of a poor class hence the curse of being black! A curse, in this context, is a magic spell which has been placed upon black people with the intention of demeaning them. Anthropologists argue that curses are the most dreaded form of magic, often called "black magic," and are believed to be universally used to dehumanize persons.[9] In my context, the principal purpose for a curse is for hatred! Sociologically and religiously, curses laid on families have been known to have plagued them for generations.

---

8. Míguez Bonino, *Doing Theology in a Revolutionary Situation*, 27.
9. Raboteau, *Slave Religion*, 17.

Marginalization of Black People as a Social Process: The Results of Slavery and Colonialism

In our everyday stories, it has become the norm to associate black people with poverty and high crime rate. This association is driven by a discourse of class that has socially disenfranchised black people and tends to associate them with failure and poverty. The reasons for such social constructions are historical. Black people have been the most economically deprived communities because of the legacy of colonialism. According to Hopkins, people in poverty typically experience persistent hunger, inadequate education and health care, and are usually alienated from mainstream social events or developments because of their prevailing condition.[10] Sociologists define poverty as a social condition of unequal and inequitable distribution of income and wealth, and the exploitative effects born out of global capitalism. In general, the causes of poverty vary from one country to the other and are ascribed to history, governance, and the dynamics of the society within it.[11] What is also true is that black people's poverty is socially conditioned through the historical processes of colonialism and civilization, which were influenced by race and class. Social formation is heavily influenced by politics, power, and economics hence these three (politics, power, and economics) have a fundamental contribution to a people's development and self-understanding. Issues of politics, power, and economics are critical to the creation of social perceptions, which in turn lead to common assumptions that categorizes people in terms of their social status, positions, and economic abilities. All these realities are critical to the current social perceptions around black people.

The experience of Professor William Julius Wilson demonstrates the living reality of the racial stigma associated with "being black":

> I am an internationally recognized Harvard professor, yet a number of unforgettable experiences remind me that, as a black male in America looking considerably younger than my age, I am also feared (not trusted and respected) . . . Several times over the years, I have stepped into the elevator of my condominium dressed in casual clothes and could immediately tell from the body language of the other residents in the elevator that I made them feel uncomfortable. Were they thinking "what is this black

---

10. Hopkins, *Introducing Black Theology of Liberation*, 18.
11. Long, *Significations*, 19.

man doing in this expensive condominium? Are we in any danger?" I once sarcastically said to a nervous elderly couple who hesitated to exit the elevator because we were all getting off on the same floor, "Not to worry, I am a Harvard professor and I have lived in this building for nine years."[12]

This experience tells of the curse of being black—an association with potential criminality! It is such stereotypes that have perpetuated salient racism into the postmodern era. The solution to these stereotyped issues lies in an honest and open dialogue on the problem of racism. Wilson points out that issues of culture and perceptions must be taken "seriously as one of the explanatory variables in the study of race and urban poverty."[13]

The experience of Wilson demonstrates how the social nature of racism views black people as potentially dangerous by "nature." In their research findings, social scientists have concluded that two types of social structures contribute to issues that perpetuate the racial and economic divide between black and white people. They are: "social acts and social processes."[14] The glaring reality about "social acts and social process" is that a polarized, frightened, and threatened society—a society built on the fallacy of the respect of human dignity, yet its actions and processes are premised on salient racism. For me, this is perhaps the most striking, and certainly the most controversial, finding of Wilson's study. Black people are disadvantaged and discriminated on the mere fact of "being black," while "white people" are simply respected on the basis of their skin! Is this much ado about nothing? The fate of being black is sealed by the social acts and social processes that are driven by the general culture of the so-called modern world—a world premised on the ideals of white culture or white class and privilege.

Liberation theologian Jose Míguez Bonino states that black and white have often been used to describe opposites: particularly truth and ignorance, good and evil, the "Dark Ages" versus "Age of Reason"—again, this a social construction.[15] Our human actions and processes are entirely driven by a learned culture and shared perceptions between the

---

12. Wilson, *More than Just Race*, 1.
13. Wilson, *More than Just Race*, 3.
14. Wilson, *More than Just Race*, 5.
15. Míguez Bonino, *Doing Theology in a Revolutionary Situation*, 26.

axioms that divide black and white people in our deeply racialized societies and communities.

Social acts are people's social conduct, their behavior, and their belief systems that are critical to their ethics and value systems. This can be exemplified by the glaring relational issues such as education, employment, and associations. On the other hand, social processes relate to "machinery of society that exists to promote ongoing relations among members of the larger group," in other words: institutional practices and culture, laws, and policies.[16] A closer analysis of these issues will reflect that most ideologies are formed around such processes. Out of these ideologies people get labeled for life through such regulative processes, hence the curses around these social structures—acts and processes that perpetuate attitudes and perceptions that lead to many social constructions dividing and dehumanizing people. What is observable from such realities is that racism against blacks is socially processed through class and privilege. This reality confirms that race is purely about people's social and cultural differences—sociologically, issues of race and class relate very well to social and economic differences between different populations of people. The discrete fallacy that claims that being "white" or "black" defines our God-given social status ignores the unique reality of human diversity! This view affirms the now commonly held view that race is indeed a social construct without biological meaning.

Social acts and social processes speak of social phenomena, social structure, and culture. What is evident is that social structure and culture are key movers of class oppression, racism, and drivers of poverty in the context and experiences of black people. But what exactly is social structure?

> Social structure refers to the way social positions, social roles, and networks of social relationships are arranged . . . A social structure could be a labor market that offers financial incentives and threatens financial punishments to compel individuals to work; or it could be a "role," associated with a particular social position in an organization such as a church, family or university (e.g., pastor, head of family, professor), that carries certain power, privilege and influence external to the individuals who occupy the role.[17]

---

16. Wilson, *More than Just Race*, 5.
17. Wilson, *More than Just Race*, 4.

Social structure is embedded in a culture; hence the need to define culture itself. Culture "refers to sharings of outlooks and modes of behavior among individuals who face similar place-based circumstances . . . or have the same social networks."[18]

Some challenges that have helped to advance the stereotype of racism, classism, and poverty relate to the insensitivity of the political and economic discourses that are structurally flawed because a particular race tends to occupy critical positions of power, privilege, prestige, influence, and authority. In other words, "economic changes and political decisions may have a greater adverse impact on some groups than others" because some racial groups are at the mercy of the more influential group.[19] Oppressed groups are more vulnerable to the socio-economic hazards of the day. In the context of a globalized economy, when there is a wave of decline those who are on the lower economic level in terms of income and status are worst affected. In most cases these are the people from the so-called "third world" countries (black/Africans, Asians, and Latinos) who still suffer the legacy of colonialism and slave history, which was the tool that created two classes of people; i.e. black and white, inferior and superior, privileged and subjugated! These classes are thus a clear result of social and economic factors which continue to haunt modernity and civilizations to date.

Issues of class and privilege have also been evident for many centuries in religious communities, hence the birth of Black Theology in the USA in the 1960s. In the Christian church, issues of "being black" were felt throughout the history of the slave trade. The roots of the dehumanization of black people and their social labeling resulting in their oppression and exploitation are located in the theology of slavery. It was slave theology that took away the humanity of black people, denied black people their personhood, and reduced black people to nothing more than a gadget to be sold in the market place. The barbaric trade in slaves lasted for centuries: between 1517 and 1840 and it is estimated that circa twenty million blacks were brutally captured from Africa and inhumanly sold and transported to the Americas as cheap labor.[20] The experience of these black people and their descendants serves as the backdrop for understanding contemporary black liberation theology—a theology

---

18. Wilson, *More than Just Race*, 4.
19. Wilson, *More than Just Race*, 6.
20. Cone, *God of the Oppressed*, 37.

of protest against the white people's religion that never affirmed black people as equally children of God without prejudice.

The predominantly white church strongly believed that the black community was not worthy to acquire a human status, basing this claim on the background that black people were a cursed generation and therefore did not deserve to be treated the same as their white counterparts.[21] At slave centers, the white Christians' interpretation of Christianity effectively robbed the slaves of any hope they might have had about their freedom. They literally used the Christian religion to pacify the slaves, making religion "opium of the people" as forwarded by Karl Marx. Christian scriptures that point to the New Jerusalem (in Christianity) where people will be walking in the streets of gold, without suffering, sickness, and oppression were employed to give a false sense of hope to the slaves. The white privileged class abused the holy Christian Scriptures for selfish ends. Some biblical verses were exploited to justify such assertions, particularly the gnostic Johannine literature, which constantly uses the comparative metaphors of black versus light: i.e. "I am the light of the world, he who follows me will not walk in darkness, but will have the light of life" (John 8:12). Anything black has thus been depicted as cursed. However, a closer look into the color black has presented a different picture. In the African context, black is a sacred color and is believed to possess some form of power and divinity that connects the living with the spirit world, hence spirit mediums wear black and white robes to symbolize their interconnectedness with the world of ancestors.

The experience of being black is visible in the manner through which black people were exploited during the slave history. Cone argues that black people were crammed into ships like sardines in a can and brought across the Atlantic Ocean for business by white people. In the process, many died at sea from dysentery, smallpox, and other diseases. Some starved themselves to death. However, to prevent this form of suicide, hot coals were applied to the lips to force the slaves to open their mouths to eat.[22] The black person was thus relegated to a poor slave, whose destiny was divinely placed in the hands of his master, the privileged "white person." This legacy is still visible in the corridors of power, across varied institutions of governance and in the general market place. The political and economic leadership of world institutions is still

---

21. Cone, *Black Theology and Black Power*, 39.
22. Cone, *For My People*, 29.

dominated by the privileged class(es) as are sporting activities, which are driven by powerful and wealthy nations. What is clear is that there is always a perception that black people are not good enough; they are a failure; they are unreasonable; and there are given to be criminal more than any other race. If this be true—one wonders whether the world has done enough to move beyond the mentality of class division and racism towards providing social reconciliation, restoration, and the healing of the memories to the millions of black people who are still haunted by the effects of class oppression, racism, slavery and colonialism.

Class System and Christian Colonialism against Ubuntu in Africa

The lack of economic progress of many black people that happens to define their poverty is a result of a class structure—a system of socio-economic stratification, most notably the social institutions, the structure of social network ties between individuals or organizations that are defined by people's enduring patterns and social relationships. The concept of a social class often assumes three general categories which are: (i) an upper class that is sociologically a powerful and wealthy class that owns and controls the means of production; (ii) a middle class that is constituted by professional workers, small business owners as well as low-level managers; and (iii) a lower class that relies on low-paying wage jobs for their livelihoods. No matter how hard we may celebrate the ideology of civilization, cases of racism and class structures have remained part of our human attitude and socialization processes. Our social setting and experiences are modeled around the levels of success and inequality in our society.

The issue of experience and social culture must be taken seriously as one of the critical variables in the study of race and poverty, since these are the pedestals that shape people's behavior and conduct. A framework that the integrates structural forces of our societies must be established whenever one engages in the study of racism and class systems since the social acts and social processes are critical in shaping human trends, behavior, and development. Social acts and processes have a pivotal influence on either promoting or debunking racial undertones, such as segregation and discrimination because issues of racism are a social construction. In this viewpoint, it becomes fundamental to promote social redemption through a holistic and inclusive social paradigm shift.

A study carried out the United States of America shows that "racism and discrimination are facts of life for many black Americans" yet the U.S. prides itself on being non-racist country.[23] This study was carried out in 2016 when the coming in of America's first black president should have de-bunked the issues of racism and those structures that continue to create unfair economic access, be there prejudice or not.[24] Many black college students in the U.S. continue to suffer stress related to racial discrimination more than other racial or ethnic groups. The sad reality is that black people in any society that is predominantly white continue to experience subtle and overt discrimination from kindergarten all the way to college level and yet, in general, the minority white people in predominantly black countries in Africa are highly respected.

The damning case of being black and being poor is quite disturbing when one looks at the extreme poverty levels in Africa while the continent is blessed with a haven of natural resources. Africa, besides its riches in the form of natural resources and rich agricultural soils, has, for many, remained a "dark continent" as was popularly referenced by the colonial settlers and white missionaries. Following this logic many white privileged persons would then start labeling African players as failed leaders. Are we to see these extreme levels of poverty as a sign of a curse? This question has for years begged to be answered and a closer look into this reflects a colonial manipulative management style, which has continued playing Africans against each other through various internal strives and conflicts. Such conflicts are driven by a clique of privileged racist classes that are driven by a neo-colonial mentality and are bent on looting the resources of Africa so that they can justify the legacy of colonialism—that Africans cannot govern themselves. It is from this context that Joseph Booth has argued in his *Africa for the African* for self-propagating and self-supporting initiatives that do not depend on handouts from a privileged class.[25]

The aspect of being black and being poor, therefore, has a sociopolitical and economic context that must be addressed in an honest and sincere thrust. There is no need to continuously label black people as failures without addressing the sorrowful vestiges of slavery and colonialism. All that we see as failure of black people in Africa today is a result

---

23. Cokley, "What It Means to Be Black."
24. Parker, Horowitz, and Mahl, "On Views of Race and Inequality," 30–32.
25. Booth, *Africa for the African*, 25–27.

of unequal distribution of resources linked to the past and our failures to address issues of class and privilege. It is no secret that colonialism left some visible and permanent marks of class and privileges. The reality we need to face is that a person's socio-economic class has wide ranging effects, even given a desire to collectively work for a better world. It can impact the schools they are able to attend, their health, the jobs open to them, whom they may marry, their treatment at all levels of society, and the systems of governance included. There are the elite few and the majority poor. There is a clique of the privileged few and a crowd of the vulnerable and disposed lot.

Sociologically, Africans are an undisputedly united, peace-loving, and are a people governed through the concept of "*ubuntu*" philosophy where one's life and success is believed to be a product of the entire community. "*Ubuntu*" (to be humane) is often translated as "I am because we are," but in a more practical translation is "the belief in a universal bond of sharing that connects all humanity."[26]

African people have been uprooted from their philosophy of "*ubuntu*" that knows no classes and are now distinguished by their material and political value. This western ideology of class has given birth to high levels of poverty resulting in high levels of corruption and crime as the poor seek to lay their hands on what they can get by all means possible for the sustenance of their livelihoods, while the privileged continue to grab everything for their personal aggrandizement. The class and privileged concepts have caused a high degree of human suffering to the majority of Africans who are marginalized by the privileged few. The case of Zimbabwe gives a fair example of the evils of class oppression where a few elite and privileged have enjoyed unlimited access to the country's rich mineral resources while the majority remains poor and disenfranchised. It is from this premise that a primer for a theology that debunks issues of class, privilege, and racism becomes necessary and efficacious.

However, any reference to the unity and tolerance of Africans to each other cannot ignore the new realities that have come with modernity where we now face issues of human rights and gender hierarchies that have become a threat to African solidarity. For Africans to be rich means to be someone who has respect for other people despite their race, gender, or background, and yet this solid ideology of life has been, for centuries, relegated out of the equation of life by the ideology of capitalism (western class ideology) that forcefully downplayed the humanist

26. Ramose, "The Philosophy of Ubuntu 49.

lifestyle of the black community and perceived it to be a curse of socialism. What is of major interest here is the fact that this African philosophy of *"ubuntu"* (to be humane) has a strong biblical parallel as demonstrated by the early Christian communities, "All who believed were together and had all things in common; they would sell their possessions and goods and distribute the proceeds to all, as any had need" (Acts 2:44–45). This calls for a theology of ubuntu in the church's march towards debunking the evils of racial and class injustices.

Debunking Racial and Class Injustices: The Role of the Church in Zimbabwe

As a black man born in a peasant rural family in Zimbabwe, I am lucky enough to have a university education that many black people of my rural village were not privileged to receive. For many black people in my rural area, having attained high school education was a great achievement. At this point one would gladly declare: "I have finished my education." To have a high school certificate was something to be proud of—it changed one's social status! And yet that paper did not have a professional skill or learning. The issue here is not whether people wanted university education or not, but the fact is that the social processes and context did not provide the environment towards such levels of education. One may ask: whose fault was this? The answer to this question is located in the social structures of the day. The legacy of colonialism and racial segregation has to shoulder the blame. The environment of my upbringing taught us that we were meant to be servants, maids, gardeners, farm workers, or factory workers in blue collar jobs. Beyond this there was a color bar—it was the white man's job! The missionary pastors did very little to assist black people to go beyond high school unless, of course, there were privileged children of African evangelists and pastors.

This is the story of black people who have grown up under the power of subjugation and colonialism—a people whose self-esteem is very low and at most is modeled around the missionary jacket. A people whose greatest achievement is to throw away their culture, their identity and follow suite in the footsteps of the white person religiously as if to be Christian means to be "white" and being "black" means to be evil. But really, I am talking primarily about African Christians—who present an image of being socially responsible, morally correct, and concerned about issues of social justice! And yet the sad reality behind the experiences of a black person is a legacy of being socialized into the culture of their colonial masters to the extent that it is seen as a privilege. Many black people will do everything to try and emulate the culture of the white person both in the religious context and the social context. In my humble submission, Christianity in Africa has tended to strengthen and reinforce issues of class and privilege. Missionary churches' outlook represents the dominant culture of the missionary context, which, to a large extent, is a class and race system. This glaring analysis, in my submission, is indeed blasphemous to the cause of the Gospel of Jesus Christ.

One wonders as to whether the missionary founded churches in Africa! To a large extent, these churches were and have remained an extension of the Western culture and civilization. These missionary churches' structures remain foreign/western, their hymns and liturgies remain colonial; their names represent the legacy of racial undertone (the Church of England, or the Anglican Church). Most of these missionary-founded churches remain class churches and a sanctuary of a privileged few: a domain of the middle-class black families. Besides being churches in Africa for the Africans, the missionary-founded churches have clung to a class and privilege structure and orientation; the hierarchal nature from secular institutions. Hymns are a mere translation of western hymnody and celebrate that culture.

In Zimbabwe, as is likely the world over, suburbs were built to perpetuate a race and class system, the rich and privileged citizens lived in affluent suburbs while the poor live in poor and congested "locations." The same system is true with the way the churches were built. The rich and the poor never mixed even in the churches! In this context, it is reasonable to assume that if churches have to make institutional accommodations to become racially diverse then they also have to make organizational adjustments to attract individuals of different levels across geographical boundaries of the existing social structures and institutions. Social distance should not be as important for racism and classism. In such a context, the Bible must be used to demystify such cases of salient racism: "There is neither Jew nor Gentile, neither slave nor free, nor is there male and female, for you are all one in Christ Jesus" (Gal. 3:28).

Learning from the memory of the early Christian communities, the church has passionately proclaimed social justice and that everybody should have the same chance for health care, educational opportunities, career advancement, and the right to work hard and prosper. Yet most of the time this has not been true of its membership's actions in their social lives and actions outside the worship environment. In the context of our social acts and social processes, one may ask: How can religious institutions, which teach about love, good neighborhoods and justice, address some of these inequalities in our social outlooks? Where would they draw their sources? The Christian scriptures are colored with various texts that speak of unity, equality, and inclusivity and these must serve as a lesson towards being a just church, a welcoming church, a family church and a haven for the salvation of all as proclaimed in the Acts of the Apostles: "All the believers were together and had everything in common. They sold property and possessions to give to anyone who had need.... They broke bread in their homes and ate together with glad and sincere hearts" (Acts 4:44–46).

What can the church do to fight structural racism and classism? A deliberate drive towards addressing the existence of structures that divide people will lead towards a vision for change that is more revolutionary than mere reform in addressing many of our human problems. This change must deal with the systematic flaws of our human structures that have promoted racism, poverty, and materialism towards the reconstruction of our societies. The church's role in the struggle against class and racial oppression has become more pronounced and critical post the birth of Independent or liberated States in Africa post the demise of colonialism. This is especially true of Zimbabwe because many Church institutions have been actively involved in Africa's liberation, independence, and freedom struggles. What is clear from these deductions is that there is great potential of social interaction within multiracial religions organizations to produce positive racial attitudes than in non-multiracial organizations.[27] The lessons for the church in Zimbabwe are the need for collective actions in the cause for social justice action.

Regarding the issue of class, the traditional institutions of family, religion, politics, economics, and education must be open forums for healthy and empowering dialogue that reflect common levels of social enjoyments. The challenges of classism tend to be associated with certain race privileges, hence my argument that race and class are social evils that haunt the ideal peaceful, prosperous, all-inclusive, and fulfilling world that we all aspire for.

---

27. Fuchs, "The Reaction of Black Americans to Immigration," 393–95.

Conclusion

As an institution that is set apart, the church must be at the forefront of the struggle against race and class systems that benefits the privileged minority at the expense of the less privileged majority. The legacy of the structures of privilege that have dominated the church and society alike should be demystified. The church should speak out against institutionalized social and economic divisions that cause social frictions. These unjust structures are not the way of the world; they are a creation of an evil system which is subject to change. I believe that God is concerned with such racial and class prejudices. I believe that God set the church apart to be means of grace to the people it serves on a very primary and personal level. Yes, I believe that God wants Christians not only to love God "in Spirit and Truth" (John 4:24) but also to be non-racist and non-classists as well as to be just and honest in all their conduct. The Christian church, therefore, cannot afford to be quiet when the evils of racism and class inequality destroy social harmony. I believe that the church must never bless poverty but fight against it with tools of justice, truth telling frankness—in spirit and truth. Yes, I believe that racism and classism have no place in our world. Driven by the Spirit of Christ, it is possible for the Christian church to eliminate racism and class injustices if believers were to be true to their faith.

Bibliography

Andreason, Robin O. "Race: Biological Reality or Social Construct?" *Philosophy of Science* 67 (2000) 653–66.

Booth, Joseph. *Africa for the African*. Edited by Laura Perry. Zomba, Malawi: Kachere Texts, 2007.

Class Action. "Class Action's Vision." https://classism.org.

———. "What about Race?" https://classism.org/about-class/what-about-race/.

Clinton, Iris. *"These Vessels . . .": The Story of Inyati, 1859–1959*. Bulawayo: Manning, 1959.

Cokley, Kevin O'Neal. "What It Means to Be Black in the American Educational System." The Conversation. October 2, 2016. http://theconversation.com/what-it-means-to-be-black-in-the-american-educational-system-63576/.

Cone, James H. *Black Theology and Black Power*. Maryknoll, NY: Orbis, 1997.

———. *For My People: Black Theology and the Black Church*. Johannesburg: Skotaville, 1985.

———. *God of the Oppressed*. New York: Seabury, 1975.

Fuchs, Lawrence. "The Reaction of Black Americans to Immigration." In *Immigration Reconsidered: History, Sociology and Politics*, edited by V. Yans-McLaughlin, 293–314. New York: Oxford University Press, 1990.

Hopkins, Dwight N. *Introducing Black Theology of Liberation*. Maryknoll, NY: Orbis, 1999.

Kraus, Michael W., Paul K. Piff, Rodolfo Mendoza-Denton, Michelle L. Rheinschmidt, and Dacher Keltner. "Social Class, Solipsism, and Contextualism: How the Rich Are Different from the Poor." *Psychological Review* 119 (2012) 546–72.

Long, Charles H. *Significations: Signs, Symbols, and Images in the Interpretation of Religion*. Philadelphia: Fortress, 1986.

Míguez Bonino, José. *Doing Theology in a Revolutionary Situation*. Philadelphia: Fortress, 1975.

Nkomazana, Fidelis. "Livingstone's Ideas of Christianity, Commerce and Civilization." *Pula: Botswana Journal of African Studies* 12.2 (1998) 44–57.

Parker, Kim, Juliana Horowitz, and Brian Mahl. "On Views of Race and Inequality, Blacks and Whites Are Worlds Apart." *Pew Research Center: Social and Demographic Trends*. June 27, 2016. https://www.pewsocialtrends.org/2016/06/27/on-views-of-race-and-inequality-blacks-and-whites-are-worlds-apart/

Raboteau, Albert J. *Slave Religion: The "Invisible Institution" in the Antebellum South*. New York: Oxford University Press, 1978.

Ramose, M. B. "The Philosophy of Ubuntu and Ubuntu as a Philosophy." In *Philosophy from Africa: A Text with Readings*, edited by P. H. Coetzee and A. P. J. Roux, 230–37. Johannesburg: International Thomson, 1998.

Wilson, William J. *More than Just Race: Being Black and Poor in the Inner City*. London: Norton, 2010.

Section IV

Organizing and Activism

10

Deep Solidarity

A Pre-requisite to Resisting Capitalism and Building Economic Democracy

ROSEMARIE HENKEL-RIEGER

Introduction

WHEN WORKING ON CLASS and labor issues one is often accused of reducing the fight against injustice to economics. This reproach overlooks that working people have never been primarily white men in blue overalls. The working class is all of us who have to work for a living, and that includes women, black and brown people, LBGTQIA+ individuals, and immigrants. Economics directly affects oppression along the lines of race, ethnicity, gender, sexuality, and origin.

As a result, fighting for economic equity is a powerful way to address injustices and oppressions in an intersectional approach. If we want structural change, we need to build the power to bring it about. This power needs to be disruptive on a large scale. Economics, class, and labor are vital to building this power. It is at work and as workers (anyone who is not independently wealthy) that we can build substantial power to fight the injustices of racism, sexism, white supremacy, patriarchy, exploitation based on ethnicity, sexual orientation, as well as economic, documentation, and felony record status. Workers have the power to impact and transform the daily workings of production and services on many levels. This includes work slowdowns, stoppages, strikes, sick outs, etc. However, these types of high-risk resistance cannot be taken lightly and have to be planned very meticulously. They can have grave consequences such as lockouts, job loss, plant shutdown, drawn-out legal battles, all of which need community support for those affected.

In this chapter I will discuss what strategies and tactics might be helpful when building solidarity and economic democracy in the context of engaging people of faith and religion. I am aware that people involved in the struggle for social and economic justice tend to have a basic understanding of the systemic barriers many poor and low-income individuals face. Nevertheless, I start by laying out what we are up against because in my work as a worker-rights activist I realized over the years that many "rank and file" folks did not always have a clear understanding. Sure, almost everyone grasps that the oppressions that many poor black, brown, and white people experience, are systemic, but it is often obscure which system lends white supremacy the upper hand, undergirds racially motivated economic inequalities, and keeps workers divided along class lines.

For this reason, I would like to name it: neoliberal capitalism, and show how it creates these multiple divisions. In my work I have found that education around economic pressures is a necessary touchstone without which moving on to a solidarity rooted in one's own awareness of privilege and power is not possible. Once we are able to analyze our own economic situation, we can then see more clearly on whose side we are.

Destabilizing Effects of Inequality

In recent years, there has been a lot of talk about increasing inequality, particularly after the 2008 "Great Recession," the Arab Spring, and the Occupy movements in 2011. Knowing that the United States is one of the top ten richest countries (actually number seven), it might be surprising to hear that despite high levels of income per capita, its income inequality as measured using the GINI coefficient is similar to the average inequality of African countries.[1] Since the United States is my context, I would like to give some insight into what effects growing inequality has had on

---

1. Santacreu, *Federal Reserve*.

working people, and why I have been part of projects that engage people of faith and churches in the worker rights struggle.

There is overall agreement that inequality creates disparities on many levels, leading to damaged social cohesion, endangered democracy, political and economic instability, and climate change inaction. In terms of the impact on the working class, the International Monetary Fund (IMF) in 2016 stated that rising inequality can lead to social erosion, lower levels of social mobility, and financial fragility.[2] Many wealthy countries such as the United States have reached levels of zero to even negative public wealth. These developments are often coupled with political polarization.

Credite Suisse, a multinational bank and investment firm, reported in their Global Wealth Report (2018) that about 64 percent (3.2 billion people) of the world's population own less than $10,000 USD, which equals 1.9 percent of total global wealth while the top 1 percent owns 47 percent of household wealth.[3] The distribution at the very top of the global wealth pyramid is extremely uneven as the Oxfam Report of 2018 shows: 26 billionaires own as much as half of the global population. Furthermore, this study shows that the combined wealth of the world's richest people increased $2.5 billion USD a day last year.[4]

In the United States, growing income and wealth inequality has been building for some time. Over the past forty years the share of national income going to the wages of the bottom 90 percent has virtually stagnated. Before 1973, wages and benefits for workers increased at about the same rate as productivity rose. However, in the years between 1973 and 2016, as productivity continued to increase at a rate of 73.7 percent, compensation only grew 12.3 percent.[5] The benefits of increased productivity did not go to the bottom 90 percent but to the top income levels. According to the Economic Policy Institute, the top 1 percent took home about 22 percent of all income in 2015.[6]

---

2. For the IMF inequality is usually not limited to income and wealth but linked closely to education and health care access, Era Dabla-Norris. et al., *International Monetary Fund*.

3. Shorrocks, Davies and Lluberas. *Credit Suisse*. See page 9: "40 percent of newly added millionaires from US alone."

4. Oxfam, *Public Good or Private Wealth*.

5. Bivens and Shierholz, *Labor Market Changes*.

6. Sommellier and Price, *New Gilded Age*.

While wages have stagnated for decades, in the United States it has been ten years since the last raise of the federal minimum wage (2009) and the average wage gap between CEOs and workers has reached a ratio of 361 to 1.[7] In 2018 the average CEO made 924 times the salary of a minimum wage worker.[8]

Twenty-three million (or 58 percent) of the nearly 40 million workers who would benefit from an increase in the minimum wage from $7.25 USD to $15 USD are women. Such a raise would impact 27 percent, or over a quarter, of the total workforce and disproportionately benefit 38 percent of African American workers and one third of Latino workers, all of whom have been disadvantaged throughout US history. Furthermore, if we look at women of color, a raise in the minimum wage would give nearly 40 percent of them a boost compared to 22 percent of male workers and 32 percent of the female workforce.[9]

Even after reaching a low in unemployment with a current rate of 3.8 percent (March 2019), American workers are still economically stressed: only 38 percent of workers are earning the middle class wage needed for dual income earners to support a family in major metropolitan areas.[10] 32 percent of jobs pay a living-wage; and 30 percent pay a "hardship" wage, which cannot support the basic necessities for adults.[11] Overall, studies show that the middle class is being hollowed out and poverty is more widespread in the United States than in India or Brazil![12] One result of wealth inequality is reduced economic mobility. The rates of absolute mobility have fallen from approximately 90 percent for children born in 1940 to 50 percent for children born in the 1980s.[13]

Possibly the most visible indicator of wealth inequality in the United States is the *Forbes* list of the 400 wealthiest Americans. In 2018, Amazon founder Jeff Bezos, Microsoft founder Bill Gates, and investor Warren

---

7. According to Oxfam's report the US pay gap is more dramatic than in most other countries. In Japan the ratio is 58 to 1; in Germany, it's 136 to 1. "Ten Years Without a Raise."

8. Babic, "Politics of Poverty."

9. Oxfarm, "Ten Years Without a Raise."

10. BLS, "United States Department of Labor."

11. Bhandari and Brown, "The Opportunity Index."

12. Powers, "Why the Term 'Middle Class' Is Meaningless Today"; Norton, "Ben Carson."

13. Chetty, et al., *Fading American Dream.*

Buffett, the three richest men in the nation, together owned more wealth than the total fortunes of the poorest half of Americans.[14]

What We Are Up Against: Capitalism

Capitalism creates class divisions by dividing people into two basic groups or classes: those that own or otherwise control the majority of the assets of production and therefore can determine the production and the sale of products and services that others need to survive, and those who must sell their labor to meet their needs. These are not arbitrary divisions but social categories/identities based on particular economic relationships. Class is a reality in which we are bound up along with all of our other identities. In this system, most of us, 99 percent of Americans, have to work for a living and sell our labor on the labor market in order to make ends meet. Of those 99 percent, 63 percent have little control over their labor as well as little security in their lives.[15]

Most of us need to work to meet our needs. We are dependent on finding a job, as most of us cannot live on what we produce ourselves or are able to trade and barter. The problem in a system such as capitalism that is based on maximizing profits is that the employer has no direct stake in the workers' welfare and, moreover, care for workers is seen as counterproductive.[16] In a situation where the labor force depends on work and the position of employers is undergirded with power and pro-corporate policies,[17] exploitation can have many facets: migrancy, temporary work, contract labor, wage-suppression, speed-up,[18] lack of benefits (such as health care, retirement), and unpredictable hours and

---

14. Collins and Hoxie, *Billionaire Bonanza*.

15. The economist Michael Zweig writes: "Class is about the power some people have over the lives of others, and the powerlessness most people experience as a result." It is, he points out, about how people are connected to each other and how we are shaped by the role we play in the big entanglement of generating products and services to fulfill our needs as humans. Using this definition, Zweig estimates that over 63 percent of Americans are working class. Zweig, *Working Class Majority*, 9.

16. This is not about greedy individuals or a few bad actors, but a systemic characteristic of capitalism. Surplus or profit is created by extracting value/labor from workers without fair compensation.

17. For more on how the labor market is tilted in favor of corporate managers and capital owners (employers for short) see: Bivens and Shierholz, *Labor Market Changes*.

18. Speed up: anytime the employer can get more work out of the worker per time unit, the more profit is gained.

wages making planning for the future impossible. Add to that the reproductive labor that mostly women do, often on top of their wage labor, and it becomes clear that workers ultimately lose control over their lives.[19] Everything revolves around work and the work schedule.[20]

Not only does capitalism create divisions between those who have to work for a wage and those who hire for a wage, but taken together with income and wealth inequality and the concentration of income and wealth gains at the very top of the top, it becomes clearer why the language of the Occupy Wall Street Movement of the 1 percent versus the 99 percent made the logic of the capitalist system so evident and therefore so dangerous to those at the top of the distribution of wealth.[21]

Authors Patel and Moore go so far as calling the time in modern history that has unfolded since the 1400s the "Capitalocene." "Using this name means taking capitalism seriously, understanding it not just as an economic system but as a way of organizing the relationships between humans and the rest of nature."[22] They emphasize how capitalism uses nature, money, work, care, food, energy, and lives to fix its problems, and it does so using these seven things in the production and consumption processes. The strategy of the processes is to keep the cost as low as possible in order to increase profit, at the expense of people and the planet.[23]

Centering profit shifts relationships (1 percent vs. 99 percent) and splits nature and society. One example where such a split is evident is climate change. We are all affected by it but not everyone contributes equally. Patel and Moore suggest that we need to "place responsibility and look to those classes and relationships that profit from this separation."[24] Capitalism's efforts at shifting relations and creating divisions make it possible to exclude massive parts of society (women, people of color, indigenous peoples), thus determining whose lives and work matter and whose do not. How do we resist falling into this trap of shifting relationships and splitting segments of society?

---

19. Patel and Moore, *History of the World*, 24. And some workers have literally no control over their work: There are more people (21 million) in forced labor in 2012 than were traded over the Atlantic (12.5 million) before slavery was abolished.

20. Chibber, *ABC's of Capitalism*, 26–34.

21. Wright, "Class and Inequality in Piketty," 38.

22. Patel and Moore, *History of the World*, 3.

23. It is human labor that is needed to produce commodities, which can be turned into money. The cheaper the labor, the greater the profit.

24. Patel and Moore, *History of the World*, 24.

Solidarity

One effective strategy of resistance is to organize: workers choosing collective over individual action. Collective action needs a foundation built on mutual obligation, the feeling of responsibility towards one another, and an understanding of being in the same boat, being peers. It is about developing class consciousness and solidarity—based on actual class structures—against the pressures at work that deliberately aim to keep us as workers divided.

As Jane McAlevey points out, workers need solidarity to win and to counter individualism that often leads to people blaming themselves for failing success in our supposedly merit-based society.[25] Solidarity is not a foreign concept for most people. This is best demonstrated in catastrophic situations: people volunteer and donate when others are in great need. But these acts usually just flare up and then die down quickly. Real organizing happens when "people connect the dots between the critical, solidarity-affirming moment and the larger system it challenges, giving the workers in crisis a new way of seeing themselves and a newly formed sense of society's political economy."[26] With this realization, "deep organizing" can take hold producing a kind of solidarity that is grounded in the workers' new understanding/consciousness of their situation.[27] This is related to what Joerg Rieger and I have termed "deep solidarity," even though we are putting greater emphasis on the oppressive economic system that welds us together.[28]

Developing deep solidarity means to recognize that neoliberal capitalism works for a few rather than for the 99 percent who have to work for a living, which puts us in the same boat. Deep solidarity is based on the realization that nothing will change unless more people come together in the struggle against oppression. Deep solidarity does not require putting people's differences aside, rather it means to deal with differences more constructively and to put them to work for a shared cause and coinciding interests. And it is important that movement spaces and organizing strategies and tactics attend to these differences.[29]

25. McAlevey, *No Shortcuts*, 199.
26. McAlevey, *No Shortcuts*, 201.
27. McAlevey, *No Shortcuts*, 201.
28. Rieger and Henkel-Rieger, *Unified We Are a Force*.
29. For more about dealing with differences in movement spaces and strategies and how differences can be overcome through coalition building see Backer and

When we pay attention to what happens where pressures are greatest—where all other forms of oppression along the lines of race, ethnicity, gender, sexuality, etc., are bundled—and to who is on the frontlines in these battles, we can develop a greater understanding of how to resist and ultimately change systemic pressures.[30] In this way we can address the various pressures that create inequality and seek to divide us.

Armed with a sense of deep solidarity it is easy to see that what "workers of all sexes, races, religions, and ethnicities have in common is that they are workers—by definition subordinate to their employers, which see them as the source of profits, status, and power."[31] We find ourselves as workers in the same boat, however, not because we are all alike and our differences do not matter; rather, we find ourselves in the same boat because of the dominant system and its efforts to use all of our work and labor for the accumulation of profit and gain at the very top.

Deep solidarity also means we are there for each other's fights and we unite to take on struggles that none of us can win alone: minority politics still matter, but it is now linked with majority politics (the politics of the 99 percent). We must build relationships for the long haul that are rooted in the principles of reciprocity, mutual respect, and an understanding that our struggles for social justice cannot be separated.

Feminist writer bell hooks describes solidarity as enduring and as formed around the common denominator of fighting oppression and says,

> Solidarity is not the same as support. To experience solidarity, *we must have a community of interests*, shared beliefs and goals around which to unite, to build Sisterhood. Support can be occasional. It can be given and just as easily withdrawn. *Solidarity requires sustained, ongoing commitment*. In the interest of continued struggle, solidarity, and sincere commitment to eradicating all forms of domination, sexist oppression cannot continue to be ignored and dismissed by radical political activists. An important stage in the development of political consciousness is reached when *individuals recognize the need to struggle against all forms of oppression*. The fight against sexist oppression is of grave political significance—it is not for women only. Feminist movement is vital both in its power to liberate us

---

Cairns, "Movement Pedagogy."
30. Rieger and Henkel-Rieger, "Deep Solidarity."
31. Yates, *Why Unions Matter*, 167.

from the terrible bonds of sexist oppression and in its potential to radicalize and renew other liberation struggles.[32]

Hooks points out that solidarity is not something that comes naturally. Though it is not a foreign concept as McAlevey says, it requires hard, intentional, and continuous work. Unity is often felt when people do not compare themselves with others' oppressions but focus on their own experiences of oppression in a non-competitive way, without falling into the trap of individualizing the solution.[33] Hooks emphasizes that when showing "concern for the collective, we strengthen our solidarity."[34]

Solidarity does not come naturally and working people do not become change agents by default; they have to be organized. Working people can only develop the consciousness, deep solidarity, and skills needed to transform society through active struggle to change systemic oppressions in the workplace upheld by the owning class. It is the workplace that is the most direct and obvious site of that struggle. Working people can only be successful when not acting as individuals who are isolated, weak, and vulnerable to being divided along lines of race, gender, religion, region, immigration status, sexuality, etc. It is when working people build solidarity that they create platforms to improve working conditions for all workers in a coordinated and sustained way. However, shared contexts—one of the basic insights of deep solidarity—cannot be assumed, they have to be discovered. In the work of organizing, we set out to create spaces for people to realize that they share economic contexts. One of our questions is how faith communities can begin to understand that they are mostly made up of working people, that most of us are workers now, and that even what is considered divine might be joining us in deep solidarity. Other communities, including labor unions and their supporters, should be able to benefit from this perspective as well.

Examples of Solidarity and the Role of Religion

In the Southern United States, religion and church continue to be influential and many people are part of a faith community and self-identify as people of faith. As most of us have to work for a living, it is easy to deduce that many workers go to church and most church members are

32. hooks, *Feminist Theory*, 40–41, my emphasis.
33. hooks, *Feminist Theory*, 56–58.
34. hooks, *Feminist Theory*, 62.

workers. As a result, bringing these two groups together in an intentional manner around worker rights and economic issues may be a promising way to create an awareness of shared interests and exploitation. Even though churches often side with the status quo, there are pockets of pro-labor "church people," and in the work I was doing for years as a labor and community organizer in Dallas, Texas, we set out to connect with them.[35] Based on these insights, we have used union- and community-led actions such as demonstrations, picket lines, protest marches, and educational events as points of contact with workers.

What became quite clear early on in our work was that in order for people to grasp that there is shared economic exploitation potential, we needed middle-class white people to hear the stories of low-wage workers, especially the first-hand workplace accounts of people of color. Using the format of public hearings with workers testifying about their job situations—and having community, labor, church, and political leaders listen and engage in trouble-shooting—turned out to be very powerful. Having these hearings in a courtroom or church sanctuary gave the events an added air of importance and urgency. Giving the audience (made up of union members, church members, activists, workers, politicians, and community members) the opportunity to address workers who shared their stories created space to reflect on our collective identity as workers.

When Walmart workers, for instance, talked about the lack of respect on the job (name-calling, constant surveillance, unpredictable scheduling and hours, repercussions for those organizing co-workers, etc.), ironworkers could relate, as their experiences of wage-theft and denial of breaks and safety equipment also indicated total lack of respect by their employers.[36] Faculty and staff at the nearby Southern Methodist University could also relate as a prominent management company proposed improving fiscal soundness of the institution by eliminating 200 mostly administrative positions. The disregard and disrespect for workers here was certainly evident, for those being laid off and for those who now had to take on extra workloads for the same pay. The slogan

---

35. This work informed the book I co-authored with Joerg Rieger, *Unified We Are a Force*.

36. As the largest retailer in the world, with retail sales at $375 billion in 2017, Walmart sets the standard for labor practices globally. While Walmart workers are unionized in Europe, South America, Japan, and South Africa, the company is fighting back and retaliating against workers in the United States for standing up for better working conditions and pay, see Federation, *Stores*.

often used in this context, "as goes Walmart, so goes the economy," makes it clear that all workers are under attack and motivates to develop the consciousness, deep solidarity, and skills needed to transform society through active struggle together.

Meeting workers who share their stories about deteriorating working conditions was an impetus for hearing participants to take the next step and join workers and union members in organized actions such as walk-outs, strikes, demonstrations, and protest marches. For workers, this type of community, as well as the support of faith communities and of fellow working class majority members, was extremely empowering. For the Walmart workers in this example, this show of support led to workers planning their own actions.

To be sure, engaging people of faith, faith leaders, and pastors was not an easy task, but when a church choir that specialized in songs of the civil rights era and resistance came to us in order to find actions and events at which to "perform," we were able to connect them to the larger worker struggles happening in the Dallas area, giving the choir the purpose for which they longed and adding the energy and unifying nature of song and music to our actions. This morphed into another solidarity-building opportunity.

In other instances, Walmart workers—many deeply religious—and activists, pastors, theologians, and students spontaneously formed prayer circles during in-store actions. This stopped customers in their tracks and managers did not know how to break up these circles without drawing negative attention from the public. This tactic proved to be a very effective way of speaking to God and to the world: customers became witnesses to the faith-based pleas for strength to change conditions at work by Walmart workers (visible by their blue work vests), clergy (wearing stoles), and community supporters (in plain clothes).

The biblical mandate for justice is a good point for connecting people of faith and the struggle for justice in the workplace. On several occasions we brought together theologians, divinity students, church members, union organizers, Walmart workers, and ironworkers, and read the Bible and talked about how God cares about justice by taking the side of the oppressed. It did not take long for participants to analyze their own faith-rooted motivations for standing up for justice, employ their faith to analyze particular injustices, and be encouraged to use their faith to inspire, lead, and organize in the struggle for worker rights.

Sustaining solidarity to take root in our everyday lives and to become second nature is what it takes to truly form deep solidarity. For this it is necessary to realize our own economic situation as working people, to start understanding how power works, to acknowledge our privileges particularly as white people, and to identify ways to use our (limited) privilege in the struggle. The respect and power that come with being (white) pastors or academics, for example, become useful in arranging meetings with corporate managers when undocumented workers requesting a meeting could not even get a hearing with the office assistant. Such meetings with the workers and management often became a first step to deconstruct white privilege and enter into pastor-worker relations of deep solidarity.

While creating these opportunities to form and sustain solidarity are not new to the struggle for worker rights and social movements in general, it reinforced a sense that no matter to what race, gender, ethnicity, degree of ability, education, sexual orientation, or age we relate, we share the identity of being workers. If we look at this shared identity solely through the lenses of race and gender, for instance, then white supremacy and capitalism win and we lose sight of the realities that connect us as workers so existentially, and we lose the capacity to build and sustain coalitions and solidarity.

Solidarity Deepening in the United States

Our economic system is killing us and the planet, and to survive we need a fundamentally new economy—one that is based on the values of solidarity, cooperation, and mutuality. But how do we get there?

Since 2016, signs of building solidarity have been emerging in the United States in the form of strikes and the larger community has shown support for the people who withheld their labor to win concessions that have gone far beyond increasing wages. The Bureau of Labor Statistics reported that in 2018 there were 20 major work stoppages involving 485,000 workers, the highest number since 1986, when 533,000 employees stopped working.[37]

One good example are the actions of educators. In 2018, West Virginia teachers disregarded their unions' advice and walked off the job for two days, protesting increasing privatization of the public school system,

---

37. BLS, "United States."

a meager one percent pay raise that was below rising cost of living increases, and the lack of overall school funding. With 35,000 teachers striking for a week, all public schools were forced to close their doors and the teachers won a five percent wage increase, health care benefit concessions, and gains in general funding for schools.

Back in 2012, the Chicago Teachers Union made major gains when they joined force with two-thirds of the parents, centering the struggle around the children and the community's needs and desires.[38] An interesting fact about this public-sector strike was the fact that unlike in previous labor struggles, no union member crossed the picket line.[39] On top of that, as a show of solidarity, tens of thousands of Chicago teachers joined the picket lines with workers of Hyatt Hotels. With this action the teachers made the public aware that the struggles of both groups were linked. After all, the owners of hotel chains that exploit their workers are also the folks destroying public education in Chicago.

The success of the West Virginia teachers initiated a wave of teacher strikes that swept across the nation to other states such as Arizona, Oklahoma, California (six-day strike), Colorado (three-day strike), and Marriott hotel workers picketing in four states. Showing that teacher concerns are community concerns has helped broaden the appeal of these labor struggles far beyond the members of unions.

The strike wave has carried on into 2019 with 31,000 "Stop and Shop" workers walking off their jobs at 240 stores across three states, making this ten-day work stoppage the largest private-sector strike in years.[40] The workers agreed on a new three-year contract that maintained health care and retirement benefits, overtime pay for Sundays, and a pay increase. Workers experienced the solidarity of their communities when customers refused to cross the picket line or brought food to strikers.[41]

Striking teachers in Los Angeles bargained for the common good and won better wages and benefits, but they also gained 300 more school nurses, more green space at every school, support for immigrant families, a stop to random police searches at schools, and more. These types of far-ranging social and racial justice concerns were brought to the bargaining

---

38. Jaffe, *Necessary Trouble*, 122–23.

39. In 2018 the unionization rate for public sector workers was 33.9 percent compared to 6.4 percent of private sector workers. BLS, "United States."

40. The grocery store chain is owned by a Dutch multinational corporation and is highly profitable. Logan, "We Should Welcome Workers."

41. Logan, "We Should Welcome Workers."

table because the teachers and the unions had been deeply involved with the on-going organizing in their communities, creating a sense of shared struggles. Obviously, this kind of solidarity does not come overnight and without great coalition-building efforts.[42] And let us not forget that besides years of selfless dedication, sacrifice, and patient organizing, when they go on strike workers give up their pay and risk losing their jobs![43]

It was not the US Congress that negotiated the end of the partial government shutdown in early 2019, but ten air traffic controllers who in a show of solidarity ultimately forced the US Government and Congress to strike a budget deal. As federal government workers, they did not have the formal right to strike but they could withhold their labor power. And that is what they did: they called in sick. This had a ripple effect all along the east coast, where flight delays started piling up in several main airports. The treat of a massive breakdown of national air travel was enough to foment a political solution putting roughly 800,000 furloughed government employees back to work after going without pay for over a month.[44] Here we see another an example of impactful solidarity!

But can such deep solidarity and the realization that our own liberation and struggles are bound up with those of others be sustained? Can there be long-term solidarity, not just a mobilizing effort that wanes when people move on to the next issue?

Challenges to Solidarity

Solidarity does not come easy and a false sense of optimism is not helpful. For these reasons, we need to realize what we are up against, and who benefits if we cannot build a just economy. Solidarity has its limits and difficulties, and so it is important to be watchful for who is included and who is left out.

Workers have been fighting for some of the most basic human rights for centuries. In the United States, some of the early efforts to squash collective organizing of workers were violently enforced by police and

---

42. Jaffe, "This Is Much Bigger Than Us."

43. Windham, *Knocking on Labor's Door*. For a closer look at the number of workers seeking to organize since the 1970s, see page 3. What she finds is that there is no decline in the number of workers petitioning to organize a union compared to the 1950s and 1960s. "What did decline, however, was workers' ability to win those union elections."

44. Zezima, "Even with the Shutdown over."

even the military. Unions were more broadly accepted in the twentieth century and they gained economic and political power for the working class until the 1950s (e.g. federal minimum wage, eight-hour workday, end of child labor). However, with the shift towards neoliberalism, the attitude towards workers has again taken a more confrontational stance that has resulted in wage stagnation, erosion of worker rights, reduced bargaining power of unions, suppressed union activity, submissive attitude of workers, speed up (more hours worked for same pay, working at higher efficiency for same pay, less paid time off, sick days), and reduced social programs.[45] The result has been the creation of more "flexible" labor pools that are readily available and easier to dispose of.

Here the so-called "gig economy" is a welcome addition: workers can feel like they are their own bosses and in control of creating income, but the reality is that as independent contractors all responsibility lies with the worker. This life quickly turns into a constant hustle for gigs on an individual basis.[46] For gig workers all sense of collective membership to the working class is distorted and solidarity goes out the door. While gig work undermines solidarity and the development of a collective worker consciousness, it also shows how necessary deep solidarity is: we cannot lose sight of how capitalism pits us against the "bosses" and their interest as well as against each other as workers, which some call "negative solidarity."[47] This is yet another way in which for example racial, ethnic, and gender divisions among working people are reinforced by capitalism and simultaneously help to reinforce capitalism.

Dividing workers is based on the logic of capital. Racism, for example, comes natural to bosses as it works in their class interest, whereas for white workers racism does not work in the same way. On the contrary, as David Roediger notes, "struggles for racial justice are sites of learning for white workers, of self-activity by workers of color, and of placing limits on capital's ability to divide workers."[48] Of course white workers lacking class consciousness or a sense of deep solidarity usually do not realize how the system gives limited advantages to white people to disguise class interests, and thus keeps them from challenging the wealthy and

---

45. Stanford, *Economics for Everyone*, 109–10.

46. Katz and Krueger, "Rise and Nature of Alternative Work."

47. Jaffe, *Necessary Trouble*, 16: "'Negative solidarity'... focusses on tearing down those who seem to have it better than you rather than demanding that your circumstances improve."

48. Roediger, *Class, Race, and Marxism*, 12.

powerful, with whom they identify based on their whiteness. And vice versa, race and gender oppression cannot be fought effectively without class mobilization: if we want resources or wealth to be redistributed or the government to reallocate spending priorities so that racial minorities and women also benefit, working people together have to confront capital and who controls it.[49]

Besides divide and control, identity politics can be used as another effective tool to prop up dominant ideology, as it can make collective opposition impossible. Identity politics, Asad Haider reminds us, does have promising roots in the way it was re-introduced into the political conversation by the Combahee River Collective, a group of black feminist scholars who focused identity more broadly than is commonly done today on the multiple identities of their realities. These included class, but also race, ethnicity, gender, etc. In contrast, unilinear definitions of identity often make us forget that only when all these identities are taken into account can the most radical solutions be considered.[50] By centering the interrelations of oppression in their work, the Combahee River Collective "understood that coalition building was crucial to [their] own survival."[51] Haider goes on to point out that race and class have been at the center of the civil rights movement making it "the closest US equivalent to the mass workers' movements in postwar Europe," but that this connection is omitted in the dominant narratives of the movement and stories of Martin Luther King, Jr., Malcolm X, Huey Newton, and others of the era.[52]

Today identity politics is often used to focus on who we are as individuals, undermining the initially intended coalition-building effect.[53] For example, the critique from both the Left and the Right of the Occupy Wall Street Movement being just a white middle class movement made it possible to discount the "99 percent" framing as a one-sided affair. A similar thing happened to the initial grassroots-dominated class and race focus at the core of the Black Lives Matter Movement. Soon after the shooting of Michael Brown in Ferguson, race and class were divided and seen as different, opposing identities. This works out well for Black and

49. Chibber, *The ABC's of Capitalism*.
50. Haider, *Mistaken Identity*.
51. Frazier, "Rethinking Identity Politics," 12.
52. Haider, *Mistaken Identity*, 15.
53. Haider, *Mistaken Identity*, 23–24.

white elites,[54] because when cross-racial coalitions are blocked, movement-building based on income, wealth, democratic control and ownership inequalities or other shared identities are even harder to initiate. Coalition forming is easily blocked.

Movements also suffer when participation is limited to individual concerns. As bell hooks points out, "when we show our concern for the collective, we strengthen our solidarity."[55] She emphasizes that women need to bond over shared strengths and resources, not shared victimization, which severely limits their agency in challenging notions of race and class, and the complexity of their experiences.[56] "Women do not need to eradicate difference to feel solidarity."[57] The clearer we are about this, the more deep solidarity becomes an option. Work and labor are what connects us, up and down the various social ladders and scales that exist among the 99 percent. Deep solidarity is built on the awareness that we all have to work to meet our needs—this includes the underemployed and the unemployed, the incarcerated, many of whom are forced into prison labor, those excluded from the economy because of illness, ability, or age, and those involved in unpaid reproductive labor.

Sociologist Charles Derber has researched social movements for decades and lays out the way forward for movements in what he terms "universalizing resistance."[58] For Derber, surviving and creating a more just world depends on the majority of people unifying popular power to transform the system, creating new communities and common struggles out of the many fractured movements and siloed efforts we currently have.[59] According to Derber, there is more resistance building because the flawed system is driving more people to take to the streets, such as on January 21, 2017, when an estimated 1 percent of Americans protested the presidency of Donald Trump. This demonstration was the called the Women's March, and over half of the demonstrators had never been part of a protest action before.

---

54. Haider, *Mistaken Identity*, 30
55. hooks, *Feminist Theory*, 62.
56. hooks, *Feminist Theory*, 46.
57. hooks, *Feminist Theory*, 64–65.
58. Derber, *Welcome to the Revolution*, xxii.
59. Derber, *Welcome to the Revolution*, 54–56.

Resisting and Building

Unifying global social movements have been meeting for decades to frame plans of a new society and economy, as neoliberal capitalism with its maximization of profit, unregulated markets, trade deals, and finance capital, privatization, austerity politics, and pillage of natural resources and human labor has mostly failed 99 percent of us, even in the so-called First World. In this spirit the solidarity economy seeks a pluralist approach (multiple paths to a just and sustainable world), built on concrete practices that already exist or are emerging and are aligned with the values of solidarity (cooperation, mutuality, sharing, reciprocity), equity (opposing all forms of oppression), participatory democracy (self-management, collective ownership), and sustainability (nature not to be owned and exploited).[60] The solidarity economy creates a real opportunity to challenge our social, political and economic contexts, and transform the ways people across the globe work, live, and cooperate. It is about resisting and building.

And in order to build we need more than a vision, we need a plan on how to shift ownership relationships, because as long as there is no real discussion and democratic decision-making about what we produce, how we produce things, and who decides what is done with the resulting profit, our economic system will create increasing wealth and income inequality.

Cooperative Developments

I took this step from resisting to building in my own work by becoming part of shaping the economy from the angle of workers owning the assets of production and facilitating worker ownership and control through the cooperative model, thus expanding the principles of deep solidarity. These efforts led me to co-found the Southeast Center of Cooperative Development in Nashville, with organizer and activist Benny Overton.[61]

Some historians regard one of the first examples of a modern social economy to be the founding of the Rochdale Society of Equitable Pioneers in the United Kingdom in 1844, claimed to be the first modern cooperative. The concept of social economy refers to an ownership type

---

60. Poirier, "Social Solidarity"; also see Kuwano, "Solidarity Economy."
61. See www.co-opsnow.org.

in which each individual has one vote, as opposed to a shareholder model in which the more shares you buy, the more voting power you have.[62]

The Rochdale Pioneers were important as they pooled their resources, set up a store that offered good food at honest prices, and based its governance on one person, one vote, and seven principles that have been passed down in slightly modified form:

1. Cooperatives are voluntary organizations, open to all persons.

2. Cooperatives are democratic organizations controlled by their members, who actively participate in setting policies and making decisions.

3. Members contribute equitably to, and democratically control, the capital of their cooperative.

4. Cooperatives are autonomous organizations controlled by their members.

5. Cooperatives provide education and training for their members and employees so they can contribute effectively to the development of their cooperatives. They are committed to informing the public about the nature and benefits of the cooperative model.

6. Cooperatives strengthen the cooperative movement by working together.

7. Cooperatives work for the sustainable development of their communities.

Following these principles, according to a definition by the International Cooperative Alliance, "cooperatives are people-centered enterprises jointly owned and democratically controlled by and for their members to realize their common socio-economic needs and aspirations. As enterprises based on values and principles, they put fairness and equality first allowing people to create sustainable enterprises that generate long-term jobs and prosperity."[63]

Cooperatives are certainly not a modern invention, as they have existed for centuries in various forms. In her work on the commons, Nobel Prize winner in economics in 2009, Elinor Olstrom, shows that humans

---

62. For more on the history of cooperatives in the United States, see Curl, *For All the People*.

63. Definition by the International Cooperative Alliance, *International Cooperative Alliance*.

have the propensity to cooperate rather than compete.[64] Humans have a long history of cooperation and many different traditions. For example, cooperative irrigation and water management were undertaken by many early civilizations, like the Sumerians in Mesopotamia, who dug canals and built dams to irrigate their fields. Native American societies were also built on community cooperation rather than individualism. In every period of American history, African Americans addressed economic, political, social, familial, and personal challenges by pooling resources and forming joint ownerships. They realized early on that collective organizing and sharing ownership were the bulwarks to resilience and survival creating a long tradition of mutual aid, as Jessica Gordon Nembhard has outlined.[65]

Worker cooperatives, cooperatives owned and self-managed by workers, rose to prominence during the industrial revolution in response to growing industrialization and mass production as industrial capitalism took hold.[66] They increased in number during economic downturns and labor crises. In the early 1800s, workers often formed cooperatives while on strike and sometimes maintained these cooperatives after the strike had ended. In the 1880s, the Knights of Labor in the United States began to urge the creation of consumer and producer cooperatives among locals, and between 1880 and 1888, 334 cooperatives were established. With increased mechanization of everything from farm labor to skilled craft work, many workers saw their livelihoods threatened. By creating their own cooperatives, they could maintain their work and have more control of their lives. However, the decline of the Knights of Labor in the late 1880s weakened the cooperatives and many closed.

The Great Depression gave way to the passage of the New Deal in the United States, which included several programs that supported the development of self-help groups, producer cooperatives, established electric and fertilizer cooperatives, as well as agricultural banks to serve agricultural cooperatives. The Federal Credit Union Act helped stabilize the imbalanced financial system by ensuring that credit would be available to people with little means. Once the Depression ended, many cooperative programs were terminated. The 1960s and 1970s ushered in a new wave of cooperatives linked to various popular social movements. This

64. Ostrom, *Governing the Commons*.
65. Gordon-Nemhard, *Collective Courage*.
66. See Wright, *Worker Cooperatives*; and for more on the history of worker cooperatives: Curl, *For All the People*.

led to the development of cooperatively owned businesses, housing, and financial institutions. A second wave of worker cooperative development started in the late 1990s. By the mid-2000s, several worker cooperative development organizations took off, using the form as a means to create good jobs for low- and moderate-income workforces, from home care to housecleaning.

Today there are increasing numbers of worker co-ops all around the world, large and small, taking on diverse forms, but all centered around the same core values and principles. Worker cooperatives are businesses owned, operated, and democratically controlled by their workers who share in the profits of their labor and practice solidarity.[67] Control is exercised on the premise of "one worker, one vote." Workers own the majority of the equity in the business and control the voting shares. They decide what is produced or what service is rendered and how this is done, how to the distribute the profit, and they put worker and community benefit at the core of their purpose. These typically small businesses can be found in every sector and industry, from engineering and manufacturing to retail and service.

One of the benefits of worker cooperatives lies in their resilience: In economic downturns, most corporations are even more narrowly focused on maintaining value for the shareholders at the expense of their employees. When they cannot maximize profits for shareholders at very high levels, corporations often sell out or shut down, terminating jobs. Co-ops on the other hand are based on generating income and providing stable employment for their members. When faced with a tradeoff between pursuing profits and maintaining employment, worker co-ops often choose preserving jobs.

Furthermore, worker cooperatives help build community wealth through local ownership. Workers who own their jobs have a direct stake in the local environment, and they have the power to decide to do business in ways that create community benefits. Worker cooperatives are likely to form relationships with other local businesses, hire local workers and workers with barriers to employment (e.g. felony records), and reinvest their profits back into the neighborhood. Worker-owners are interested in generating profit, but they are also invested in ensuring that they

---

67. Ranis, *Cooperatives Confront Capitalism*, 44. Political scientist Peter Ranis points out that worker cooperatives can create a sense of class consciousness based on their experience in the process of production.

work in a healthy environment, have job stability, safe business practices, and fair wages and benefits. Solidarity is built into the model.

Ultimately, we are shifting ownership relationships of the assets of production and democratizing or centering economic decisions in the community, taking the questions of the economy (What and how do we produce? Who gets what we produce? What is done with the surplus?) to the community for answers. In a capitalist economy, by contrast, all answers are based on whatever maximizes profits for shareholders. As participants and supporters of the solidarity economy, our solutions focus on spreading out wealth, income, and ownership in the broadest sense.

Engaging People of Faith

Our next challenge is to connect the principles of shared ownership and control of the assets of production to the faith-rooted values of the church. This task does not seem too difficult on the surface, as cooperatives have been started by churches, share common values, and there is a common history and tradition of taking part in broad ownership structures.[68]

For example, Mondragon, the world's largest network of worker-owned industrial cooperatives, was founded by Father José María Arizmendiarrieta, a young Catholic priest who came to Arrasate-Mondragón, a town of 8,500 inhabitants in the Basque Country in 1956. Father José started a community-run, self-governed, self-financed training school to help the youth receive job training, technical skills, and lessons in participatory humanism based on Christian values. Creating a way for fair employment, this priest's cause was to *socialize knowledge in order to democratize power*. He was convinced that people needed the right framework of participatory democracy and skills in order to create power. Today, the Mondragon Cooperative Corporation is made up of 268 businesses with 101 cooperatives and a total of $14 billion USD in revenue, operating in 70 countries worldwide, including 5 businesses in the United States.[69] The Mondragon Cooperative Corporation employs about 74,000 employees with about 40 percent being worker-owners. Mondragon's more than sixty-year-old mission is to generate wealth for

---

68. See Schneider, "Truly, Much Can Be Done," for more on cooperatives and the Catholic church.

69. Mondragon, *Mondragon*.

society through business development and job creation under the "one worker, one vote" cooperative framework.

The Southeast Center for Cooperative Development is interested in bringing community economic engagement to faith communities, because we believe that looking at economic justice through a theological lens can be empowering. We cannot build deep solidarity without acknowledging our own economic situation as the working majority. These discussions will help us connect our theology to meaningful action in the community, shaping what change can look like when we start building a new economy.

Churches, particularly African American churches, have long been the hubs for economic participation. For many workers, churches have been the place to make important employment connections. Our cooperative project seeks to address the challenges that particularly people of color, women, and low-income individuals face in building wealth and income by gaining access to quality jobs with dignified wages and benefits. As we look to create a more equitable economic system, democratizing decision-making power in the workplace can be achieved by increasing shared ownership through cooperative economic development.[70]

The co-op model provides a framework for churches to help foster economic activity that produces not only financial resources but also meaningful work, starting with the most exploited. Charitable efforts that seek to support communities can now be combined with constructive efforts that promote meaningful work enriching communities in need, churches, and individuals. Concretely, churches can provide experts from the congregation with skills in various business-related fields, offer mentorship programs, or just check in regularly with newly forming cooperatives. Faith communities with underutilized space or land can house or accommodate a cooperative start-up, and interested church members can become part of actively incubating cooperative businesses. On the financial side churches can use their financial resources to make loans, donations, and invest long-term in the local cooperative ecosystem.

Our goal is to grow and amplify faith-based voices and action (theory and practice), beginning in minority neighborhoods where the pressures are greatest, built on a robust moral, faith, and socio-economic understanding of how inequality and concentration of wealth by the few is hurting many of us, particularly minorities and women. We seek

---

70. Schneider, *Everything for Everyone*, 225.

transformational change not only by calling out injustice but also calling into collaboration for generative change. We want to reclaim space in the larger inter-faith community for deeper discussions about economic justice and how shared ownership and collective control in the economy can become solutions by building community wealth through the cooperative model. Only when we start to shift ownership relationships to a broad-based model can we democratize the economy and transfer wealth and decision-making power to those who have been economically sidelined and excluded.

Conclusion

The notion of deep solidarity, being there for each other's fights and uniting to take on struggles that none of us can win alone, is a prerequisite for broad-based economic change. It is a foundation on which we build relationships for the long haul, rooted in the principles of cooperation, reciprocity, and mutual respect. Deep solidarity gives us the conviction that our struggles for social justice cannot be separated. This is what will sustain us in our fight for economic democracy and for "commoning" ownership relationships.

Bibliography

Babic, Mary. "Six Simple Reasons We Should Raise the Minimum Wage Right Now." Oxfam America. https://politicsofpoverty.oxfamamerica.org/2019/02/6-simple-reasons-we-should-raise-the-minimum-wage/.

Backer, David, and Kate Cairns. "Movement Pedagogy: Beyond the Class/Identity Impasse." *Viewpoints Magazine* (December 2017). https://www.viewpointmag.com/2017/12/21/movement-pedagogy-beyond-class-identity-impasse/.

Bhandari, Ryan, and David Brown. "The Opportunity Index: Ranking Opportunity in Metropolitan America." Third Way. https://www.thirdway.org/report/the-opportunity-index-ranking-opportunity-in-metropolitan-america.

Bivens, Josh, and Heidi Shierholz. "What Labor Market Changes Have Generated Inequality and Wage Suppression?" Economic Policy Institute. https://www.epi.org/publication/what-labor-market-changes-have-generated-inequality-and-wage-suppression-employer-power-is-significant-but-largely-constant-whereas-workers-power-has-been-eroded-by-policy-actions/.

Bureau of Labor Statistics. "Economic News Release." https://www.bls.gov/news.release/union2.nro.htm.

———. "The Economics Daily, 20 Major Work Stoppages in 2018 Involving 485,000 Workers." https://www.bls.gov/opub/ted/2019/20-major-work-stoppages-in-2018-involving-485000-workers.htm.

———. "Labor Force Statistics from the Current Population Survey." https://data.bls.gov/timeseries/lns14000000.

Chetty, Raj, David Grusky, Maximilian Hell, Nathaniel Hendren, Robert Manduca, and Jimmy Narang. "The Fading American Dream: Trends in Absolute Income Mobility since 1940." *Science* 356 (2017) 398–406.

Chibber, Vivek. *The ABC's of Capitalism: Understanding Capitalism*. New York: Jacobin Foundation, 2018.

Collins, Chuck, and Josh Hoxie. "Billionaire Bonanza 2018: Inherited Wealth Dynasties in the 21st-Century U.S." Inequality. October 30, 2018. https://inequality.org/great-divide/billionaire-bonanza-2018-inherited-wealth-dynasties-in-the-21st-century-u-s/.

Curl, John. *For All the People: Uncovering the Hidden History of Cooperation, Cooperative Movements, and Communalism in America*. Oakland: PM, 2012.

Dabla-Norris, Era, et al. "Causes and Consequences of Inequality: A Global Perspective." https://www.imf.org/en/Publications/Staff-Discussion-Notes/Issues/2016/12/31/Causes-and-Consequences-of-Income-Inequality-A-Global-Perspective-42986.

Derber, Charles. *Welcome to the Revolution: Universalizing Resistance for Social Justice and Democracy in Perilous Times*. New York: Routledge, 2017.

Fernández Campbell, Alexia. "The Largest Private Sector Strike in Years Is Over. Supermarket Workers Won." *Vox*. April 22, 2019. https://www.vox.com/2019/4/22/18511066/stop-shop-workers-union-strike-contract.

Frazier, Demita. "Rethinking Identity Politics." *Sojourners* 12 (1995) 12.

Gordon-Nemhard, Jessica. *Collective Courage: A History of African American Cooperative Thought and Practice*. University Park: Pennsylvania State University Press, 2014.

Haider, Assad. *Mistaken Identity: Race and Class in the Age of Trump*. Brooklyn: Verso, 2018.

hooks, bell. *Feminist Theory: From Margin to the Center*. Boston: South End, 1984.

International Cooperative Alliance. https://www.ica.coop/en.

Jaffe, Sarah. "This Is Much Bigger Than Us, Than Our Union, Even Than Our City." *The Nation* (January 23, 2019). https://www.thenation.com/article/la-teachers-strike-utla-victory-agreement.

———. *Necessary Trouble: Americans in Revolt*. New York: Nations Books, 2016.

Katz, Lawrence F., and Alan B. Krueger. "The Rise and Nature of Alternative Work Arrangements in the United States, 1995–2015." *Industrial and Labor Relations Review* 72 (2019) 382–416.

Kuwano, Emily. "Solidarity Economy: Building an Economy for People & Planet." *The Next System Project*. May 1, 2018. https://thenextsystem.org/learn/stories/solidarity-economy-building-economy-people-planet#production.

Logan, John. "We Should Welcome Workers' 'Powerful Victory' in the Stop & Shop Strike." https://thehill.com/blogs/congress-blog/labor/440271-we-should-welcome-workers-powerful-victory-in-the-stop-shop-strike.

McAlevey, Jane. *No Shortcuts: Organizing for Power in the Gilded Age*. New York: Oxford University Press, 2016.

Mondragon. "Mondragon: Cooperative Experience." https://www.mondragon-corporation.com/en/co-operative-experience/faqs.

National Retail Federation. "Stores—Top Retailers 2018." https://stores.org/stores-top-retailers-2018.

Norton, Ben. "Ben Carson Blasted North Korea for Spending More on the Military than the Hungry: Has He Looked at His Own Country?" https://www.salon.com/2015/12/18/ben_carson_blasted_north_korea_for_spending_money_on_the_military_instead_of_the_hungry_has_he_looked_at_his_own_country/.

Ostrom, Elinor. *Governing the Commons: The Evolution of Institutions for Collective Action*. Cambridge: Cambridge University Press, 1990.

Oxfam. "Public Good or Private Wealth." https://s3.amazonaws.com/oxfam-us/www/static/media/files/bp-public-good-or-private-wealth-210119-en.pdf.

———. "Ten Years without a Raise." https://www.oxfamamerica.org/explore/research-publications/ten-years-without-a-raise.

Patel, Raj, and Jason Moore. *A History of the World in Seven Cheap Things: A Guide to Capitalism, Nature, and the Future of the Planet*. Oakland: University of California Press, 2017.

Poirier, Yvon. "Social Solidarity Economy and Related Concepts Origins and Definitions: An International Perspective." http://www.ripess.org/wp-content/uploads/2017/09/Solidarity-Economy-and-other-Concepts-Poirier-July-2014.pdf.

Powers, Benjamin. "Why the Term 'Middle Class' Is Meaningless Today." https://www.huffpost.com/entry/why-the-term-middleclass_b_8885636.

Ranis, Peter. *Cooperatives Confront Capitalism: Challenging the Neoliberal Economy*. London: Zed, 2016.

Rieger, Joerg, and Rosemarie Henkel-Rieger. "Deep Solidarity: Broadening the Basis of Transformation." In *HTS Teologiese Studies/Theological Studies* 73 (November 2017). https://hts.org.za/index.php/hts/article/view/4578/10727.

———. *Unified We Are a Force: How Faith and Labor Can Overcome America's Inequalities*. St. Louis: Chalice, 2016.

Roediger, David. *Class, Race, and Marxism*. Brooklyn: Verso, 2017.

Santacreu, Ana Maria. "How Does U.S. Income Inequality Compare Worldwide?" https://www.stlouisfed.org/on-the-economy/2017/october/how-us-income-inequality-compare-worldwide.

Schneider, Nathan. *Everything for Everyone: The Radical Tradition That Is Shaping the Next Economy*. New York: Nation, 2018.

———. "Truly, Much Can Be Done": Cooperative Economics from the Book of Acts to Pope Francis." In *Care for the World: Laudato Si' and Catholic Social Thought in an Era of Climate Crisis*, edited by Frank Pasquale, 145–66. Cambridge: Cambridge University Press, 2019.

Shorrocks, Anthony, et al. "Why Wealth Matters. The Global Weatlh Report." https://www.credit-suisse.com/corporate/en/research/research-institute/global-wealth-report.html/.

Sommellier, Estelle and Mark Price. "The New Gilded Age: Income Inequality in the U.S. by State, Metropolitan Area, and County." Economic Policy Institute. https://www.epi.org/publication/the-new-gilded-age-income-inequality-in-the-u-s-by-state-metropolitan-area-and-county.

Stanford, Jim. *Economics for Everyone: A Short Guide to the Economics of Capitalism*. Halifax: Fernwood, 2008.

Windham, Lane. *Knocking on Labor's Door: Union Organizing in the 1970s and the Roots of a New Economic Divide*. Chapel Hill: University of North Carolina Press, 2017.

Wright, Chris. *Worker Cooperatives and Revolution: History and Possibilities in the United States*. Bradenton, 2014.
Wright, Erik Olin. "Class and Inequality in Piketty." In *Twenty-First Century Inequality and Capitalism: Piketty, Marx and Beyond*, edited by Lauren Langman and David A. Smith, 58–61. Studies in Critical Social Sciences 116. Leiden: Brill, 2018.
Yates, Michael D. *Why Unions Matter*. New York: Monthly Review, 2009.
Zezima, Katie. "Even with the Shutdown Over, Some Federal Employees Still Can't Afford Diapers as They Await Paychecks." https://www.washingtonpost.com/national/even-with-the-shutdown-over-some-federal-employees-still-cant-afford-diapers-as-they-await-paychecks/2019/01/27/e1fc5dae-2262-11e9-90cd-dedboc92dc17_story.html/.
Zweig, Michael. *The Working Class Majority: America's Best Kept Secret*. Ithaca, NY: Cornell University Press, 2011.

11

Invited, Invigorated, and Invented Spaces
A Trans-development Approach

SITHEMBISO S. ZWANE

Introduction

THE TRIPLE CHALLENGE OF unemployment, poverty, and inequality that persist unabated in most communities is repugnant in the postcolonial context. The neoliberal economic paradigm perpetuated by the Global North, with serious social, economic and political repercussions for the Global South, is a cause for concern. Most countries, especially in the so-called Third World, have adopted neoliberal capitalist policies that promote capital rather than labor intensification because of the fourth industrial revolution. Economic inequalities and extreme poverty among people are not accidental but systemic, designed to ensure neoliberal economic hegemony. The development of unorthodox economic and religious emancipatory methods is fundamental in challenging the dominant social, economic, political, and religious narrative of "development." When the marginalization and economic exclusion of the working class becomes unbearable, alternative methods for the re-appropriation of the concept of development are inevitable.

What is Development?

The concept of development is broad and finds hegemonic expression in modernization theory which contends with dependency theory.[1] The concept has been contested because it is a process that affects people differently, depending on how they have been shaped by it. Amartya Sen argues, for instance, that development is "a process of expanding the real freedoms that people enjoy."[2] Pertinent questions that arise are: what freedoms and which development? The dominant neoliberal understanding of development does not seem to incorporate the real freedoms that people enjoy. On the contrary, it creates a conducive environment for structural and systemic oppression of the people.

Sen states that development refers to the removal of major sources of economic unfreedom, which includes the exclusion of communities from meaningful participation in decision-making processes.[3] Sen's fundamental argument is that real freedoms are intricately associated with functioning and capability. The limitation of this definition is that it is not overt about the ideological and structural causes of the major sources of unfreedom that hinder functioning and capability. The critical phrase is "freedoms that people enjoy," which relates to issues about choices that people have within a structural and systemic context. However, poverty is not homogeneous but relative to each context, hence the diversified response to it. Critical to a process of development should be the liberation of those who are suffering and vulnerable to structural and systemic marginalization.

According to Jerry Pillay, development is associated with "upwards" progress from situations of ignorance and poverty to knowledge and riches.[4] It is evident from Sen and Pillay's definitions that development as progress is neither generic nor universal in nature. Furthermore, Gilbert Rist states that development involves a variety of practices that have the potential to conflict with one another.[5] Development can either mean liberation or oppression, hence the reference to a variety of practices associated with the concept. The most pertinent critique of the concept of development comes from liberation theology in Latin America.

1. See Larraín, *Theories of Development*.
2. Sen, *Development as Freedom*, 3.
3. Sen, *Development as Freedom*, 3.
4. Pillay, "Church and Development," 15.
5. Rist, *History of Development*, 13.

According to Edward J. Martin, Gustavo Gutierrez identifies three critical areas that characterize the failures of development paradigm in the so called Third World countries. First, in Martin's view Gutierrez argues that development is a form of tokenism and does not provide fundamental changes to the structural and systemic dimensions of economic development.[6] Second, Gutierrez states that development is exploitative in its very form because it directs finances and resources to anti-democratic countries under the disguise of ensuring stability.[7] Ultimately, Gutierrez argues that the anti-democratic regimes implement repressive policies that have the propensity to undermine democracy.[8] Third, Gutierrez indicates that development is paternalistic, which means that decisions about what is good or ethical for Latin America and the Third World are not made by those in the periphery or the poor themselves, but by the elites and the so-called developed countries in New York, London, or Bonn.[9]

The effectiveness of development depends on the meaningful participation of communities in decision-making processes. I subscribe to the notion that development as a concept is not inconsequential and can be re-appropriated to advance the interest of those marginalized by it. The concept is not a fundamental problem, however, its appropriation and application is.

The Concept of Space in Participatory Community Development

French theorist Henri Lefebvre argues that space is a social product. It is not simply available as a neutral container waiting to be filled, but is a dynamic, humanly constructed and contested process of control and domination.[10] Lefebvre contends that space is not readily available to those who need it, but linked to a struggle waged through a structural and systematic process of coercion, power, and control. Space is characterized by how time is allocated and utilized as a form of domination. Robin

---

6. Gutierrez, *Theology of Liberation*, 26 cited in Martin, "Liberation Theology," 73.
7. Gutierrez, *Theology of Liberation*, 26, cited in Martin, "Liberation Theology," 73.
8. Gutierrez, *Theology of Liberation*, 26, cited in Martin, "Liberation Theology," 73.
9. Gutierrez, *Theology of Liberation*, 26, cited in Martin, "Liberation Theology," 73.
10. Lefebvre, *Production of Space*, 24.

Petersen argues that time can become a central source of domination.[11] Furthermore, argues Petersen, "the clock dominates not only the factory life, but all of social existence."[12] The power to determine time within a particular space is an indication of power and control, and it is contested.

Space is a politically contested concept in many respects. According to Andrea Cornwall, a space "can be emptied or filled, permeable or sealed; can be an invitation to speak or act. Spaces can also be clamped and closed, voided of meaning, or depopulated as people turn their attention elsewhere."[13] The concept of (contested) space is discussed extensively in this chapter as a contested notion in terms of voices that are privileged in participation, especially with regard to gender and class.[14] Cornwall's description of space underscores Lefebvre's argument that space is a contested notion, subject to appropriation in certain contexts. This, therefore, suggests that there is no universal, generic or homogeneous appropriation of space. Cornwall introduces two concepts of space that contend with each other. There are "invited" (oppressive or controlled) spaces and "invented" (liberated or popular) spaces. In between these two spaces, I argue, "invigorated" spaces facilitate community participation from the invited to invented spaces through a redemptive religious narrative.

Cornwall indicates that "invited" spaces are more durable, taking the shape of irregularized institutions.[15] In this case the government or donors invite the community into a space that is controlled or manipulated, undermining proper deliberations that enable decision-making processes to be implemented. Faranak Miraftab argues that invited spaces are the ones occupied by the grassroots and their allied non-governmental organizations, but which are legitimized and controlled by the donors and government interventions.[16] The elites organizing these spaces are often in cahoots with their allied grassroots organizers, disguised as the vanguard of the working class. Their grassroots allies could be any structure that is manipulated or regulated by the authorities in

11. Petersen, "Time, Resistance and Reconstruction," 238.
12. Petersen, "Time, Resistance and Reconstruction," 240.
13. Cornwall, "Introduction," 1.
14. See Cornwall, "Making a Difference?"; Cornwall and Gaventa, "Bridging the Gap"; Cornwall, "Making Spaces, Changing Places"; Cornwall, "Whose Voices?"; Cornwall, "Introduction"; Cornwall and Brock, "What Do Buzzwords Do for Development Policy?"; and Cornwall and Coelho, *Spaces for Change?*
15. Cornwall, "Introduction," 2.
16. Miraftab, "Invited and Invented Spaces," 1.

the marginalization of the working class. Invited spaces in this context serve the interest of those with close proximity to power and resources in both the public and private spheres. Invited spaces undermine progressive forces and adversely entrench economic and political hegemony that dehumanizes and undermines people's agency and praxis. Invited spaces, characterized by exclusion, deprive the community of the ability to participate in development processes.

Invigorated spaces contend with invited spaces. Invigorated spaces are meant to provide much-needed capacity to members of the working class to challenge their non-participation and exclusion from development processes. The focus of invigorated spaces is capacity-building of those excluded or marginalized by neoliberal development processes. Invigorated spaces contribute to the building of agency within religious and social movements, enabling them to challenge marginalization and exclusion. The invigorated spaces of agency created by the Ujamaa Centre for Biblical and Theological Community Development and Research, the focus of this chapter, contend with invited spaces.[17] The Ujamaa Centre builds resilience among controlled and marginalized working class groups, enabling them to speak prophetically and theologically against their oppressors. These controlled and manipulated groups are recognized and given a voice within the invigorated spaces of participation.

Furthermore, invigorated spaces facilitate the creation of invented spaces of resistance that have the potential to lead to participatory community development. Cornwall argues that the "popular" or "invented" spaces are "those arenas in which people join together often with others like them in collective action, self-help, initiatives or everyday sociality."[18] The invented spaces are created by controlled, manipulated, and marginalized working class groups in the community. These groups include, in terms of the scope of this chapter, but are not limited to, the African Initiated Churches (AICs), social movements, unemployed youth, abused women, the HIV positive, sex workers, the LGBTQI+ community, and those with disability. Organized working class groups in the community

---

17. A Community Development and Research Centre with a Faith Based focus located within the School of Religion, Philosophy and Classics (SRPC) in the College of Humanities at the University of KwaZulu-Natal, Ujamaa critically engages with the dominant theological narratives in the public realm using alternative redemptive theologies of resistance and liberation that promote community participation and development.

18. Cornwall, "Introduction," 76.

engage in collective action, mobilizing other social agents to challenge social, economic, and political injustices in the public realm. Miraftab argues that invented spaces are those that "are occupied by the grassroots and claimed by their collective action by directly confronting the authority and the status quo."[19] These spaces are critical in redefining the concept of development from below.

Invited Spaces: Neoliberal Development

Invited spaces are characterized by contestation between the dominant economic narrative premised on neoliberal development on one hand and people's struggles yearning for economic justice on the other. According to Remy Herrera, the process of development economics is designed to demonstrate that the world's poor economies can progress and develop.[20] The assumption is that these economies are underdeveloped and need to embark on a neoliberal economic trajectory in order to migrate from underdevelopment to development. The world's poor economies are encouraged to adopt new economic strategies to ensure that growth and investment happens. Herrera refers to neoliberalism as the "return to power, that is, by the most powerful (US mainly) world capital owners."[21] Furthermore, Elizabeth Martinez *et al.* define neoliberalism as the set of economic policies that have become widespread during the last three decades.[22] These economic policies have been imposed on a number of developing countries in Africa and Latin America. Both the former and the latter have resisted the imposition of neoliberal economics. The latter being the most radical in challenging the economic atrocities of neoliberalism.

Jorge Larraine states that the beginning of a capitalist economic system dates back to the seventeenth century.[23] Larraine traces the history of capitalist development and the critical theories that shaped it. He provides a detailed account of three important phases, namely the age of competitive capitalism (1700–1860), the age of imperialism

---

19. Miraftab, "Invited and Invented Spaces," 1.
20. Herrera, "The Neoliberal 'Rebirth' of Development Economics," 2.
21. Herrera, "Neoliberal 'Rebirth' of Development Economics," 3.
22. Martinez, "What Is Neoliberalism?" 1.
23. Larraín, *Theories of Development*, 6.

(1860–1945), and late capitalism (1945–today).[24] In each of these phases there is contestation between modernization and dependency theories. The proponents of neo-classical economics within modernization theory, Adam Smith, Walter Rostow, and Talcott Parsons, argue vehemently for a non-interventionist approach to the regulation of the market and the economy.[25]

The proponents of modernization theory popularized concepts like the "big push" and "take off" to persuade developing countries to embrace economic liberalization. The modernization theory articulated by Smith and David Ricardo as the natural and absolute mode of production was challenged by Karl Marx who argued for an alternative socialist economic theory.[26] Marx rejected capitalism as the only natural and absolute economic system for global development. Andre Gunder Frank, influenced in part by Marxian thought, advocated for dependency theory, and subsequently world systems theory, as alternatives to modernization theory.[27] Modernization theory finds expression in neoliberal economic narratives designed to ensure economic growth, investments, and the accumulation of capital through the processes of privatization, deregulation, and trade liberalization. Herrera argues that the "heart of neoclassical economics and the source of its claim to being a science is general equilibrium theory."[28] This theory attempts to show that when every buyer and seller in the marketplace acts out of self-interest, competition will produce a unique set of prices and quantities that will create a perfect match between the supply and demand.[29] The core assumption of this theory is the "trickle down" effect of investment and growth, contributing to unfulfilled promises of a better life for the poor. Neoliberal economic theory maintains that labor secures its fair share of wealth when workers' wages equal their contribution to the product.[30] The rationale is that global markets influenced by aggressive competitiveness will produce adequate wealth for the majority of people on an international scale.[31] Marx-

24. Larraín, *Theories of Development*, 6–8.

25. Smith, *Wealth of Nations*; Rostow, *Process of Economic Growth*; Parsons, *Social System*.

26. Marx, *Capital*.

27. Frank, *Capitalism and Underdevelopment*; Frank, *Critique and Anti-Critique*.

28. Herrera, "Neoliberal 'Rebirth' of Development Economics," 5.

29. Herrera, "Neoliberal 'Rebirth' of Development Economics," 5.

30. Martin, "Liberation Theology," 72.

31. Martin, "Liberation Theology," 72.

ist theory rejected this view, arguing that social relations are intimately connected with forces of production and that the wealth derived from capital through the labor of workers is often unjustly expropriated by the capitalist class.[32] The notion of a fair share of wealth is an elusive and unrealistic proposition within a neoliberal economic paradigm because it is premised on self-interest, greed, and profit maximization.

In order to achieve profit maximization, the neoliberal capitalist economic system requires cheap labor, which is achieved through the exploitation of the working class. Companies often increase working hours without compensation for overtime, flouting labor relations legislation and undermining the needs and rights of the workers in the process. They also tend to adopt capital intensification rather than labor intensification as a method to increase productivity. The management of conglomerate companies privatize the gains and socialize the losses, which contradicts the logic of a fair share of wealth between management and the workers. When companies experience losses, the workers are retrenched as a means to mitigate against the losses.

South Africa was not exempted from the neoliberal economic ideology affecting economies in the Global South. According to Paul Williams and Ian Taylor, "neoliberalism in South Africa became prominent in the ANC pronouncements such as the 1990 Discussion Document on Economic Policy; the 1992 draft policy guidelines; and both the 1994 Reconstruction and Development Programme (RDP) and the 1996 Growth, Employment, and Redistribution (GEAR) programmes."[33] These documents were influenced by the financial processes of the International Monetary Fund (IMF) and the World Bank (WB), aimed at restructuring economies, especially those of the developing countries. Williams et al. underscore that the adoption of GEAR as a neoliberal macro-economic policy framework for South Africa was an imposition from the WB and the IMF respectively.[34] The limited participation of the community in the processes of GEAR suggested a shift in macro-economic policy.[35] Neoliberal economic ideology thrives on self-interest, designed to maximize the accumulation of wealth at the expense of the poor and the vulnerable. This economic ideology resonates with the Western concept

32. Martin, "Liberation Theology," 72.
33. Williams and Taylor, "Neoliberalism and the Political Economy," 22.
34. Williams and Taylor, "Neoliberalism and the Political Economy," 33.
35. See Bond, *Elite Transition*; Bond, *Looting Africa*; and Bond, *Talk Left, Walk Right*.

of individualism and is incompatible with the African spirit of Umuntu umuntu ngabantu (a person is a person because of others). This African idiom finds expression in the redemptive religio-cultural narrative of Contextual Bible Study (CBS) within the invigorated spaces of agency.

Invigorated Spaces: Contextual Bible Study (CBS) Methodology

Invigorated spaces contend with invited spaces through the Contextual Bible Study (CBS) as a tool for social and economic justice. The dialogical methodology of the CBS creates a conducive environment for communal reading of the Bible between the "trained" (socially engaged scholar) and "ordinary" (organic intellectual) readers of the Bible. However, this does not suggest that the collaborative reading is without contestation. It means that the Ujamaa Centre's praxis of Contextual Bible reading is a conduit for participatory community development.

The Ujamaa Centre has been actively contributing to participatory community development from a biblical and theological perspective for the past 30 years in South Africa and abroad. The Centre is overtly committed to social justice and liberation theology as the fundamental principles of the gospel. It works mainly with the marginalized and organized sectors of the community, especially working class religious and social movements. The Contextual Bible Study praxis has been widely used both in the community and within the academy as a tool for social justice and inclusion of the poor and marginalized.[36] The liberation trajectory is evident in the CBS praxis through its dialogical pedagogical process that affirms the role of ordinary readers of the biblical text. This dialogical process of contextual Bible reading enables the community to confront the established powers that marginalize the poor. Furthermore, the CBS process is embedded in the biblical-theological method of See-Judge-Act, developed by Cardinal Joseph Cardjin in the 1930s in Belgium where he was working as a chaplain. There are six important pillars of CBS that contribute to participatory community development.

First, in the CBS process the Bible is read in the community, by the community, and for the community. Participants sing, preach, and pray as

---

36. See Cochrane, *Circles of Dignity*; Haddad, "African Women's Theologies of Survival"; Dube, "Reading for Decolonization"; West, *Academy of the Poor*; and Ukpong, "Parable of the Shrewd Manager."

a community in their homes and places of worship. According to Gerald West, "the CBS always begins with an act of community, whether singing, praying, an icebreaker or some other opportunity to experience a sense of being part of a community."[37] The Bible is owned by the community and not by an individual who is an expert. However, the participants from the community seldom find public spaces where their contribution in recognized.

Second, in the CBS process the Bible is read in the context of the working-class communities who are the oppressed. In 2009, the Ujamaa Centre invited prospective casual laborers who were primarily from the religious and social movements into a CBS workshop and began to read Matthew 20:1–16, the parable of the workers in the vineyard with them. Gerald West and Sithembiso Zwane argue that the Ujamaa Centre "activates the Bible as weapon of struggle for economic liberation, wresting it from the hands of those who use it to stigmatize and blame the unemployed for what is a systemic predicament."[38] This is an important contextual reading of the text with working class religious and social movements affected by structural chronic unemployment and abject poverty.

In his analysis of the socio-economic context of Jewish Palestine, William Herzog argues that "the fact that the agora (marketplace) is filled with day laborers at all hours of the day indicates a situation of high unemployment."[39] Unemployment is not a new phenomenon in our contemporary context but has existed for centuries because of unjust economic systems. According to Marcus Borg, the parable of the workers in the vineyard can be read as a narrative about God's generosity challenging an unjust system.[40] The story reflects various dimensions of economic systems, especially the contestation between socialism and capitalism.

Third, in the CBS process the Bible is a reflection of contestation. West argues that the Bible itself is a site of (class) struggle with competing interests seeking recognition.[41] The CBS in this context is a fundamental socio-economic and theological concept of "struggle" which affirms the

---

37. West, "Do Two Walk Together?," 434.
38. West and Zwane, "Why Are You Sitting There?" 181.
39. Herzog, *Parables as Subversive Speech*, 59.
40. Borg, *Jesus*, 183.
41. West, "Reading With the Marginalized," 241.

God of life against the idols of death.[42] The God of life is concerned with the oppression of the poor and the marginalized.

Fourth, in the CBS process the Bible has always been read critically to encourage the oppressed and marginalized working class to apply socio-historical and literary tools to the (re)reading of biblical texts.[43] Critical reading takes the form of theological discernment as its fundamental component. In the re-reading process, criticality takes into consideration the ideo-theological and political situation of the context, the "behind the text," "on the text," and "in front of the text" processes of reading that analyze issues of class, race, gender, and culture in the interpretive reading process.[44] Criticality means the ability to interrogate the socio-historical context of the text to find resonance with the contemporary context. Criticality creates a conducive environment for meaningful collaboration.

Fifth, in the CBS process the Bible is read collaboratively by both the "ordinary reader" and the "trained reader" in a dialogical interpretive communal process. Both the "ordinary reader" (working class) and the "trained reader" (socially engaged scholar) provide unique experiences in the collaborative contextual reading. The "ordinary reader" brings the experience from below that constitutes an important narrative of the oppressed or marginalized community, while the "trained reader" provides the socio-historical resources to engage with the reality of the oppressed "ordinary reader" of the text in the community. West argues that, "the socially engaged biblical scholar is called to read the Bible with ordinary reader, but not because they need to be conscientized and given interpretations relevant to their context. No, socially engaged biblical scholars are called to collaborate with them because they bring additional interpretive resources which may be of use to the community group."[45] The difference is that biblical scholars who are proponents of liberation hermeneutics understand the importance of participation in building people's agency in the reading process. Therefore, their participation is not a form of domination but rather of collaboration, which provides the basis for participatory community development. The participation of communities

---

42. West, "Reading With the Marginalized," 241.
43. See Nadar, "Beyond the 'Ordinary Reader.'"
44. See West, *Academy of the Poor*.
45. West and Dube, *Bible in Africa*, 601.

in their own development is progressive and significant in changing the status quo.

Sixth, in the CBS process the Bible is read for change and the empowerment of the working class to participate in development processes. The working class communities that "read with" the Ujamaa Centre find comfort in the collaborative reading process as a tool for economic and political participation that is emancipatory and transformative.[46] The invigorated spaces facilitate invented spaces of resistance in subversive re-appropriation of development within the working class AICs and the Abahlali social movement.

Invented Spaces: Re-Appropriating Development

The invigorated spaces that contend with invited spaces facilitate the invented spaces of resistance and protest. The CBS builds biblical and theological capacity and leadership among the AICs and Abahlali, enabling them to challenge dominant narratives of neoliberal economic development. The CBS offers resources to religious and social movements to re-appropriate development from below. The CBS as a tool for socio-economic and theological emancipation contributes to the AIC's and Abahlali's struggle for socio-economic justice. The AICs and Abahlali re-appropriate development through communal religio-cultural and socio-economic practices in the invented spaces.

The AICs in Africa are fast becoming a dominant religious force as more groups emerge in different working-class communities, articulating the importance of their cultural identity in the postcolonial context. It is only in the AICs that one can find a leader working as a gardener, security guard, or a salesperson during the week and as a bishop on Sunday. The AICs represent the black working-class struggle that formed the fundamental basis for a black theology of liberation in South Africa prior to 1994.

According to Itumeleng Mosala, a black theology of liberation has to take into consideration its cultural hermeneutics of struggle from a critical re-appropriation of black culture, just as African theology must consider political hermeneutics that arise from the contemporary social struggles of black people under apartheid capitalism.[47] Mosala's assertion

---

46. West and Dube, *Bible in Africa*, 26.
47. Mosala, "Relevance of African Traditional Religions," 99.

raises the question, What do the AICs offer in terms of a re-appropriation of development in the postcolonial context? In Mosala's argument it is evident that the starting point for black and African liberation hermeneutics is respect for a cultural identity and historical ideology that is progressive and relevant to contemporary African society. However, Mosala is conscious of the fact that not all African traditional cultures and ideologies are progressive and relevant to contemporary society.[48] It is therefore imperative that any cultural or ideological contribution be interrogated and appropriated progressively to advance the interest of the community rather than the individual. Mosala argues that critical to black theology, which includes the AICs, is the "social, cultural, political and economic world of the working class and peasantry."[49] He provides an elaborate contextual reality of the role of black theology as articulated by the AICs within African Traditional Religion (ATR). He advances black hermeneutics as the basis for his class analysis of the AICs resistance against Western capitalist apartheid. The importance of Mosala's analysis is the historical and cultural contribution of the AICs as the principle for challenging Western capitalist apartheid.

However, AICs have evolved and are not homogenous in their approach to resistance. The AICs do not offer a generic cultural response to Western capitalist apartheid, nor do they have similar biblical or theological orientations. The so-called "Messianic" AICs are traditional and do offer conventional cultural approaches to Western capitalist apartheid. The Ethiopians, Spirit, or Zionist type churches combine both traditional and progressive approaches to social, economic and political issues.[50] The common trend among the AICs, which I will use for the purposes of this chapter, is the communal approach, which serves the interest of the community rather than the individual.

For Mosala, AICs use pre-colonial African resources as a sociocultural protest against dominant Western capitalist models.[51] Sibusiso Masondo concurs with Mosala and argues that AICs contribute significantly as preservers, developers, and promoters of African culture.[52]

48. Mosala, "Relevance of African Traditional Religions," 99.

49. Mosala, "Relevance of African Traditional Religions," 21.

50. See Sundkler, *Bantu Prophets in South Africa*; Anderson, "Hermeneutical Process"; Daneel, *African Initiated Churches in Southern Africa*; and Oosthuizen, "African Independent Churches in South Africa."

51. See Mosala, "African Independent Churches (AICs)."

52. Masondo, "African Indigenous Churches," 7.

I concur with both Mosala and Masondo that the AICs, especially the "Messianic" ones, can use their cultural identity and history as a weapon against economic and political imperialism imposed by Western apartheid capitalism. Masondo argues that AICs, like Shembe and Lekganyana, utilize African resources for the development of their people.[53] These African resources include, but are not limited to, traditional medicines that mitigate against sickness and dark forces. Western practices disguised as development tend to trivialize the role of indigenous knowledge systems generated by these churches complementing Western medical methods. The AICs are still among the few religious institutions that encourage communal sharing of social and economic resources, which build communities. They contribute meaningfully to the processes of decolonization. They organize and participate actively in *izitokufela* (communal savings clubs), ilima (communal agricultural practices), and *omasingcwabisane* (communal burial societies) in the community. These socio-economic and cultural practices underscore the importance of communal participation in development processes.

The AICs in their different formations contribute to a re-appropriation of development by challenging the dominant religious discourses that advocate for a prosperity gospel in the midst of unemployment, poverty, and inequality. The AICs in partnership with Ujamaa Centre, argue that the book of Acts 4:32–37 offers a subversive re-appropriation of development, premised in a socialist understanding of participatory community development.[54] Religion in this context is a public good that challenges the neoliberal capitalist ideology of self-interest. In this context, religion is redemptive and not the "opium of the people," as Marx argued.

The AICs concept of development is also articulated through their role in strengthening democracy and social cohesion in the public realm. These churches have been used as sites for education and democracy. Phillip Öhlmann *et al.* conducted a study among the AICs which indicates that they contribute to community relief, feeding schemes and donations, counseling for people living with HIV and AIDS, and youth services and education.[55] Such a contribution is often assumed to come from mainline churches as part of their diaconal projects. In this case,

---

53. Masondo, "African Indigenous Churches," 7.
54. West and Zwane, "Why Are You Sitting There?," 182.
55. Öhlmann, Frost, and Gräb, "African Initiated Churches," 7.

it is the AICs who are providing communal support to the community from their own limited resources, redefining the concept of development.

Öhlmann et al. believe that AICs understanding of development is conceptualized and expressed through their lived experiences of unemployment and poverty as existential problems in people's daily lives.[56] These existential needs that AICs are responding to in the community are the challenges imposed by the failures of development.[57] Furthermore, Öhlmann et al. argue that the AICs receive inadequate recognition as development actors but are active in development-related activities in many ways.[58] The AIC's lived experiences offers a unique reflection and analysis on the challenges of unemployment and poverty created by a capitalist economic system. Barbara Bompani states that AICs might not be active in the national political landscape like mainline churches, but they are actively involved at a local level.[59] The traditional economic and cultural ethos of the AICs contributes significantly to contemporary re-appropriation of development through a redemptive cultural, religious and socio-economic narrative. Like the AICs, the role of social movements in the processes of re-appropriating development is fundamental.

Abahlali Basemjondolo[60]

Social movements have contributed immensely to the South African political landscape, strengthening democracy and social development. Movements such as the Jubilee Campaign, the Treatment Action Campaign (TAC), the Anti-Privatization Forum (APF), the National Association of People Living with HIV (NAPWA), and the Rural Network (RN) have contributed to re-appropriation of development.

In this chapter I will draw from the activist work of Abahlali based in Durban, South Africa. Abahlali have used their activism to challenge authorities and unjust systems through various forms of resistance. The invasion of the Abahlali's space ignited a sense of solidarity among the

---

56. Öhlmann, Frost, and Gräb, "African Initiated Churches," 9.

57. See Bompani, "African Independent Churches in Post-Apartheid South Africa"; Bompani, "Religion and Development from Below."

58. Bompani, "Religion and Development from Below," 9.

59. Bompani, "African Independent Churches in Post-Apartheid South Africa," 4.

60. A Shackdwellers Social Movement based at Kennedy Road in Durban, KwaZulu-Natal, South Africa.

movement members, characterized by the philosophy of Ubuhlali, which advocates for human dignity in the midst of indignity. Nigel Gibson argues that, "Abahlali represents a new stage of poor people's politics marked by the principle that the poor can think critically."[61] Abahlali Basemjondolo can be characterized as organic intellectuals capable of articulating their ideological position against any form of domination and exclusion. Antonio Gramsci's analysis of the term intellectual indicates that every social group has the ability to create their own identity and ideology, which gives it homogeneity.[62]

According to Richard Pithouse, Nigel Gibson ascribed the general ideological collapse of the ANC partly to their failure to develop a radical intellectual praxis matching the challenges of the democratic transition.[63] Pithouse concurs with Gibson about the ANC's inability to protect the marginalized and vulnerable in the postcolonial dispensation as the contributing factor to its ideological capitulation. Patrick Heller lamented the vanguardism of the ANC and argued that "a once strong social movement sector has been incorporated or marginalized by the ANC's political hegemony."[64] Despite constant post-liberation state repression, Abahlali remained resolute against the economic and political empire that consistently marginalized and violently harassed their members at Kennedy Road.

According to Pithouse, Abahlali confronted repression, violence and illegal evictions from their shacks in the Kennedy Road location where most members in Durban are residents.[65] Bhattacharya and Jairath argue that social movements are a force to express the voice of the people against the ruling authority.[66] Furthermore, Bhattacharya et al. argue that such a social movement "contributes to people's praxis, which is a process of building people's power for development as an alternative to the existing dominant power, that is, the elite praxis."[67] The CBS Praxis becomes a tool for people's movements like Abahlali to engage in dialogue with the authorities as a conduit to deconstruct and transform oppressive

61. Gibson, *Fanonian Practices in South Africa*, 222.
62. See Gramsci, "The Intellectuals"; Gramsci, "Hegemony, Intellectuals and the State."
63. Pithouse, "Abahlali Basemjondolo," 244–45.
64. Heller, "Moving the State," 159.
65. Pithouse, "Abahlali Basemjondolo," 260–1.
66. Bhattacharya and Jairath, "Social Movements," 303.
67. Bhattacharya and Jairath, "Social Movements," 304.

structures and systems of power and control.[68] Praxis is an instrument of reflection and action that creates a conducive environment for persons unjustly dealt with, deprived of their voice, and cheated at work, to challenge their oppression.[69] Bhattacharya et al. state that "the inherent power in these movements, in any act of resistance to structures of power, opens up political spaces of contention."[70] Both the AICs and Abahlali offer re-appropriation of development from below through redemptive cultural, religious, and socio-economic resistance.

The Land and Human Dignity Campaign Project

Abahlali are affected by socio-economic injustices, especially the critical issue of access to land in South Africa. They are deprived of land especially in the urban areas where they reside as workers. The contestation between Abahlali and the Thekwini Metropolitan Municipality is primarily on the issue of land and housing (human settlement). The indignity of the shacks ("informal settlement") that they are subjected to attest to their economic marginalization. The irony of this economic marginalization, argues Pithouse, is that there is a deliberate attempt to regulate the movement of poor Africans into the city, contributing to the increase in building of shacks as a form of resistance by social movements.[71] Social movements have been organizing communities of the working class poor to participate in the Human Dignity of Shack Dwellers Campaign Project, aimed at boycotting local government elections. They organize an annual campaign entitled "Unfreedom Day," lamenting the post-1994 situation of the working poor. This campaign coincides with South Africa's Freedom Day, which is April 27. The Municipality has tried in vain to discourage Abahlali's campaign for social and economic justice for the past two decades. Pithouse argues that the Municipality uses colonial and apartheid spatial design strategies in the building of houses for the poor, forcing people to relocate away from the city and their places of work.[72] The dominant narrative is that Abahlali refuses to occupy the houses allocated to them by the Municipality. This propaganda creates a

68. See Freire, *Pedagogy of the Oppressed*.
69. Freire, *Pedagogy of the Oppressed*, 50.
70. Bhattacharya and Jairath, "Social Movements," 303–4.
71. Pithouse, "Abahlali Basemjondolo," 107.
72. Pithouse, "Abahlali Basemjondolo," 107.

perception that social movements are counter revolutionaries, refusing to cooperate with the political leadership of the Municipality.

Abahlali are offering an alternative perspective through the building and mobilization of social movements to challenge the government's policy narrative on land reform, especially in the local government. Social movements like Abahlali are mobilizing like-minded progressive forces to challenge apartheid legislations that deprive the majority of black working-class access to land and human dignity in rural and urban areas. Edward Lahiff argues that "the negotiated transition to democracy in South Africa (1990–1994) left much power and wealth of the white minority, including land ownership intact."[73] The land question in South Africa is both historical and ideological in nature. The white minority continues to own large parcels of land, while the black majority remain landless in their own country of birth. The post-1994 socio-economic context indicates that 86 percent of total agricultural land is in the hands of white people in South Africa.[74] The Ingonyama Trust in the state of KwaZulu-Natal regulates the remaining land.[75] The Ingonyama Trust Act deals with the administration of land on behalf of its members in the tribes and rural communities under the King of the Zulu Nation. Both Abahlali and the Rural Network social movements are part of the KwaZulu-Natal urban and rural land respectively. Abahlali are campaigning for access to urban land for human settlement while the Rural Network seeks to protect rural land for agricultural and residential purposes.

These social movements have influenced land policy reform beyond their respective rural and urban communities. They made submissions on land expropriation without compensation, contributing to the amendments of section 25 of the Constitution of South Africa. The presidential advisory panel on land reform appointed by President Cyril Ramaphosa has re-affirmed the failures of the previous "willing buyer, willing seller policy" of the government.[76] Due to these failures, the panel recommended that the government must ensure equitable redistribution of land through a diversified land redistribution program.[77] Abahlali and the Rural Network have been advocating for land reform for the past ten

73. Lahiff, "Willing Buyer, Willing Seller," 1578.

74. Lahiff, "Willing Buyer, Willing Seller," 1578.

75. See Center for Law and Society: Rural Women's Action Research Programme, "Land Rights"; Juda-Chembe, "The Ingonyama Trust."

76. "Final Report," 52.

77. "Final Report," 52.

years in South Africa. The recommendations of the panel are a step in the right direction in terms of land reform. The struggles of Abahlali and other social movements like the Rural Network contributed immensely towards these progressive recommendations by the Presidential advisory panel on land reform and agriculture. The recommendations of the panel indicate that there will be a fundamental change in policy as a result of the mobilization and submission made to the advisory panel by social movements.

Abahlali are forming collaborative networks and solidarity groups based on a fundamental need for social and economic justice. During the Apartheid era, communities were united against a common enemy, which was an illegitimate colonial government that polarized society based on racial supremacy. Similarly, contemporary social movements are in solidarity against the minorities occupying large parcels of land, depriving the majority access to land. The hierarchical binaries of male and female, white and black, rich and poor, literate and illiterate are evident in the ownership of land in South Africa post 1994.

Conclusion

The CBS as an ideo-theological praxis invokes religious resilience and resistance among the AICs and Abahlali. The dominant religio-cultural and socio-economic narratives imbedded in the invited spaces of neoliberal development are interrogated in the subversive process of re-appropriating development. The participatory CBS process invigorates spaces of agency and resilience among the AICs and Abahlali, enabling them to speak theologically and prophetically to oppressive structures. The biblical and theological conceptual contribution of the CBS facilitate invented spaces of resistance, disrupting conventional religio-cultural and socio-economic development that undermines community participation.

Bibliography

Anderson, A. "The Hermeneutical Process of Pentecostal-Type African Initiated Churches (AICs) in South Africa." *Missionalia* 24.2 (1996) 171–85.

Bhattacharya, Niloshree, and Vinod K. Jairath. "Social Movements, 'Popular' Spaces, and Participation: A Review." *Sociological Bulletin* 61 (2012) 299–319.

Bompani, Barbara. "African Independent Churches in Post-Apartheid South Africa: New Political Interpretations." *Journal of Southern African Studies* 34 (2008) 665–77.

———. "Religion and Development from Below: Independent Christianity in South Africa." *Journal of Religion in Africa* 40 (2010) 307–30.

Bond, Patrick. *Elite Transition: From Apartheid to Neoliberalism in South Africa.* Scottsville, South Africa: University of KwaZulu-Natal Press, 2005.

———. *Looting Africa: The Economics of Exploitation.* New York: Palgrave Macmillan, 2006.

———. *Talk Left, Walk Right: South Africa's Frustrated Global Reforms.* Scottsville, South Africa: University of Kwa-Zulu-Natal Press, 2004.

Borg, Marcus J. *Jesus: Uncovering the Life, Teachings, and Relevance of a Religious Revolutionary.* San Francisco: HarperSanFrancisco, 2006.

Center for Law and Society: Rural Women's Action Research Programme. "Land Rights under the Ingonyama Trust." 2015. http://www.cls.uct.ac.za/usr/lrg/downloads/FactsheetIngonyama_Final_Feb2015.pdf.

Cochrane, James R. *Circles of Dignity: Community Wisdom and Theological Reflection.* Minneapolis: Fortress, 1999.

Cornwall, Andrea. "Introduction: New Democratic Spaces? The Politics and Dynamics of Institutionalised Participation." *IDS Bulletin* 35.2 (April 2004) 1–10.

———. "Making a Difference? Gender and Participatory Development." Institute of Development Studies. https://www.ids.ac.uk/publications/making-a-difference-gender-and-participatory-development.

———. "Making Spaces, Changing Places: Situating Participation in Development." Institute of Development Studies. https://www.ids.ac.uk/publications/making-spaces-changing-places-situating-participation-in-development.

———. "Whose Voices? Whose Choices? Reflections on Gender and Participatory Development." *World Development* 31 (2003) 1325–42.

Cornwall, Andrea, and Karen Brock. "What Do Buzzwords Do for Development Policy? A Critical Look at 'Participation,' 'Empowerment' and 'Poverty Reduction.'" *Third World Quarterly* 26 (2005) 1043–60.

Cornwall, Andrea, and Vera Schattan P. Coelho, eds. *Spaces for Change? The Politics of Citizen Participation in New Democratic Arenas.* Claiming Citizenship 4. London: Zed, 2007.

Cornwall, Andrea, and John Gaventa. "Bridging the Gap: Citizenship, Participation and Accountability." *PLA Notes* 40, January 1, 2001.

Daneel, M. L. *African Initiated Churches in Southern Africa: Protest Movements or Mission Churches?* Boston: African Studies Center, Boston University, 2000.

Dube, Musa W. "Reading for Decolonization (John 4:1–42)." *Semeia* 75 (1996) 37–59.

"Final Report of the Presidential Advisory Panel on Land Reform and Agriculture." South African Government. https://www.gov.za/sites/files/gcis/documents/201907/panelreportlandreform_1pdf.

Frank, Andre Gunder. *Capitalism and Underdevelopment in Latin America: Historical Studies of Chile and Brazil.* New York: Monthly Review, 1969.

———. *Critique and Anti-Critique: Essays on Dependence and Reformism.* New York: Praeger, 1984.

Freire, Paulo. *Pedagogy of the Oppressed.* London: Bloomsbury Academic, 2000.

Gibson, Nigel C. *Fanonian Practices in South Africa: From Steve Biko to Abahlali BaseMjondolo*. New York: Palgrave Macmillan, 2011.
Gramsci, Antonio. "Hegemony, Intellectuals and the State." In *Cultural Theory and Popular Culture*, edited by John Storey, 69–75. New York: Prentice Hall, 1997.
———. "The Intellectuals." In *Contemporary Sociological Thought*, edited by Sean P. Hier, 108–237. Toronto: Canadian Scholars, 2005.
Gutiérrez, Gustavo. *A Theology of Liberation: History, Politics, and Salvation*. Translated and edited by Sister Caridad Inda and John Eagleson. Maryknoll, NY: Orbis, 1973.
Haddad, Beverly. "African Women's Theologies of Survival: Intersecting Faith, Feminism, and Development." University of KwaZulu-Natal Press, 2000.
Heller, Patrick. "Moving the State: The Politics of Democratic Decentralization in Kerala, South Africa, and Porto Alegre." *Politics & Society* 29 (2001) 131–63.
Herrera, Rémy. "The Neoliberal 'Rebirth' of Development Economics." *Monthly Review* 58 (May 2006). https://monthlyreview.org/2006/05/01/the-neoliberal-rebirth-of-development-economics/.
Herzog, William R., II. *Parables as Subversive Speech: Jesus as Pedagogue of the Oppressed*. Louisville: Westminster John Knox, 1994.
Jerry Pillay. "The Church and Development in the New South Africa: Towards a Theology of Development." PhD diss., University of Cape Town, 2000.
Juda-Chembe, Phyllis Kedibone. "The Ingonyama Trust and Its Implications for Rural Women Regarding Land Acquisition: Sizani Ngubane Responds to Kedibone Chembe." *Agenda* 32.4 (2018) 90–95.
Lahiff, Edward. "'Willing Buyer, Willing Seller': South Africa's Failed Experiment in Market-Led Agrarian Reform." *Third World Quarterly* 28 (2007) 1577–97.
Larraín, Jorge. *Theories of Development: Capitalism, Colonialism, and Dependency*. Cambridge, MA: Polity, 1989.
Lefebvre, Henri. *The Production of Space*. Translated by Donald Nicholson-Smith. Democracy and Urban Landscapes. Cambridge, MA: Blackwell, 1991.
Marx, Karl. *Capital: A Critique of Political Economy*. Translated by Ben Fowkes. New York: Vintage, 1977.
Masondo, Sibusiso T. "The African Indigenous Churches' Spiritual Resources for Democracy and Social Cohesion." *Verbum et Ecclesia* 35.3 (2014) 1–8.
Martin, Edward J. "Liberation Theology, Sustainable Development, and PostModern Public Administration." *Latin American Perspectives* 30.4 (2003) 69–91.
Miraftab, F. "Invited and Invented Spaces of Participation: Neoliberal Citizenship and Feminists' Expanded Notion of Politics." *Wagadu* 1 (Spring 2004) 1–7.
Mosala, Itumeleng. "African Independent Churches (AICs): A Study of Socio-Theological Protest." In *Resistance & Hope, South African Essays in Honour of Beyers Naude*, edited by John W. de Gruchy and Charles Villa Vicencio, 103–11. Grand Rapids: Eerdmans, 1985.
———. "The Relevance of African Traditional Religions and Their Challenge to Black Theology." In *The Unquestionable Right to Be Free: Essays in Black Theology*, edited by Itumeleng J. Mosala and Buti Tlhagale, 91–112. Johannesburg: Skotaville, 1986.
Nadar, Sarojini. "Beyond the 'Ordinary Reader' and the 'Invisible Intellectual': Shifting Contextual Bible Study from Liberation Discourse to Liberation Pedagogy." *Old Testament Essays* 22 (2009) 384–403. http://www.scielo.org.za/pdf/ote/v22n2/09.pdf.

Öhlmann, Philipp, Marie-Luise Frost, and Wilhelm Gräb. "African Initiated Churches' Potential as Development Actors." *HTS Teologiese Studies/Theological Studies* 72.4 (2016) 1–12. https://hts.org.za/index.php/hts/article/view/3825/8883.

Oosthuizen, G. C. "The African Independent Churches in South Africa: A History of Persecution Proselytism in Religion-Specific Perspective." *Emory International Law Review* 14 (2000) 1089–120.

Parsons, Talcott. *The Social System*. London: Routledge, 1991.

Petersen, Robin Mills. "Time, Resistance and Reconstruction: Rethinking Kairos Theology." PhD diss., University of Chicago, 1995.

Richard Pithouse. "Abahlali Basemjondolo and the Struggle for the City of Durban in South Africa." *Cidades* 6.9 (2009).

Rist, Gilbert. *The History of Development: From Western Origins to Global Faith*. New York: Zed, 2008.

Rostow, W. W. *The Process of Economic Growth*. Oxford: Clarendon, 1960.

Sen, Amartya. *Development as Freedom*. New York: Knopf, 1999.

Smith, Adam. *The Wealth of Nations*. Middletown, DE: Shine Classics, 2014.

Sundkler, Bengt. *Bantu Prophets in South Africa*. London: Lutterworth, 1948.

Ukpong, Justin S. "The Parable of the Shrewd Manager (Luke 16:1–13): An Essay in Inculturation Biblical Hermeneutic." *Semeia* 73 (1996) 189–210.

West, Gerald O. *The Academy of the Poor: Towards a Dialogical Reading of the Bible*. Interventions 2. Sheffield: Sheffield Academic, 1999.

———. "Do Two Walk Together? Walking with the Other through Contextual Bible Study." *Anglican Theological Review* 93 (2011) 431–49.

———. "Reading With the Marginalized, the Value/s of Contextual Bible Reading." *Stellenbosch Theological Journal* 1 (2015) 235–61.

West, Gerald O., and Musa W. Dube Shomanah, eds. *The Bible in Africa: Transactions, Trajectories, and Trends*. Leiden: Brill, 2000.

West, Gerald, and Sithembiso Zwane. "'Why Are You Sitting There?': Reading Matthew 20:1–16 in the Context of Casual Workers in Pietermaritzburg, South Africa." In *Matthew*, edited by Nicole W. Duran and James P. Grimshaw, 175–88. Texts@ Contexts. Minneapolis: Fortress, 2013.

"What Is Neoliberalism?" *Corpwatch*. https://corpwatch.org/article/what-neoliberalism.

Williams, Paul, and Ian Taylor. "Neoliberalism and the Political Economy of the 'New' South Africa." *New Political Economy* 5 (2000) 21–40.

12

Transcendence in the Time of Neoliberalism

A Theological Reflection on the Employer–Employee Relationship and the Theological Struggle for Everyday Life

KARL JAMES E. VILLARMEA

IN THE CURRENT NEOLIBERAL order, the politico-juridical Employer–Employee Relationship (EmRel) is the most prominent material and consequential operation of transcendence. Under the Philippine constitution and jurisprudence, EmRel defines the nature and parameters of labor work. In other words, it operates and functions as the sovereign power over workers.

This sovereign power operates more significantly, however, as an economic procedure that has become the primary feature of neoliberalism that exposes workers to the zone of bare life (Giorgio Agamben). In a world where work is *a priori* to basic commodities, the operation of EmRel assumes therefore transcendental importance to survival and flourishing, and in this particular respect, acquires theological significance.

Thus the theological wager of this chapter is this: a theological analysis of EmRel allows us to understand better the material operation of the system that makes death come too soon for many (Gustavo Gutierrez) and through which we can imagine new horizons of theological engagement at present.

Theology, Labor, and the Everyday Life: An Introduction

I commenced in the writing of this chapter on the day that the Silliman University Faculty Association (SUFA), the sole and exclusive bargaining unit in the university for the faculty, sat down at the negotiation table to negotiate for a supplemental CBA (Collective Bargaining Agreement) for the next two School Years, 2019–2020 and 2020–2021, with the Administration of Silliman University. First signed in 2017, this supplemental CBA is a necessary feature of the labor law in order to account for inflationary rates and other factors that might not have been considered previously but are now necessary for the well-being and welfare of workers. While supplemental, this is thus equally important and essential.

As part of SUFA's Negotiating Panel, this is a most important and critical time for me and the union. I consider the task of negotiating on behalf of all faculty for what is just and fair a sacred task. Negotiated terms from this negotiation have transcendental value for members of the Collective Bargaining Unit (CBU). The condition of life for the faculty for the next two years will depend on the negotiated benefits. Based on our most recent experience that led us to stage a strike for three days in July 2017, this kind of negotiation can last for several months if not for over a year. It was not easy—and will not ever be. Negotiation for a new or supplemental CBA demands a lot from members of the negotiating panel. In addition to time, this process entails emotional, spiritual, mental, and physical rigor as this requires marathon meetings, multiple mediation and conciliation processes, crunching figures and analysis of the environment, and colossal amounts of patience and self-control in order to maintain a conducive and decent atmosphere for the negotiating parties.

Indeed, I write this theological reflection not in a vacuum but in a world of worries and struggles. In this particular time and space, I am not only a teacher and theologian but also a laboring animal (Hannah Arendt) who happens to also represent and negotiate on behalf of the rank and file faculty members of Silliman University for better living and working conditions. So I labor to write and to think not simply to fulfill duties, professional or otherwise, but to respond to and be responsible to others and to the world. Echoing what feminist theologian Rosemary Radford Ruether described many years ago as the "use of intelligence,"[1] I reflect not just to understand and represent the world but to reflect so that I can (re)orient my thinking to the *praxis* of transformation toward the flourishing of the common and shared life.

In this chapter, I do this reflection by way of looking closely at what I have observed in the labor world, an operation that many also describe as transcendence, namely, the Employer–Employee Relationship (EmRel henceforth). As a theologian, this operation strikes me immediately—as I will discuss below—as theological not simply because of its terminology but primarily because its basic feature and operation correspond to the idea of sovereignty of God in classical theology. In my mind, this deserves a closer look because it seems it can provide important insights for *orthopraxis* (right practice) not only for labor organizers but also for theologians. As I try to demonstrate below, this theological analysis is particularly important for union/labor work, for this allows organizers to understand better the role of faith in labor justice; and this theological analysis on the experience of labor workers is essential to contemporary theology in its constructive and emancipatory task.

Here, my personal circumstances provide initial materials for this reflection as they become subsequent sources for insight and orientation to my work as a union leader and as a theologian. Thus I situate this theological reflection on transcendence not in terms of its philosophical or literary or theological currency but based on my material situation where transcendence is deeply implicated and concretely interwoven with my own life and all workers (the proverbial 99 percent). I do not approach the transcendent as it is typically approached in the debate of post-secularity nor even in the current landscape of the field of philosophy of religion. Instead, I situate it in its sociological dimension as also indicated by Carl Schmitt in his famous thesis: "All significant concepts of the modern theory of the state are secularized theological concepts, not only because of their historical development—in which they were transferred from theology to the theory of the state, whereby, for example, the omnipotent God became the omnipotent lawgiver—but also because of their systematic structure, the recognition of which is necessary for a *sociological consideration of these concepts*."[2] In short, I locate theology in

---

1. Ruether, *Sexism and God-Talk*.

2. Schmitt, *Political Theology*, 36 (italics mine). This transfer, while particularly referring to the concept of sovereignty—"The omnipotent God became the omnipotent

its sociological incarnation, and more particularly, through its political theology articulation. As a union leader, I localize it further in the sphere where I experience its most intense manifestation and concrete operation: in the reality and experience of workers.

Employer–Employee Relationship: Transcendence

During our annual Labor Education Day in 2017, our resource speaker who also happens to be our Union (SUFA) lawyer, reminded us that the Grievance Mechanism as provided for in the Labor Code only works when the parties involved are legally established through a relationship. This is the first and sole determination before anything else is considered. According to him, this relationship is the relationship between an employer and employee, commonly known as EmRel. In this relationship, neither party determines or can determine what the status of the relationship is or what the respective parties say it should be. This relationship is a fact of law, defined and prescribed by law.

The topic that concerned us during this LED (Labor Education Day) was how to determine the help or the kind of advice to be extended to any request of assistance from workers who are not necessarily members of the Union. So what our lawyer was saying was that any complaint (using the Grievance Mechanism as an example) was only valid and legitimate under the Labor Code if the complainant fell under the prescription and definition of an employee. In other words, the validity of a complaint to seek redress of a labor issue against an employer depends on the status of the complainant in relation to Employer–Employee Relationship. While this is already enlightening, the theological significance of this relationship occurred to me a year later when this relationship between employer and employee was discussed as a topic itself in a seminar I attended.

At the end of November 2018, I attended a three-day seminar on Labor Law, organized by the University of the Philippines, in the School of Labor and Industrial Relations. Here a well-known labor lawyer argued that in labor law, there is one legal principle that determines the standard or the conditions of employment. This is the Employer–Employee Relationship. According to him, this relationship establishes the legal and contractual obligations between the employer and employee,

---

lawgiver," can also be understood as migration, or theologically put, the outpouring of substance into another, *kenosis*.

and thus effectively, it is the legal basis for what creates the conditions in employment. It provides the legal ground and umbrella cover for all other terms and parameters of employment. Simply put, this relationship defines and prescribes the status of employment. For this reason, this is considered a transcendental relationship in labor law.

Truth be told, what first got my attention in this presentation is the word transcendence that describes and qualifies the Employer–Employee Relationship. As a theologian, the word does not only ring a bell but it also signals theological things that imply many of its first principles in the field of epistemology and ethics—just like in labor law. Moreover, as explained by the presenter, the concept itself as employed in the legal world implies regulative and normative principles, which at the same time are productive operations that result in the production and categorization of juridical subjects, which in this particular case are workers and employees. And more intriguing for me is the idea that, like in theology, transcendence in labor law signifies terms of possibilities particularly as they relate to human life by way of its operation.

In the end, this encounter led me to probe transcendence as understood in Philippine jurisprudence via a theological investigation in order to explore and confirm my initial hunch that this could offer new insights to the work in labor organizing and theology in the time of neoliberalism.

Transcendence and Power in the Social World: When Theology Incarnates in the Material World

As a theologian, I usually place the discussion of transcendence in the field of epistemology; particularly, I consider it within the binary frame of transcendence-immanence defined within a space-time continuum. Or to put it in the postmodern rendering of Robyn Horner that puts this binary relationship in a non-separate schema: "transcendence is always in the transcendence-in-immanence."[3] In short, epistemologically, transcendence is always part of and interwoven in the question of immanence.

In terms of its epistemological value, I deem transcendence as that which exceeds our conceptual control. It is that which we cannot grasp. Or to put it directly in its theological significance: it is the mystical, out of reach in terms of experience and what exceeds reason. Or as Hans Schwarz

---

3. Horner, "Betrayal of Transcendence," 61.

puts it: "Everything that cannot be the object of experience belongs to transcendence, including everything that cannot enter consciousness through sense experience."[4] In other words, I count transcendence as an epistemological repository of all that is beyond or outside; and therefore its primary significance resides in this qualification in the field of epistemology, which has deep significance and profound consequence for theology.

Transcendence, however, cannot simply and exclusively belong to the field of epistemology, nor its specific formulation in theology. We learn from the theoretical schema of Michel Foucault that knowledge is always interwoven with power. It is a product of a configuration of power and it produces the same for and in the social world. Knowledge represents and reproduces social investments, economic interests, political agendas, and cultural practices. In short, it is not separate from the operation of power. As Foucault puts it: "Power produces knowledge," in the specific sense that, "(p)ower and knowledge directly imply one another; that there is no power relation without the correlative constitution of a field of knowledge, nor any knowledge that does not presuppose and constitute at the same time power relations."[5]

While this is evident in all areas of the social world, the knowledge/power coupling is more interesting and illuminating when cast in the Judeo-Christian biblical tradition. For it is here that we see transcendence not only as part of the operation of power but it is also, decisively, allied with legitimate and legitimizing power. According to Schwarz, in this tradition, transcendence is associated with power, or more precisely, God's mighty power.[6] As further intensified in the Reformed tradition, it is closely identified with the sovereignty of God. Transcendence is linked with legitimate and legitimating power in the highest order. It is deeply-intertwined with and implicated in the highest source of power. Transcendence, in short, has its maximum potential and highest potency in the Christian tradition.[7]

Many contemporary theologians have found this situation acutely problematic; not only because of its epistemological implications but also because of its theological-political consequences. Knowledge bound with

4. Schwarz, "Transcendence," 56.
5. Foucault, *Foucault Reader*, 175.
6. Schwarz, "Transcendence," 56.
7. As this discussion indicates, this genealogy is limited to the tradition of Augustinian-Latin thought.

sovereign power in the highest order only seems to produce totalitarian and anti-democratic politics. Historically, this became the basis of a deeply hierarchical-monarchical social order and ecclesiological structures that have only established patterns of unjust human relationships and tyrannical institutions.

Thus, in recent years, postmodern theological thinkers have softened the force and efficacy of this transcendence/power coupling. Horner, for instance, puts this sensibility in this way, "transcendence is...that which will not yield a content or a determination but which, nevertheless, *affects* us."[8] Perhaps in their attempt to reimagine the God differently, postmodern theological thinkers try to dissociate traditional attributes of power and transcendence from God. Or, in their attempt to think ethical life and democratic politics differently, they disassociate any legitimate and legitimating power with knowledge/God.

What is also important in the genealogical account of this chapter is the way in which transcendence/power remains operative and how the Christian paradigm provides us with thought-patterns through which to think and understand the efficacy and the effect of it to the social world. As I will demonstrate below, employing the theoretical schema of political theology, the material operation of transcendence in the world remains potent. Its power remains efficacious. Indeed, its historical and genealogical roots anchored in the biblical tradition remain effective and lethal in the present. Transcendence is not simply an "outside, beyond, unknown/uncontrollable, mystery," which Regina Schwartz also rightly observes, has been "beyond question, beyond critique," and in whose name, she claims, "crimes have been committed."[9] Transcendence is also, importantly, a concrete operation of power. Nothing illustrates this point better than the experience and situation of workers in the current neoliberal order. Transcendence and its associated power is incarnated and made operational in the juridical principle of Employer–Employee Relationship (EmRel). In the world of workers, this is the "beyond question, beyond critique" principle and in whose name "crimes have been committed" against workers.

---

8. Horner, "Betrayal of Transcendence," 76 (italics mine).
9. Schwartz, "Introduction," vii.

Transcendence/Power in the World of Workers

Nothing in the world of workers better embodies the coupling of transcendence/power in the traditional attribute of the transcendental power of God than EmRel. Source of legitimate and legitimating power, it is the juridical principle that determines all other legal principles related to employment and defines the parameters of work for workers. In the world of workers, EmRel is the transcendental legal principle ("beyond question, beyond critique") whose power encompasses and shapes their life-world. It defines and qualifies their lives. It is the condition that conditions their condition.

In Philippine jurisprudence, the transcendental relationship of employer–employee as a legal principle is embedded in the Labor Code where it is enshrined to primarily define and qualify employment. According to one of the foremost Filipino legal luminaries in the field of labor law, Cesario A. Azucena Jr., under Book III of the Labor Code, a condition of employment is operational and effective if "there exists between the parties *the relationship of employer and employee.*"[10] In other words, it is the underlying and qualifying principle of law. For this reason, in the legal circle, the relationship of employer–employee is commonly known as the transcendental relationship. It is the across-the-board legal ground that establishes the terms and parameters as it is also the enabling legal principle for the determination of the kind of employment workers have or will have under the law.

Moreover, according to Azucena, the relationship does not only bind legally but also creates legal "obligations related to social security, workmen's compensation, security of tenure, and unionization, and, of course, the benefits under Title I of . . . Book III."[11] That is, it makes employers legally obligated to the employees in particular and to the relationship in general. It imposes legal commitments to employer. In other words, it is a performative legal principle; a law that has also its own enabling mechanism that binds employers and employees to a legal relationship.

Put differently, EmRel is the legitimate and legitimating power that at the same time is the enabling power of the conditions of employment. What this concretely means is that the legal or the non-legal status of the worker as employee ultimately depends on his or her relationship to EmRel, whether he or she is part or not-part of the relationship. Under

10. Azucena, *Everyone's Labor Code*, 76 (emphasis mine).
11. Azucena, *Everyone's Labor Code*, 76.

this juridical order, EmRel qualifies his or her status as worker. This is the transcendence in labor law in whose name crimes against workers are committed.

Evidenced in the movement of EnDo (end of contractualization), the qualification of the definition of terms of employment for employees is vital to their lifeline.[12] It literally means their life and death. On the one hand, employment under EmRel guarantees that one has statutory benefits, which protect workers from calamitous events (i.e., health, changes in life circumstances, etc.) and security of tenure that ensures sustainability of livelihood and all other benefits necessary and indispensable to a meaningful and comfortable life. Under EmRel, while not an economic insurance of a good and abundant life, there is at least a legal guarantee of basic human rights afforded to workers that enhance their ability to demand better economic arrangements. This guarantee provides the necessary *a priori* condition for succeeding possibilities, i.e., the capacity to provide basic commodities to family, etc.

On the other hand, in the current economic order, not to be part of EmRel is to expose one's life to harsher conditions. Outside of the employment condition of EmRel, employees are most vulnerable to debilitating economic forces. Existential and physical well-being is always under threat under this condition. In the "enchanted world,"[13] this is akin to being outside the sphere of God or membership of the church, which offers protection from demonic forces that bring certitude of death. In the "disenchanted world,"[14] outside of EmRel, there is an exposure to forces that make workers more vulnerable to harsh conditions of having unstable work. This is the zone where a worker's life is at its barest, a zone not protected by the transcendental politico-juridical power of EmRel. In the schema of Giorgio Agamben, this is the zone where subjects are *homo sacer*,[15] the place where contractual workers, day laborers, and project workers—the neoliberal *homo sacer*—are exposed from wanton discretion and prerogative of employers and abuse of power to unfair and unjust labor practices, and detrimental and dangerous working conditions. As the situation of the factory workers in Valenzuela City, Philippines,

---

12. The hiring of workers in 5-month-long cycles to avoid granting them regular status that is due on the sixth month of employment.

13. Taylor, "Place for Transcendence?," 1.

14. As appropriated by Charles Taylor in the tradition of Max Weber and Marcel Gauchet.

15. Agamben, *Homo Sacer*.

illustrates, this is a zone that makes the situation of life filthy, or in our language salty (because here life survives on a daily consumption of cheap instant noodles and dried fish).[16]

In this zone of abandonment, to employ an idea developed by Joao Biehl and cast it in this context of workers, life here is at its most precarious.[17] This is where individuals are left to themselves, to fend off for themselves whatever comes on their way. A situation which is one physical injury away from insurmountable debt or inevitable hunger. This is the life of contractual workers and day wage laborers in the Philippines, whose numbers are increasing by the day.[18]

In short, EmRel has acquired the transcendental principle of "beyond critique, beyond question" and now assumes an operative legal doctrine which defines and determines life, which subsequently becomes the providential power in the lives of workers. It is in this respect that the terms that mostly define what "being a human" today is are not anymore based on metaphysical definitions according to the God-human connection; rather what it means to be a human is primarily now based on a politico-juridical determination according to the terms of EmRel.[19]

Employer–Employee Relationship as a Neoliberal Apparatus

Many observers today describe the current age as the age of neoliberalism. Neoliberalism is this general idea that society and its institutions work best when it works according to market principles. And this is what

---

16. Valenzuela City is the plastic capital of the Philippines, where I spent a few days with the factory/manufacturing workers to learn more about their plight and their working conditions. This experience was made possible through the Council of World Mission (CWM) in their project titled "Re-Imagining Liturgy in the Context of Empire."

17. This theme is developed in his study of a place called *Vita* in Brazil. See Biehl, *Vita*. While the focus is different, the operation involved in this abandonment is strikingly similar. And the situation is eerie, especially now that this zone is declared as "war zone" in the War on Drugs of President Rodrigo Roa Duterte.

18. In a report in 2018, the Department of Labor reported that there are now more 3337 companies reportedly to be found engaged or suspected to be into labor-only contracting, see CNN Philippines Staff, "DOLE Reveals Top 20 Companies."

19. Perhaps in this neoliberal time this means that a theological anthropology must now be based on the marginal idea of "laboring animal" and not anymore on the influential idea of "*zoon politikon*." See Arendt, *Human Condition*.

we experience now: a growing numbers of "taking over" of businesses and adoptions of financial practices and principles in most of our public institutions. We see increasing numbers of business executives with more managerial expertise than educational expertise running educational institutions. Public services are now in the hands of private entities and corporations.[20] Or even in churches, we do not call pastors anymore; we *hire* them. And so on and so forth.

This particular historical epoch is not only limited to Western countries. The neoliberal turn is taking place in most countries in the world. The colonial infrastructures during the era of colonialism from the eighteenth century to the turn of the twentieth century, which largely remain intact and operational, have made neoliberalism a default governmental idea and practice in the former colonies. The hegemony of Western countries and financial institutions like the World Bank (WB) and the International Monetary Fund (IMF) ensures that neoliberalism is the paradigm by which the political economy of the world operates.

It is in this context that the transcendental power of EmRel acquires potent force and becomes more lethal. From my point of view, the material and consequential operation of this transcendental juridical principle of EmRel can be first demonstrated and clarified through the productive machine model of Michel Foucault that Agamben develops into what he calls an apparatus.[21]

In *What is an Apparatus?*, Agamben describes the Foucauldian productive machine that (re)produces subject-workers as apparatus. He defines an apparatus in this manner: it is "literally anything that has in some way the capacity to capture, orient, determine, intercept, model, control, or secure the gestures, behaviors, opinions, or discourses of living beings. Not only, therefore, prisons, madhouses, the panopticon, schools, confession, factories, disciplines, *juridical measures* and so forth…but also the pen, writing, literature, philosophy, agriculture, cigarettes, navigation, computers, cellular telephones…and language itself."[22]

---

20. There is a growing literature on this matter. For major theoretical discussions, see, for instance, Harvey, *Brief History of Neoliberalism*; Brown, *Undoing the Demos*, Spence, *Knocking the Hustle* for a material discussion on the intersection of class and race in neoliberalism.

21. For an overview discussion on how subjects are produced in the theoretical schema of Foucault, see, for instance, Foucault, "The Subject and Power."

22. Agamben, *What Is an Apparatus?*, 14 (emphasis mine).

In other words, an apparatus encompasses human life. No human life is not influenced or controlled or determined by some apparatus. We are captured and produced by this machine in one way or another. Accordingly, we are subjectified or de-subjectified by different apparatuses.

In the current neoliberal order, the force of juridical measure which Agamben mentions but does not discuss, and which I consider as the most significant apparatus today viewed from the perspective of, and experienced by, the working class, is the legal principle in labor law: the Employer–Employee Relationship. According to the definition of the Agambenian apparatus, this is the legal apparatus that defines and determines the term of subjectivities of workers, particularly its juridical status in the constituted and constitutional order. The kind and quality of life of the so-called proverbial 99 percent, the working class, almost entirely depends on it for security and insurance against economic uncertainty.

More relevantly, in Philippine jurisprudence, this apparatus acquires transcendental status. EmRel is unassailable, beyond question and beyond critique. Even if its operation affects the majority of the people, it is not up for democratic process or constitutional amendment. It is simply posited as the transcendental principle that defines and legitimizes the status of workers, and which all other labor laws follow. Akin to the theological principle of natural law, EmRel is that which must remain as it is because it is so. It cannot be amended or revised through people's initiatives. It is an assumption that must be simply accepted as it is. It is out of reach—the "beyond"—yet it is concrete as it holds power over people.

In short, EmRel is the transcendental apparatus that (re)produces and ultimately determines juridical measures that classify the juridical status of workers, prescribing them what they can have and not have under this juridical order. Via Foucault-Agamben, this is the politico-juridical machine that produces subjects and subjectivities. But what makes this power more severe is that in the age of neoliberalism it becomes the legitimate and legitimating source on how "the laboring animals" are economically categorized and defined. When the economy assumes the logic and language of the political, this apparatus becomes the most consequential apparatus for day-to-day life. In this manner, EmRel is the transcendental power in the neoliberal order to which workers have to bow down and to which workers ultimately pray and aspire to become a part of, a power that provides for their financial security and economic insurance. Along this line that we can see EmRel is also what Paul Tillich calls the Ultimate Concern.[23]

Labor-Only Contracting, the Abandoned Workers, and the Sovereign Employers: When the Natural and Material Converge

What makes EmRel more potent and lethal among other politico-juridical apparatuses, however, is that it is through this apparatus, that the natural ("law of nature," i.e., beyond question) is also material ("operation of economy," i.e., determines value and wages). Here is where the transcendental becomes concrete and operational—posited as "beyond" yet considered as "material." And through this apparatus, more importantly, the economic condition of the 99 percent is produced and decidedly determined and subsequently made operational. In short, it is through its incarnation released through its operation that this apparatus becomes serious and critical for workers at present.

In my experience as a union leader and with my work in organizing university unions and helping faculty form their own faculty association in the Visayas region, the convergence of the natural and the material in EmRel is manifested most concretely and violently when it excludes workers from its coverage, that is, when they are placed outside this relationship.[24] As I will further discuss this point (inclusion-exclusion mechanism) below, this exclusionary mechanism of inherent power and operation of EmRel exposes workers to discriminatory and exploitative work situations. Outside EmRel, workers are not guaranteed security, tenureship, and other benefits. They do not have, for instance, a secure source of income and health insurance. In other words, its exclusionary power places workers in a precarious situation, namely, the labor-only contract situation.

---

23. While this chapter presents this issue differently in terms of looking at the "religious" in its material operation particularly through EmRel, Tillich's approach to this question through the lens of theological existentialism nevertheless provides us with another layer to see how this problem has a religious content. Indeed, both approaches see this issue as "religious." See Tillich, *Dynamics of Faith*, particularly chapter 1 on Faith and Ultimate Concern for his discussion on how this existentially structures human life.

24. Composed of many islands, Visayas is located in the middle region of the Philippines. Outside Manila, the capital city, this is the region of the country where important universities are also located.

In the neoliberalized order, the abandoned workers are those who are under the labor-only contract.[25] Legally defined as "an arrangement where the contractor or subcontractor merely recruits, supplies or places workers to perform a job, work or service for a principal," labor-only contracting is only for a short or temporary period. Thus, unlike workers under EmRel, workers on labor-only contracting find themselves in a very limited and disadvantageous condition of employment. Moreover, in several industries like manufacturing and packaging and distribution, labor-only contractual workers receive the most hazardous and risky assignments in the work place. In the factories in Valenzuela, Philippines, for instance, they work at night time, the so-called graveyard shift, without extra or overtime pay. Regular workers work in the day time. In other words, they are the most vulnerable class of workers—the excluded and exposed class—and hence the most exploited.

In Philippine jurisprudence, under certain conditions, labor-only contracting is allowed; but it is not legally permitted.[26] Thus employers still manage to employ this labor practice legally. Even in higher education, which has its own versision of labor-only contracting in *adjunctification* or *part-timization* of teachers, this kind of labor practice is becoming more a norm rather than an exception. As argued by the End of Contractualization (ENDO) Movement, there is a pattern of normalization of this particular kind of labor employment.

In a recent case decided by the Court of Appeals, the second highest court of the land sided with the Philippine Long Distance Telephone Company or PLDT (principal contractor) and the Meralco Industrial Engineering Services Corporation or Miescor (the subcontractor who does the work on behalf of the principal) against the line installation workers of Meralco. Overturning the previous decision rendered by the Labor Secretary Silvestre Bello III, which ordered PLDT to regularize almost

---

25. Labor-only contracting has different modes and arrangements, i.e., seasonal workers, daytime labor, or household/domestic work. Another important in relation to the thesis of this chapter but beyond its scope is the situation of overseas foreign workers who provide billions of annual remittances to the country.

26. This is a gray area in labor law. Article 3 of the Labor Code of the Philippines entitled "Declaration of Basic Policy" states that "The State shall assure the rights of workers to self-organization, collective bargaining, security of tenure, and just and humane conditions of work" (emphasis mine). Thus, for instance, the End of Contractualization (ENDO) Movement lobbies for a legislation to redress this issue, that is, the implementation of the Basic Policy of the Labor Code to ensure the rights of workers to "security of tenure."

9,000 workers and required the same to pay about P66 million in unpaid benefits and P2.3 million of back wages, the Court of Appeals maintained that PLDT and MIESCOR did not engage labor-only contracting. While this case is now elevated to the Highest Court of the Republic, the decision of the Court of Appeals remains in effect. The workers remain employed under labor-only contracting. This landmark case demonstrates the normalization of this exclusionary mechanism of EmRel and the exposure of workers to uncertain working situation.

What is more important in this particular situation is not that employers can skirt around this prohibition because they have brilliant lawyers. Rather, the reason for their ability to make the law inoperative (i.e., make the law not applicable to them or skirting around it) is that they are the sovereign power in a world populated with laboring animals. That is to say, they are able to determine whom to include and whom to exclude in the Employee-Employer Relationship. Unlike the Schmittian sovereign power however, the source of this sovereign power is not based on the constitutional politico-juridical order. Rather, it stems from their classed status as employer-capitalists who now, as in the case PLDT and MIESCOR, can exercise their power to employ on their own accord. In other words, their sovereign power is based on their economic status.

In my experience as a union leader, widespread practice of *adjunctification* or *part-timization* demonstrate this operation of sovereign power over the lives of "contractualized" teachers. Even the Department of Labor and Employment, a government agency tasked to ensure the well-being of workers, can only yield to this sovereign power of the employer-capitalist class (i.e., senior executive university officials) to employ workers (teachers) on contractual basis.

In the time of neoliberalism, naturalization of this sovereign executive power reaches its most violent form because now the symbolic and practical coincides.[27] Ideology is no longer false consciousness but fully appropriated and implemented to its logical effect and conclusion. It touches on our bodies and defines not only what our bodies can do but what our bodies can have.

27. While I approach this issue differently from the theoretical work of Pierre Bourdieu, he is instructive here. See, for instance, Bourdieu, *Language and Symbolic Power* where he indicates that language is not simply a means of communication but a medium of power. What this does to this analysis is that it substantiates further the idea that ideology is a product and mechanism of power that is not simply a reflection and representation of a social order but employed to enhance further political and economic interest.

The Sovereign Power of EmRel in the Time of Neoliberalism: The Inclusion and Exclusion of Subjects

In political theology, the naturalized form of sovereign power operates through the executive discretion of a sovereign (or in the case of modern democracies, a President of the Republic). In labor, the naturalized form of power of EmRel materializes in the form of Management Prerogative (a principle in labor law that grants employers the right to "reasonable returns on investments; the right to expansion and growth; the right to exercise powers essential or necessary to carry out its purposes stated in the articles of incorporation; the right to regulate all aspects of employment.")[28]

While different in kind, what is telling here is that both of these forms of power have been significantly employed in recent history particularly at the neoliberal turn of the current global order. Not limited to localized situations, the exercise of these powers is rather widespread. In the *State of Exception*, Agamben suggests, for instance, that the inherent sovereign power in Western democracy has become a primary approach utilized in governance.[29] This is the reason why we see the rise of totalitarian tendencies among many Western democracies and its corollary phenomenon of populism.

In my experience with labor work and union organizing, the power of EmRel through Management Prerogative (MP) has become the primary principle of employers in the management of human productivity and the maximization of profit. For instance, employer and management can invoke this principle in order to assert its right to protect and advance its interests. One example of this is changing of working conditions without workers prior consent and assent, a practice that is rampant and common in many sectors and industries—a management strategy to fully utilize human resources available to produce the most possible goods. In a local university, the Administration unilaterally decided to change the schedule already published in the official school calendar because it wanted their teachers to render community service and do research for one week out of the three weeks already scheduled as university holiday break.

In short, these forms of power are more intense, as they are often employed to promote and to carry out the idea that collective and common life is best managed through market principles. As I indicated above,

28. Azucena, *Everyone's Labor Code*, v.
29. Agamben, *State of Exception*, 1–31.

this is most severe in the life of the 99 percent, especially for those who are in the labor sector and the most vulnerable in this sector, the labor-only contract workers. For them, the power of EmRel is not abstract. Management Prerogative is not simply a management style but a mode and means of strategic power over their lives. It determines the kind and quality of life they will have, both in the short and long term.

Another key in this analysis is the operative power of EmRel to include and exclude subjects, which in in the field of political theology is an attribute that properly belongs to sovereign power.[30] This is the power that subjectivizes and de-subjectivizes. Thus in the current order, this concrete operation to include and exclude is significant not only in thinking about the semblance of power between the politico-juridical and economic order, but also, importantly, in looking at the material operations of a sovereign power that concretely affects the lives of workers.

EmRel is not only a legal principle that is "beyond critique, beyond question" but it is also an operation that follows the logic of the sovereign and functions like one. Along the schema of Schmitt, I suggest that it is precisely this sovereign feature that makes EmRel the primary operative power that produces neoliberal subjects. In the experience and reality of workers, this is the sovereign power that defines and qualifies their lives.

The idea of sovereign power, as developed earlier by Carl Schmitt, is substantially clarified and articulated recently by Giorgio Agamben. In *Homo Sacer*, Agamben, describes the primary operation of sovereign power as one that creates a situation of exception, a situation different from a normal situation. To put it spatially, the situation of exception is an outside of an order. It is a creation from such an order but separate and distinguishable insofar as it is a suspension of operative norms of such order. Simply put, it is an outside that is nevertheless related to the inside. Thus, for instance, in a politico-juridical order, which Agamben observes in his analysis of sovereign power, "the exception maintains itself in relation to the rule in the form of the rule's suspension. *The rule applies to the exception in no longer applying, in withdrawing from it.* The (situation) of exception is thus not the chaos that precedes order but rather the situation that results from its suspension."[31] In other words, sovereign power is an operation of power that creates distinction, and which subsequently

---

30. As defined in the work of Schmitt in *Political Theology* and particularly developed by Agamben.

31. Agamben, *Homo Sacer*, 17–18.

maintains it. And in both not mutually exclusive spheres, it remains effective.

Applied to our analysis of EmRel, this operation is also how the primary operation of EmRel basically works. As a "sovereign power" in the world of labor, EmRel creates two spheres for workers, namely, coverage and non-coverage; this is equal to the inside and outside of the politico-juridical order discussed above. Specifically, the non-coverage here is the outside and by its legal definition and juridical operation, it is created and maintained relative to the sphere of coverage.

In the analysis of Agamben, this sovereign power produces not only the conditions (for him, politico-juridical) but also subjects. In the same case of EmRel, it produces economic and working conditions and subjects—workers. More relevantly, this power also de-subjectivizes: *homo sacer* for Agamben; labor-only contract workers for EmRel. In EmRel, workers outside its coverage are de-subjectivized subjects insofar as these workers are exposed to extra judicial and economic forces, i.e., contractualizations.

In this labor situation, de-subjectivized subjects are also what Agamben calls *homo sacer*—defined as those who "can be killed, but not sacrificed."[32] In this analysis, they are legally excluded but remain part of the law, but as its abandoned subject. That is to say, they are people whose life is bare, exposed to the harsh conditions outside the law. This is the condition of labor-only contract workers, the subjects of the current neoliberal regime. They are subjects in terms of being subjects who are de-subjectivized. Abandoned, they are part as non-part of the transcendental relationship that exposes them to the harsh condition of being not part of it.

In the situation of workers, being de-subjectivized means having no tenure of security, which EmRel would have provided. They are stripped off of their basic human rights and the rights of workers. They are the abandoned subjects. Under labor-only contracting a worker is always under the mercy of employers. He or she can be fired from his or her job without just cause or due process. Without security of tenure, labor-only contract workers can only depend on luck and must be in complete subservience to employer-capitalists even if it means giving up their basic rights. This is made more difficult in a very patriarchal society like the Philippines because male workers are the breadwinners of the family. The

---

32. A figure in Roman Law which Agamben used to reflect "bare life" under the current politico-juridical order. See discussion in Agamben, *Homo Sacer*, 8–11.

loss of job on average equals the loss of income for a family of six. In 2018, it was estimated that there were more than 1.3 million labor-only contract workers in the Philippines.[33] They and their families are the *homo sacer* in the country today.

Under neoliberalism, the politico-juridical procedure that Agamben pointed out is only intensified in the economic sphere. The sovereign power that he identified is more active in people's lives and particularly in the life of workers. Like prisoners in Guantanamo Bay or stateless refugees or migrant children at the border, labor-only contract workers only have bare life. In contrast to Arendt's thesis, in this age it is not the social but the economic that has taken over the political, as the potency and the lethal of power EmRel is more active and operative in everyday life. This is the reign of neoliberalism.

The Struggle for Labor Justice in the Time of Neoliberalism

As indicated above, one problem I see in the current neoliberal order is its politico-juridical economic apparatus. What is problematic with this apparatus is that, since it is posited as a transcendental principle without going through any democratic procedures and public considerations, it is not responsible and accountable to the general public.[34] Accepted as natural—like the natural law of theology, its procedure is simply presumed legitimate. So while it is out of sight like the natural law of theology, in the case of EmRel, the operation of this apparatus is consequential to many lives. In other words, what we have today is an operation of power that is primarily made operative without any democratic support from the people who are affected by it.

In this neoliberal situation, the task of struggle for life and justice could then primarily be about direct engagement with this apparatus. What I hope to specifically suggest here, however, is that beyond the simple binary of good and evil and genealogical criticism, this engagement

---

33. Rey, "Jollibee."

34. This point is along the lines of Joseph Stiglitz who points out that this is the problem in the current suprainternational monetary institutions like International Monetary Fund and World Bank. In other words, what we have today are systems of power that operate outside the democratic space. See Stiglitz, *Globalization and Its Discontents*. For a full-blown theological discussion on this global issue, see Katherine Tanner, Tanner, *Economy of Grace*.

is based on the *praxis* of demand and negotiation that labor organizers and union leaders have demonstrated in their struggle for greater justice for workers. In their praxis, we see how the oppressed and exploited are not simply passive victims and objects of power but also, importantly, agents and possessors of power. They see the operation of power in a non-monolithic and non-totalizing manner. Power is always complex; relation (i.e., employer–employee) is always asymmetrical. Thus they employ power strategically toward beneficial ends. For them, to address oppressive and exploitative labor situations (the power relation of workers) is always time-bound, need-specific, and negotiable. Claims and demands are not essentialized. In other words, through and with them, we can learn that the *praxis* of demand and negotiation opens up possibilities for new ways of relating and living. Contrary to negative stereotyping that this kind of work is paralyzing because it does not provide liberation from a circuitous negative situation, such praxis is an active affirmation of hope that things can happen and can change for the better. It maybe that this struggle for a better life is tactical and strategic, but this is not about an ideological assertion or for doctrinal purposes. Rather this is ultimately about finding a way where there seems none—a negotiated settlement satisfactory to parties involved *in the meantime*. A *praxis* of constant negotiation and improvisation of engagements with powers based on labor demands, in the end, is an instantiation of what is possible at present. Theologically put, this is prayer-in-praxis. One particularly illustrative case here is how labor organizers and union leaders struggle to advance the rights and welfare of employees. They negotiate the terms of possibility based on the current situation, demanding better terms and conditions that could enhance the quality of their lives. They do not say a prayer for what must come. They do what must come.

At this particular juncture that I also see how theology can offer us a cue on how to deepen the *praxis* of demand and negotiation particularly relative to the issue of sovereignty and its material and consequential operation in the social world. For to demand and negotiate for what is possible, better working conditions that create new and better possibility for workers, might not be enough to enact a more just and humane world. Labor demand and negotiation is still within the closed-circuit relationship between the employer–employee, indeed, under the logic and within the grammar of sovereignty (EmRel). As theologians like Jürgen Moltmann, Johannes Metz, and Dorothee Soelle, or even theoreticians like Michael Hardt and Antonio Negri or Gilles Deleuze and Felix Guattari have pointed out, this logic and grammar of sovereignty, which as I have suggested underpins the transcendental relationship of EmRel, only reinforce and perpetuate the unjust structures and exploitative practices of our constituted order. For one, this sovereignty resides not in the 99 percent but in the 1 percent.

Thus, here I further suggest the need to re-conceptualize and enhance the labor frame of demand and negotiation with a theological key of collaboration in order to think of *praxis* that could allow us to move beyond the closed-circuit logic and grammar of EmRel. The binary either/or logic leads us nowhere but to the continuous (re)production of the state of exception and *homo sacer*.

From Negotiation to Collaboration: Towards a Political Theology of Labor From Below

As I write, the Silliman University Faculty Association (SUFA) enters into a critical stage of Collective Bargaining Agreement negotiation with the Silliman University Administration—under Conciliation-Mediation facilitated by the National Conciliatory and Mediatory Board of the Republic of the Philippines. We are now in the last stretch before the union will exercise its constitutional right to stage a strike or work stoppage. As a panel member, I cannot accept any terms that put the quality of life of teachers in jeopardy. I must negotiate for a better term that is adequate for the needs of the time, even if it means ultimately using our "nuclear option."

This experience with the union tells me that the human situation is the situation of workers today, a situation of constant struggle to define and redefine the terms of life. In the current neoliberal order, the struggle of many workers is to fight for the inclusion in EmRel; to be part of, and to have subsequently better negotiated terms under, a Collective Bargaining Agreement. It is becoming clearer to me that providential power through the lens of workers is a "power" that must be negotiated, at all cost and by all means. Transcendence is not a given. It is negotiated. It must be negotiated. Otherwise, this power will only work against the interest of the working class. This is the danger when it is simply posited as "natural" and then employed by as the ruling power. Like God as Father or God as Heterosexual in Christian theology, EmRel cannot be left to operate on its own. It must be questioned. Here labor organizers and union leaders are like constructive liberation theologians. They make EmRel not a tool for the oppressor nor an instrument of oppression. Rather they make this "transcendental power" life-affirming. Indeed, one of the theological wagers of this chapter is this: to do god-talk today is akin to the work of a labor organizer. The task is to organize and to negotiate for a better "god" on behalf of the Collective Bargaining Unit—the people. Thus theologians today do not have to go outside or assume a different role—all they need to do is be theologians in order to advance the work of liberation theology.[35] In the site of labor work, union, and labor justice, one must remain a theologian as the struggle here is a struggle to negotiate for a god, a god that allows us to survive and flourish particularly in the time of inflationary hikes.

However, more valuable than the above lesson, I see the trap of EmRel—the relationship that defines and prescribes who and what we are us/faculty and them/administrators of Silliman University—which always leads us to an endless cycle of antagonism and deep distrust as more problematic. Under this relationship, we may be able to negotiate for a better term. But every two years we repeat this logic and perform the previous drama of negotiation all over again—the repetition of the same. In my eyes, this is the drama that tells us the same story year in and out—industrial dispute and labor relations. And what this does to the collective body, in our particular case, is that it makes us not ask anymore the more important and deeper questions that have to do, for instance, with our institutional mission and our professional vocation as teachers. In this endless cycle of the same, creative and constructive energies are put aside. Apathy and indifference reign. In other words, theologically put, this situation is the situation of the old—the world that Paul of Tarsus indicates particularly in his letters to Rome and Corinth is perishing. Indeed, this situation of repetition does not open the horizon for new things to appear, as things remain the same. The logic of this situation makes us enact the same old world. Sameness of the present order only brings staleness and decay.

---

35. This is opposed to the position of Ivan Petrella when he suggests: "To work in liberation theology today could mean to work outside of it, by finding ways the epistemological and practical-moral elements can infiltrate, subvert, and transform other bodies of knowledge. Here the liberation theologian need not carry the label of 'theologian' and works best under a different disciplinary guise" (150). See Petrella, *Beyond Liberation Theology*.

This is also what happens in the larger world of labor. The logic of repetition and sameness reigns in. And worse, it assumes a violent operation that perpetuates the exclusionary regime of domination. EmRel might secure and grant rights and privileges of some workers but it also at the same disqualifies the same for other workers. Based on the either/or logic, EmRel is an apparatus that saves some and damns others. Framed theologically, EmRel is the apocalyptic neoliberal apparatus that embodies the logic and theological grammar of the religious right and the establishment—a paradigm from above, from the powers that be—framed in the strict distinction of friend-enemy.[36] Others are friends and some are enemies. Negotiation might advance the interest of workers—but this only means salvation for the privileged few of the class. In this black-and-white scenario, some are destined to have security of tenure; some are not.

Here, therefore, I would like to add a few thoughts on how the labor framework of demand and negotiation can be enhanced with collaboration, understood theologically through Pauline thought, in order to demonstrate how to perhaps dislodge ourselves from the logic and grammar of the sovereignty of EmRel.

As a unionist, I must first emphasize here as well that this kind of collaboration is based on existential and material recognition that there are better or alternative terms of existence. It is about working together to better the working conditions for the 99 percent. In short, I situate this collaboration among and with the workers of the world—that is from below. That it is about working together that things happen. From here and this situation of collaboration we see power emerging as common, one that instantiates a kind of hope for what could or might be, indeed a new kind of life.

In *Beyond Liberation Theology*, Ivan Petrella suggests that the work of liberation theologians today is to infiltrate, subvert, and transform other bodies of knowledge. His example for this kind of work is the work Paul Farmer, a medical anthropologist at Harvard Medical School, who rethinks medical anthropology from the experience and reality of the majority of humankind; indeed a scholar who struggles to reshape his own discipline around the "concerns and issues that affect the majority of humankind."[37]

---

36. This kind of idea is powerfully articulated by Carl Schmitt, whose work became influential to many neoconservative thinkers. See Schmitt, *Concept of the Political*.

37. Petrella, *Beyond Liberation Theology*, 150.

My attempt in this article is to also articulate a theological position not dissimilar from the position of Petrella. But what I am not emphasizing here is the situation of the work of liberation as primarily in the field of knowledge. I think rather the work of liberation must be situated in the field of social movements and political organizations. Here theologians are not in disguise; they work as they are—to provide critical insights and theological analysis to the inner logic of politico-juridical and economic apparatuses to political movements and organizations. So, theologians remain religious scholars but now their concern is the general condition of laboring animals. Thus the work is not about liberation theologies carving out a small space for theology in a secular world. This work is about developing a more expansive view of theological work that commits to a particular purpose of improving the working condition of workers. It is about organizing unions and labor groups in a setting that tries to diminish and actively eliminate organizations that represent the laboring animals.

In other words, what I hope to indicate here is the kind of work that theologians as well as labor organizers and union leaders undertake, and about which we also read in the messianic writings of Paul of Tarsus: the work of organizing assemblies or cell groups that instantiate not apocalyptic consciousness but a kind of messianic life and whose principles are based on persuasion and not appeal to authority or even revelation. Any theologian working in the labor movement knows that workers understand the Pauline messianic notion that the old world of domination is coming to an end as the incoming of the new is much better than any other one. And this comes about easily because workers in the labor movement already share and live a life of togetherness, envisioning the new and embodying the possibilities of what could be in organizing, in demanding, in negotiating with powers that be. For them, the nearness of the new life is therefore just looming over the horizon, about to burst forth. Like the messianicity of Paul, their shared life and their work to enhance their collective life is about doing and living out the new, displacing the old by way of infecting it with their commitment to companionship with one another. Theologians of labor live and breathe with them in this life of togetherness. Perhaps this is a way to establish a political theology of labor—companionship of and with the lowly.[38]

---

38. I also understand this companionship as deep solidarity. On deep solidarity, see Rieger and Henkel-Rieger, *Unified We Are a Force*.

Thus, in the meantime, I go back and sit again at the negotiating table to negotiate on behalf of the Collective Bargaining Unit of Silliman University a Collective Bargaining Agreement that allows us, faculty of the university, to survive and flourish during inflationary hikes and economic uncertainties. But perhaps it is also about time to cross the table and together look for alternative way of being and doing, indeed, of relating to one another that is outside the labor law. In this way, the new which is embodied in the messianic politics of Pauline communities and which is embodied today in us workers and unionists infects the old.

Bibliography

Agamben, Giorgio. *Homo Sacer: Sovereign Power and Bare Life*. Stanford, CA: Stanford University Press, 1998.

———. *State of Exception*. Chicago: University of Chicago Press, 2005.

———. *What Is an Apparatus?: And Other Essays*. Stanford: Stanford University Press, 2009.

Arendt, Hannah. *The Human Condition*. Chicago: University of Chicago Press, 1969.

Azucena, Cesario Alvero, Jr. *Everyone's Labor Code: Essential Textbook and Updated Reviewer*. 9th ed. Manila: Rex Book Store, 2018.

Biehl, João Guilherme. *Vita: Life in a Zone of Social Abandonment*. Berkeley: University of California Press, 2005.

Bourdieu, Pierre. *Language and Symbolic Power*. Edited and introduced by John B. Thompson. Translated by Gino Raymond and Matthew Adamson. Cambridge, MA: Polity, 1991.

Brown, Wendy. *Undoing the Demos: Neoliberalism's Stealth Revolution*. Cambridge, MA: MIT Press, 2015.

CNN Philippines Staff. "DOLE Reveals Top 20 Companies Found or Suspected to Be Engaged in Labor-Only Contracting." CNN. https://cnnphilippines.com/news/2018/05/28/DOLE-labor-only-contracting-companies-contractualization.html.

Foucault, Michel. *The Essential Foucault: Selections from Essential Works of Foucault, 1954–1984*. Edited by Paul Rabinow and Nikolas Rose. New York: New Press, 2003.

———. *The Foucault Reader*. Edited by Paul Rabinow. New York: Pantheon, 1984.

Hans Schwarz. "Transcendence." In *New and Enlarged Handbook of Christian Theology*, edited by Donald W. Musser and Joseph L. Price. Nashville: Abingdon, 2003.

Harvey, David. *A Brief History of Neoliberalism*. New York: Oxford University Press, 2005.

Horner, Robyn. "The Betrayal of Transcendence." In *Transcendence: Philosophy, Literature, and Theology Approach the Beyond*, edited by Regina M. Schwartz, 61–81. New York: Routledge, 2004.

Petrella, Ivan. *Beyond Liberation Theology: A Polemic*. Reclaiming Liberation Theology. London: SCM, 2008.

Philippines. *The Labor Code: With Comments and Cases*. Manila: Rex Book Store, 1999.

Rey, Aika. "Jollibee, Dole, PLDT among Top Companies 'Engaged' in Illegal Contracting." Rappler. http://www.rappler.com/nation/203529-jollibee-dole-pldt-labor-only-contracting.

Rieger, Joerg, and Rosemarie Henkel-Rieger. *Unified We Are a Force: How Faith and Labor Can Overcome America's Inequalities*. St. Louis: Chalice, 2016.

Ruether, Rosemary Radford. *Sexism and God-Talk: Toward a Feminist Theology*. Boston: Beacon, 1993.

Schmitt, Carl. *The Concept of the Political*. Chicago: University of Chicago Press, 1996.

———. *Political Theology: Four Chapters on the Concept of Sovereignty*. Chicago: University of Chicago Press, 2005.

Schwartz, Hans. "Transcendence." In *New and Enlarged Handbook of Christian Theology*, edited by Donald W. Musser and Joseph L. Price. Nashville: Abingdon, 2003.

Schwartz, Regina M. "Introduction." In *Transcendence: Philosophy, Literature, and Theology Approach the Beyond*, edited by Regina M. Schwartz, vii–xi. New York: Routledge, 2004.

Spence, Lester. *Knocking the Hustle: Against the Neoliberal Turn in Black Politics*. North Charleston: CreateSpace, 2015.

Stiglitz, Joseph E. *Globalization and Its Discontents*. New York: Norton, 2003.

Tanner, Kathryn. *Economy of Grace*. Minneapolis: Fortress, 2005.

Taylor, Charles. *A Secular Age*. Cambridge, MA: Belknap, 2007.

Tillich, Paul. *Dynamics of Faith*. New York: Harper, 1958.

Contributors

Jin Young Choi is Professor of New Testament and Christian Origins and the Baptist Missionary Training School Professorial Chair in Biblical Studies at Colgate Rochester Crozer Divinity School (Rochester, New York).

Juan M. Floyd-Thomas is Associate Professor of African American Religious History at Vanderbilt University Divinity School and teaches in the Graduate Department of Religion at Vanderbilt University (Nashville, Tennessee).

Kwok Pui-lan is Dean's Professor of Systematic Theology at Candler School of Theology, Emory University (Atlanta, Georgia).

Chin Ming Stephen Lim is an adjunct lecturer at Ming Hua Theological College (Hong Kong).

Rosemarie Henkel-Rieger is cofounder of Southeast Center for Cooperative Development (Nashville, Tennessee).

Sifiso Mpofu is a former lecturer in Counseling at United Theological College (Harare, Zimbabwe).

Keun-Joo Christine Pae is Associate Professor of Religion and Women's Gender Studiesat Denison University (Granville, Ohio).

Joerg Rieger is Distinguished Professor of Theology, Cal Turner Chancellor's Chair in Wesleyan Studies, and the Director of the Wendland-Cook Program in Religion and Justice at Vanderbilt University Divinity School and he teaches in the Graduate Department of Religion at Vanderbilt University (Nashville, Tennessee).

Marcus Trammell is Associate Director of the Wendland-Cook Program in Religion and Justice (Nashville, Tennessee).

Karl James E. Villarmea is Associate Professor in the Religion and Peace Studies Department at Silliman University (The Philippines).

Gerald O. West is Professor of African Biblical Interpretation at the University of KwaZulu-Natal (South Africa).

Sithembiso S. Zwane is a lecturer in the Theology and Development Programme in the School of Religion, Philosophy and Classics at the University of KwaZulu-Natal (South Africa).

Scripture Index

OLD TESTAMENT

Genesis
1:1–2:3	4
2:2	4
2:7	4
2:8–9	4
13:13	127
13:8–13	127
19:1–38	127

Numbers
25:1	127

Deuteronomy
23:2–5	127

Joshua
21:45	57

Ruth
1:15–19	130
1:4, 22	132
2:2, 6, 21	132
4:5–6	131–32
4:10	132, 133
4:17	136

1 Samuel
8:11	116

2 Samuel
13:1–22	xiv, 119
13:4	113–16
13:11	116
13:12	116–19
13:12–13, 16, 19	118
13:20	118

1 Kings
5	115
11:1	127
11:28	115
12:6	115
12:7	116
12:8	115
12:8–11	115
12:8–14	116
12:10–11	116
21:1–16	xiv, 107–10, 111, 112, 119
21:1–19	115
21:5	113–16
21:15–16	116
21:17	118
21:17–20	112, 113
21:19	118
21:20b	116
21:25	114

Ezra

9–10	127

Nehemiah

13:23–27	127

Psalms

	4

Isaiah

16:2–3	127

Jeremiah

48:6	127

NEW TESTAMENT

Matthew

9:9–13	97
10:9	92
20:1–15	90
20:1–16	221
20:2	94
23:1–6	15

Mark

1:21, 45	90n13
1:30–31	96
2:1–3:6	93n27
2:13–17	97
3:6, 10	94
5:24–34	96
6:3	90n16
6:8	92
6:36–37	96
6:56	90n13
7:24–30	96
10:21	96
10:29–30	96n38
11:15–19	93
11:16	93
11:19	90n13
11:27–33	93n27
12:1–12	93n27
12:13–17	93n27
12:14	94
12:16	95
12:18–27	93n27, 95
12:28–34	93n27
12:35–38	93n27
12:38–44	87
12:41–44	xiii
12:41	92, 93, 94
12:44	96
13:3	94
13:14	99
14:3–9	96
14:7	97
14:50, 52	99
16:8	99

Luke

2:7–10	13
11:3	97
16:20, 22	97n42
21:1, 4	92, 94n30
21:4	92

John

4:24	180
8:12	173
14:6	165

Acts of the Apostles

2:44–45	177
2:44–46	179
4:32–37	225

Galatians

3:28	178

APOCRYPHA

2 Maccabees 3:6, 10	94

QUR'AN

4.135	15
4.75	18
15.6	4
49.9	15n23

General Index

A
Abahlali Basemjondolo, xv, 226–28, 233
Abrahamic religions, xii, 4–6, 10–12, 14–18, 20
Absalom, biblical figure, 118–19
activism, x, xv, 45, 49–50, 69–70, 76, 226
advocacy, 39, 49, 66, 134
AFL-CIO, 10, 71, 83
Agamben, Giorgio, 234, 242, 244–45, 249–52, 258
Ahab, biblical figure, 108, 112, 114, 119
AIC (African Initiated Churches), xv, 216, 223–26, 228, 230, 232
Allah, Islamic figure, 15, 18
antislavery, 59–60
antiwar, theory, 149–50
antiwork, theory of, xvi
apartheid, 107, 110–11, 114, 223–25, 228–29
apocalyptic, 78, 80, 94, 256–57
Arendt, Hannah, 235, 243, 252, 258

B
belief, Christian, 38–39, 47, 57–58, 71–73, 78, 80
biopower, 144
Black Manifesto, the, xiii, 29, 45–55, 57, 60, 62–68
Black, theology and politics, 44–55, 57–68, 110–11, 116–17, 120, 164, 169–70, 172–73, 175, 179–81, 200, 232, 259
blackness, 58, 63, 165
Boaz, biblical figure, 128, 131, 133, 135
body(ies), 45, 64, 101, 125–29, 144–45, 148–52, 154, 161, 169, 248, 255–56
Bonhoeffer, Dietrich, 9, 20
borders, nation-state, 36, 62, 148, 159
Bourdieu, Pierre, 92, 98–99, 103, 248, 258
bourgeoisie, 27, 147
Buddhism, 37

C
Caesar, Roman emperor, 93–95
capital, 27, 30, 36, 51, 58, 60, 63, 65, 70, 90, 101, 148, 189, 199–200, 202–3, 212, 217–19, 243, 246
capitalism, 14, 16, 19, 26, 38–39, 185–86, 189–91
Capitalocene, 190
caste, xii, 3, 92
Catholicism, 75–76, 206
CBS (Contextual Bible Study), 106–10, 112–15, 117–19, 220–23, 227, 230
chattel slavery, 44, 47, 52, 55, 58, 60–61, 63, 89
China, xii, 2, 25–37, 40–43, 135
Christ, Christian figure, 12, 33, 39, 73, 79, 162, 178, 180

church, xv, 9–10, 31–33, 37–39, 49–50, 54–55, 58, 61, 64–66, 76–78, 80, 83–84, 146, 161–62, 171–73, 177–80, 193–95, 206–7
citizenship, 100, 153, 160, 163, 231–32
class, xi–xv, 1–2, 7
classless, 63, 166
collective bargaining, 10, 39, 197, 199, 235, 247
colonialism, x, xv, 102, 107, 129, 165, 169, 172, 174–77, 179, 244
commons, the, 203–4, 210
communalism, 209
communism, 57, 156–57
communist, 27, 29–30, 32, 35, 42, 53
Cone, James H., 47, 63, 67, 172–73, 180
Confucian, 26, 37–38, 41
congregation, 46, 70, 207
conscientize, 133, 160, 222
conservative, xiii, 53, 70–71, 77–78, 80
constitutional, 245, 248, 254
consumerism, 13
consumerist, 38
consumption, 89, 116, 190, 243
contractual, 130, 237, 242–43, 247–48
contractualization, 242, 258
cooperative, xii, 39, 202–5, 207–8
cooperatives, business, 2, 29, 203–7, 209
Copeland, M. Shawn, 60, 67
corporations, 7, 11, 14, 19, 101, 150, 205, 244
covenant, 14–15
creation, theology of, 4, 33

D
debt, 58, 62, 89, 122, 243
decolonization, 220, 225, 231
democracy, theory of, 26, 39, 65, 186–87, 202, 206, 208, 214, 225–26, 229, 249

denomination, Christian church, 9, 47–48, 51, 72
deregulation, 101, 218
development, 212–14, 216–20, 223–28,
dignity, vii, xii, 38, 57, 92, 126, 136, 158, 165, 170, 227, 229
discrimination, x, 35, 60, 64, 148, 154, 158–59, 164, 174–75
doctrine, 95, 243
Dorrien, Gary, 39, 41
Douglass, Frederick, 59, 67
Du Bois, W. E. B., x, xvi

E
economy, capitalist market, 11, 33–34, 36–38, 41–43, 57–60, 80–81, 93–97, 101–2, 195–96, 198–99, 201–2, 206–10, 244–46
education, xiii, 35, 37, 61, 64, 71, 74, 79, 114, 155, 159, 166, 169, 171, 177, 179, 186–87, 196–97, 203, 225, 247
egalitarian, 30, 81, 112, 115, 125
emancipatory, 45, 106, 212, 223, 236
embodied, 63, 72, 88, 118, 258; See also biopower; body(ies)
empire, v, 4–5, 20–21, 87–96, 98, 103, 122, 146, 163, 243
employees, 30, 58, 196, 198, 203, 205–6, 211, 238, 241–42, 253
employer, xv, 15, 58, 126, 130, 144, 154, 189, 208, 237, 241, 248–49, 251, 253
enslaved, people, 44–45, 55–56, 58, 62, 64, 91, 148
epistemic, 123, 161
epistemology, 161, 238–39
equality, 21, 64–65, 77, 83–84, 153, 179, 203; See also equitable; equity
equitable, 207, 229
equity, vii, 39, 185, 202, 205
Esack, Farid, 14–15, 21
Esperanza, theatrical play, xiv, 122–23, 127–37, 139

ethnicity, x, xii–xiii, xv, 3, 9, 13, 16, 66, 109, 135, 168, 185, 192, 196, 200
ethnocentrism, 3, 137
evangelical, 9, 31, 41, 73, 75
evangelicals, 77–78
Exodus, biblical story, 11–12
expropriation, xiv, 60, 92, 98, 106, 229
extraction, of labor, wealth, and sexuality, 64, 116, 144–45, 151, 156

F
feminist, x, 98, 110–11, 122, 145, 147, 200, 236
financial capitalism, xi, 37, 64–65, 69, 187, 204–5, 207, 219, 244–45
foreign, worker, xiv, 123–26, 129–33, 135–37, 247
Foucault, Michel, 119, 239, 244–45, 258
fundamentalism, 124, 135; See also fundamentalist
fundamentalist, 75, 80–81, 134

G
Galilean, 90–91, 97
Galilee, 88, 90–91, 102; See also Galilean
gender, 8–9, 16–17, 35, 40, 63, 66, 100–102, 106–7, 110–11, 122, 147–49, 153–55, 166–67, 176, 192–93, 196, 199–200, 215, 222
Gramsci, Antonio, 227, 232
Gutiérrez, Gustavo, 214, 234

H
hegemony, 149, 212, 216, 227, 244
heteropatriarchal, 83, 147–48, 161
heterosexism, 3
heterotopia, 119
Honig, Bonnie, 132, 136, 138
hooks, bell, 192–93, 201, 209
Horsley, Richard A., 5, 91, 103

I
ideology, 38, 72, 79–80, 88, 150, 166, 174, 176, 200, 219, 224–25, 227, 248
IMF (International Monetary Fund), 187, 219, 244
immigrants, x, 81, 136, 144, 185
imperialism, 26–27, 29, 31, 98, 148, 217, 225
indigenous, 110–11, 224–25, 232
individualism, 38, 73–74, 191, 204, 220
industrialization, 30, 156, 204
inequality, xii, xv, 17, 34, 39, 89, 165–66, 174, 186–88, 190, 192, 202, 212, 225
intercultural, 119–20
interracial, x, 52
interreligious, 21, 48
intersectional, x, xii, xiv–xv, 109, 185
intertextual, 106–7, 119
Islam, xii, 4, 10, 12–15, 17–18, 21, 75
Islamic, ii, 17, 20–21
Israel, 17, 57, 104, 114–16, 119, 127, 131, 133, 137
Israelite, 127, 131, 135

J
Japan, 26, 28–29, 157, 159, 188, 194
Jerusalem, 87, 90–91, 93–95, 104, 115, 173
Jesus, Christian figure, xiii, 4–5, 8, 12, 15, 17, 28, 31–33, 38, 40, 70, 81, 83, 87–88, 90, 92–99, 101–4, 146, 178, 221, 231–32
Jew, 91, 178
Jewish, xiii, 12, 14–15, 17, 21, 48, 66, 83, 88, 90–91, 93, 95, 98, 103, 221
Jezebel, biblical figure, xiv, 108, 110–15, 120
Josephus, Jewish scholar, 90–91, 98, 103
Jubilee, 226
Judea, 88–91, 102

Judeans, 90–91
jurisprudence, 234, 238, 241, 245, 247
justice, xii, 9, 14–16, 21, 28, 31, 38, 44–45, 56, 58–59, 61–62, 64–65, 80, 84, 118, 122, 143, 146–47, 160–61, 177–80, 186, 192, 195, 197, 199, 207–8, 217, 220, 223, 228, 230, 236, 252–53, 255
justice, economic, 9, 14–16, 28, 38, 44–45, 58–59, 61–62, 64–65, 80, 84, 147, 160, 177–79, 186, 207–8, 217, 223, 228, 252–53
justice, racial, 55–64, 149–52, 177–79, 199–200

K
Kairos, 110, 117–18, 120, 233
Korea, ix, 145, 149–50, 155–59, 163, 210
Korean, 93, 144–45, 149–51, 154–59, 163

L
labor, xi–xv, 1–2, 7
land, xiv, 29, 48, 58, 89, 91–92, 94–95, 106–7, 109, 111–12, 127–28, 130–31, 135, 148, 165, 207, 228–30, 247
Latino(s), 3, 154, 172, 188
Latinx, 65
law, 56, 235, 237–38, 241–42, 245–49, 251–52, 258
liberalism, 26, 49
liberation, 12–14, 49–51, 220–24, 253, 255–57
liberation theology, ix, 28, 49–50, 88, 117–18, 160, 172–73, 213–14, 218–20, 223–24, 255–58
liberationist, 88, 110, 122
Luther King Jr., Martin, x, xvi, 49, 53, 56, 67, 146, 200

M
Mammon, 37, 39

marginalization, economic, xv, 100–101, 212–13, 216, 228
market, 14, 34, 36–37, 189–90, 208, 243–46; See also capitalism
Marx, Karl, 1–2, 32, 60–61, 74–75, 99–102, 218–19
Marxism, v, xvi, 27–28, 44, 47, 58, 199, 210
masculinities, 107, 113, 120
materialism, theory of, 124, 138
McAlevey, Jane, 191, 193, 209
messianic, 224–25, 257–58
migrant, workers, 26, 34–35, 37, 71, 79, 99, 252
migration, x, 70–71, 131
militarism, xiv, 143–46, 151, 160–62
militarization, 156, 162
military, xiv, 88, 91, 94, 143–46, 148–61, 199
minjung, theology, 93, 102
misogyny, 38
mission, Christian, 27, 66, 98, 144, 206, 255
Moabite, 127, 131–33, 135–37
modernity, 10, 124, 172, 176
modernization, 34, 37, 156, 158, 213, 218
Mondragon, the Cooperative Corporation, 206, 209
Moses, biblical figure, 5, 12, 17
Muhammad, Islamic figure, 5, 12–13, 17, 57
multitude, xiii, 88, 91–93, 96, 98, 101; See also *ochlos*, Greek term
Muslim, 14, 38

N
Naboth, biblical figure, v, 105–6, 108–9, 111–12, 114, 117, 120
necropolitics, theory, xiv, 143–45, 149–52, 155, 157–62
neoliberalism, theory of, vi, 217, 219, 231, 233–34, 243–44, 249, 252, 258
Niebuhr, Reinhold, 28–29, 42, 75

nonviolence, theory of resistance, 46, 146

O
Occupy Wall Street, the economic and political movement, 3, 16, 21, 186, 190, 200
ochlos, Greek term, xiii, 88, 92–93, 96–99, 101–2; See also multitude
organizers, xi–xii, 11, 215–16, 236, 253–55, 257
organizing, political, economic, and racial justice, x, xii, xv, 10–11, 19, 27, 39, 190–91, 193–94, 198, 204, 228, 246, 249, 257

P
pacifism, theory of, 28, 146–47
Palestine, 88, 91, 94, 101, 221
Passover, Jewish holiday, 12–13
patriarchy, xiii–xiv, 64, 80, 93, 95–96, 100, 102, 113–16, 185
Paul, Christian figure, 4–5, 21, 81, 103, 181, 219, 233, 246, 255–59
Pauline, 89, 103, 256–58
peacebuilding, theory of, 143, 163
peacemaking, 147–48, 160
Pentecostalism, 72, 74, 84
Petrella, Ivan, 134, 139, 255–58
Philippines, ix, 128, 130, 133, 145, 159, 237, 242–43, 246–47, 251–52, 254, 258, 262
populism, theory of, 80, 249
populist, 38, 75
postcolonial, theory, xiii–xiv, 5, 110–11, 144, 212, 223–24, 227
postmodern, theory, 165, 170, 238, 240
poverty, xiii, 59, 62, 64, 89–90, 92, 97–98, 155–57, 164–66, 168–72, 174–76, 179–80, 212–13, 225–26
praxis, theory, 58, 65, 105–6, 216, 220, 227, 230, 236, 253–54

prisoners, 89, 147, 152, 252
prisons, 61, 244
privilege, xiv–xv, 63–64, 126, 133, 135, 165–66, 170–72, 176, 178, 180, 186, 196
production, theory of, 11, 29–33, 101–2, 115–17, 174, 189–90, 202, 204–6, 218–19, 238; See also labor
profit, 8, 162, 190, 192, 202, 205, 219, 249; See also capitalism; market
proletarian, 152, 156
proletarianization, 145, 152–53, 160
proletariat, 27, 99, 145
prophet, xiv, 13, 53, 112, 117
prophetic, traditions, 4, 45, 47, 50, 55, 62, 66, 110, 117–18, 127
prostitution, xiv, 144–45, 149, 156–61

Q
Qur'an, Islamic text, 4, 13–16, 18, 20

R
race, x, xii–xv, 44–47, 49, 63–66, 107–10, 123, 143, 145, 149–60, 166–74, 176, 178–81
racialized, xiv, 54, 63, 143–45, 148, 156, 162, 171
racism, x, xiii, 3, 7, 45, 47, 60, 158, 164–68, 170–72, 174–76, 178–80, 185, 199
rape, 106, 113, 146, 160
reconciliation, act and theory of, 7, 32–33, 55, 147, 174
redistribution, economic, 30, 46, 101, 229
reparations, xiii, 45–47, 50, 52–67
reproductive, rights and labor, 81, 96, 190, 201
resistance, movements of, xii, 13, 91, 146, 160, 191, 195, 201, 216, 223–24, 226, 228, 230
revolution, movements of, 8, 28, 30, 50, 92, 204, 212
Rieger, Joerg, xii, 39–40, 81–82, 100, 191–92, 194

Rome, Empire of, 88–91, 94–95, 103, 255

S
Schneider, Nathan, 206–7, 210
Schüssler Fiorenza, Elisabeth, 104, 109, 120
scriptures, Christian, Jewish, and Islamic, 77, 81, 83, 173, 179
secular, 51, 65–66, 146, 178, 257
secularization, 8
segregation, racial, x, 48, 54, 60, 174, 177
sexuality, x, xii–xv, 3, 9, 13, 16, 40, 63, 66, 100–101, 145, 147–48, 151–53, 156, 160, 185, 192–93
Shanghai, city of, 26–27, 31, 34, 41
sin, theological category, 6–7, 14, 31, 45, 73, 127
Singapore, v, ix, xiv, 41, 102, 122–26, 128–31, 133, 135, 137–39
slavery, xiii, xv, 12, 44, 47, 51–52, 55–56, 58–61, 63, 68, 89–91, 164, 167, 172, 174–75, 190
socialism, political and economic, 26, 28, 39–40, 177, 221
solidarity, xv, 3, 12–16, 20, 39–40, 63, 71–72, 81–82, 98, 112, 114, 119, 122, 176, 186, 191–93, 195–99, 201–2, 205–9, 226, 230, 257
sovereign, political condition of, 146, 159–60, 162, 234, 240, 248–52
spiritual, 12, 28, 33, 36, 45, 66, 161, 235
strike, 26, 110, 114, 197–98, 204, 209, 235, 254; See also resistance, movements of
surrogate labor, 144, 155–56; See also labor; reproductive, rights and labor

T
Tamar, biblical figure, v, xiv, 105–7, 113, 116, 118–19, 121
Tillich, Paul, 246, 259

transtextual, 113, 123, 129, 136
transnational, x, xv, 36, 40, 59, 101, 122, 147, 155
Trump, Donald J. (45th President of United States), 25, 35–36, 38, 41–42, 80, 201, 209

U
ubuntu, xv, 176–77
undocumented, immigration status, 3, 196
union, xiii, 19, 51, 69–71, 74, 76–77, 79, 83–84, 127, 194–95, 197–99, 208–9, 235–37, 246, 248–49, 253–55, 257

V
vanguard, 46, 215
violence, acts of, 28, 30, 91, 100, 106, 134, 146–49, 160–61, 227

W
war, xiii–xiv, 91–92, 96, 99, 143–50, 152–53, 155, 157, 160–62, 243
wealth, economic term, 36–38, 64, 88–90, 95, 166, 168–69, 187–90, 200–202, 205–10, 218–19, 229
Wilmore, Gayraud, 54, 68
womanist, theology, x
women, xiii–xiv, 10, 17–18, 27, 35, 48, 60, 63–64, 79, 81, 83, 88, 91, 95–96, 98–102, 106, 110, 112, 114–15, 120, 122, 125–27, 130–31, 133, 135, 137, 145–46, 149, 151, 154, 156–60, 185, 188, 190, 192, 200–201, 207, 216
worker, xiv–xv, 4, 17, 75, 100, 126, 129–30, 186–89, 194–96, 199, 202, 204–7, 241–42, 251
worship, act of, 5, 10, 13, 46, 53, 179, 221

Y
Yahweh, biblical figure, 116, 118

www.ingramcontent.com/pod-product-compliance
Lightning Source LLC
Chambersburg PA
CBHW071241230426
43668CB00011B/1538